ON THE GENEALOGY
OF MODERNITY

FOUCAULT'S SOCIAL PHILOSOPHY

ON THE GENEALOGY OF MODERNITY

FOUCAULT'S SOCIAL PHILOSOPHY

NYTHAMAR FERNANDES DE OLIVEIRA

Nova Science Publishers, Inc.
New York

Senior Editors: Susan Boriotti and Donna Dennis
Coordinating Editor: Tatiana Shohov
Office Manager: Annette Hellinger
Graphics: Wanda Serrano
Editorial Production: Vladimir Klestov, Matthew Kozlowski and Maya Columbus
Circulation: Ave Maria Gonzalez, Vera Popovic, Luis Aviles, Melissa Diaz, and Jeannie Pappas
Communications and Acquisitions: Serge P. Shohov
Marketing: Cathy DeGregory

Library of Congress Cataloging-in-Publication Data
Oliveira, Nythamar Fernandes de.
  On the genealogy of modernity : Foucault's social philosophy / Nythamar Fernandes de Oliveira.
     p. cm.
  Includes bibliographical references and index.
  ISBN 1-978-1-60456-390-0 (softcover)
  1. Foucault, Michel, 1926-1984. 2. Kant, Immanuel, 1724-1804. 3. Nietzsche, Friedrich Wilhelm, 1844-1900. 4. Genealogy (Philosophy) 5. Social sciences--Philosophy. 6. Philosophy, Modern. I. Title.
  B2430.F724O45 2011
  194--dc23
                                        2011042429

Copyright © 2012 by Nova Science Publishers, Inc.
     400 Oser Ave, Suite 1600
     Hauppauge, New York 11788-3619
     Tele. 631-231-7269   Fax 631-231-8175
     e-mail: Novascience@earthlink.net
     Web Site: http://www.novapublishers.com

All rights reserved. No part of this book may be reproduced, stored in a retrieval system or transmitted in any form or by any means: electronic, electrostatic, magnetic, tape, mechanical photocopying, recording or otherwise without permission from the publishers.

The publisher has taken reasonable care in the preparation of this book, but makes no expressed or implied warranty of any kind and assumes no responsibility for any errors or omissions. No liability is assumed for incidental or consequential damages in connection with or arising out of information contained in this book.

This publication is designed to provide accurate and authoritative information with regard to the subject matter covered herein. It is sold with the clear understanding that the publisher is not engaged in rendering legal or any other professional services. If legal or any other expert assistance is required, the services of a competent person should be sought. FROM A DECLARATION OF PARTICIPANTS JOINTLY ADOPTED BY A COMMITTEE OF THE AMERICAN BAR ASSOCIATION AND A COMMITTEE OF PUBLISHERS.

Printed in the United States of America

Contents

About the Author		vii
Preface		ix
Introduction		**1**
	1. Zur Genealogie der Moderne, or the Foucauldian Problematic	1
	2. Kant, Nietzsche, and the Foucault-Habermas Debate	5
	3. Seven Theses on Truth, Power, and Ethics	9
Chapter One	Kant's Critique and the Truth of Modern Man	**13**
	Introduction	13
	1. Critique, Archaeology, and Human Nature	17
	2. Kant and the Limits of Representation	24
	3. The Critique of Metaphysical Reason	30
	4. Aesthetics and Ethics in the Third Critique	35
	5. Conclusion: The Critique and the End of Man	42
Chapter Two	Hegel's Critique of Kant	**47**
	Introduction	47
	1. Kant's Conception of *Moralität*	50
	2. Hegel's Conception of *Sittlichkeit*	55
	3. Kant, Hegel, and the Foundation of Ethics	61
Chapter Three	Nietzsche, Genealogy, and the Critique of Power	**67**
	Introduction	67
	1. Critique and Genealogy: Of Truth and Method	70

	2. *Human Nature and the Will to Power*	77
	3. *Nietzsche's Critique of Kantian Morality*	84
	4. *Nietzsche and the Critique of Subjectivity*	88
	5. *Conclusion: The Critique of Modernity*	93
Chapter Four	Aestheticism in Nietzsche and Foucault	**99**
	Introduction	*99*
	1. *Genealogy, Nihilism and History*	*103*
	2. *Nietzsche's Genealogy of Christianity*	*106*
	3. *Aestheticism and Moral Subjectivation*	*114*
Chapter Five	Foucault's Genealogy of Modernity	**117**
	Introduction	*117*
	1. *Foucault, Habermas and the "Questions of Method"*	*121*
	2. *Truth, Archaeology, and Genealogy*	*125*
	3. *Modernity and the Critique of Power*	*131*
	4. *Subjectivity and the Genealogy of Ethics*	*146*
Conclusion: Truth, Power, Ethics		**155**
List of Abbreviations		**165**
	1) *Immanuel Kant*	*165*
	2) *Friedrich Nietzsche*	*166*
	3) *Michel Foucault*	*167*
	4) *Others*	*168*
Index		**171**

ABOUT THE AUTHOR

Nythamar Fernandes de Oliveira was born in Rio de Janeiro, earned his Ph.D. from the State University of New York at Stony Brook, and teaches ethics and political philosophy at Porto Alegre, Brazil. He is the author of the *Tractatus ethico-politicus* (1999).

PREFACE

> We must try to trace the genealogy, not so much of the notion of modernity, as of modernity as a question. (M. Foucault, "The Art of Telling the Truth" PPC 89)

This book was born out of a reflection on a text by Habermas on Foucault, and to paraphrase the latter, this study first arose "out of the laughter that shattered all the familiar landmarks of *our* thought, the thought that bears the stamp of our age and our geography." (OT xv) Both Foucault's *Order of Things* and Habermas's *Philosophical Discourse of Modernity* provide us with a veritable archaeology of our modern condition insofar as they deal with the mapping of the discursive coordinates that have framed our modern and postmodern conceptions of truth, power, and ethics. Moreover, both thinkers deal with the cultural-historical setting of a "genealogy of modernity," in their attempt to problematize the modern articulations of "critique" and "power." Although a genuine interest in this "cross-fertilization between French and German thought" played some role in my research, I have found the theme of a "genealogy of modernity" noteworthy both for its appraisal of the history of modern philosophy and for its properly philosophical claims. To be sure, it is the very fate of the "philosophical discourse" which is at stake in Habermas's criticism of Foucault's genealogy of modernity. For Habermas, it seems that Foucault's genealogy is doomed to fall short of the rigorous, coherent patterns of rationality required by any discourse that claims to be philosophical. According to Habermas, such is indeed the postmodern predicament: the more philosophy strives to overcome its metaphysical foundations, the easier it falls prey to skepticism, irrationalism, or another form of dogmatism. On the other hand, even without addressing the riddles of Chinese encyclopaedias and their heterodox taxonomies, Habermas's critique of Foucault has renewed a problematic that underlies our modern condition, from Kant to Nietzsche, namely, the question of what and who we humans claim to be. By calling into question *our* familiarity with our own systems of classifications that distinguish the Same from its Other, Foucault's overall project can be fairly regarded as an attempt to address the question of "who we are" -- in epistemic, political, and ethical terms. Furthermore, the question of who we are, according to Kant, Nietzsche, and Foucault, could not have been asked before the emergence of modernity and its conceptions of subjectivity, self-consciousness, and reflective thought. Habermas has convincingly shown that Hegel's conception of self-determination was even more decisive to a critical understanding of our modern *ethos*. In this study, I will focus on the genealogy of modernity as it has been articulated by the original contributions of Kant, Nietzsche, and Foucault, in their respective conceptions of truth, power, and ethics. It is my contention that Foucault's works, from the archaeology of *Les mots et les choses* to the hermeneutics of subjectivation in the *Histoire de la sexualité*, indeed address this major question, as it bears both on the threshold of modernity and on the aftermath of its crises and eventual collapse.

From the outset, I invoke Habermas's text, in particular the two lectures on Foucault, almost as a pretext to recast Foucault's genealogy of modernity. But it must also be added that, thanks to Habermas's provocative essays on Foucault, the so-called *Methodenstreit* between modernists and postmodernists can go beyond mere verbiage and misunderstandings. What has struck philosophers everywhere as a *dialogue de sourds* may finally yield some substantial food for thought, in the very midst of another *fin-de-siècle* crisis of identity. Whether modernity is an unfinished project or not refers us back to the same problem that, as both Foucault and Habermas saw it, signaled the end of German idealism at the close of last century. Whether practical reason was capable or not of carrying out the universalist, emancipatory ideal of an autonomous, come-of-age humanness is precisely what links us today to the critical times of Kant, Hegel, Marx, and Nietzsche. For Habermas, it is Hegel rather than Kant who sets the paradigm for modernity, just as Nietzsche is the turning-point leading into postmodernity. Foucault would not disagree with Habermas when he asserts that "Hegel was the first philosopher to develop a clear concept of modernity" (PDM 4), even though Kant is said to have set the paradigm for our modern *ethos*. Habermas assumes of course that Hegel's "principle of subjectivity" is grounded in Kant's practical philosophy, regarded as "the standard (or authoritative) self-interpretation of modernity." (PDM 19) By reexamining the Kantian critique of metaphysics, Nietzsche's genealogy of morals, and Foucault's own genealogical critique of modern subjectivity, I will seek to show that in order to articulate a philosophical discourse on modernity one must not only refer to cultural, historical events associated with modern conceptions of truth, power, and ethics, but one must also undertake an analysis of how these different axes concur to determine what we call "modernity." Such is in effect the genealogical thrust of this study, which is explicitly based upon Foucault's readings of Kant and Nietzsche, so as to show that critique and genealogy constitute a highly original contribution of Foucault's social philosophy to the study of modernity. The "genealogy of modernity" is shown to constitute the major thesis of a Foucauldian "philosophical discourse of modernity" which, contrary to Habermas's criticisms, does not evade questions of truth, normativity, and value, but rather problematizes them. The genealogy of modernity is itself made possible by the articulation of the three axes of truth, power, and ethics that determine the historical a priori of our modern ethos as the condition of who we are, that is, the formation of modern subjectivity with its regimes of veridiction and jurisdiction, modes of subjectivation and practices of freedom.

INTRODUCTION

1. *Zur Genealogie der Moderne*, or the Foucauldian Problematic

Three domains of genealogy are possible. First, an historical ontology of ourselves in relation to truth through which we constitute ourselves as subjects of knowledge; second, an historical ontology of ourselves in relation to a field of power through which we constitute ourselves as subjects acting on others; third, an historical ontology of ourselves in relation to ethics through which we constitute ourselves as moral agents. (1983 Interview with Dreyfus and Rabinow, BSH 237;FR 351)

The main purpose of this study is to articulate a philosophical discourse that addresses the methodological problematic lying at the critical intersection of archaelogy and genealogy in Michel Foucault's conception of modernity. Both archaelogy and genealogy were described by Foucault as critical methods employed in the analyses of discursive formations and social institutions, respectively. Both proved to be decisive in his formulation of a thorough understanding of how modern "man" was born, how the subjects of modernity came into being.[1] My major thesis is that the "genealogy of modernity" not only constitutes one of Foucault's greatest contributions to the "history of systems of thought," but it also stands for what might be regarded as *the* Foucauldian *philosophical* problematic par excellence, namely, the destiny of human nature after the crisis of modern metaphysics, in particular, after the undermining of modern subjectivity. "Destiny" translates here the prosaic Greek term *daimon*,

---

[1] Throughout this book, I will employ an inclusive language, except for those contexts where the universalist ideal of human nature requires to be expressed in supposedly neutral terms -- *anthropos, homo, l'homme, der Mensch*, man, etc.

which would be diversely conceived as human flourishing (*eudaimonia*), final purpose (*Endzweck*), and self-overcoming (*Selbstüberwindung*) in Aristotelian, Kantian, and Nietzschean conceptions of the human *ethos*, respectively. The fate of human nature implies thus a "historical ontology of ourselves," as subjects of truth, power, and ethics in self-constituting modes of being that characterize modern individuals, in opposition to, say, their Ancient and Medieval counterparts. Foucault himself stated that the overall goal of his work was not "to analyze the phenomena of power, nor to elaborate the foundations of such an analysis," but rather "to create a history of the different modes by which, in our culture, human beings are made subjects." (BSH 208)[2] The question of who we are translates thus, for Foucault, a basic question that is raised, at once, qua philosophical and qua historical question. Who are we, *die Moderne*, self-constituted subjects of modernity? Since "there is no pre- and post-archaeology or genealogy in Foucault" (BSH 104), the three axes of *savoir* (knowledge), *pouvoir* (power), and *subjectivation* will be discussed in this study in relation to a genealogy of modern subjectivity, in light of Foucault's readings of Kant (critique) and Nietzsche (power). Foucault's own conception of human nature is thus articulated along the three methodological fields of archaeology, genealogy, and interpretive analytics, as a "radical hermeneutics" of modern subjectivation. It is therefore my assumption that Foucault's reading of Kant and Nietzsche is precisely what accounts for his critique of philosophical anthropology, which, although similar to Martin Heidegger's in many respects, still makes room for an articulation of ethics and political philosophy. What Foucault has termed the "critical enterprise" (OD 28) is precisely what allows for the conception of genealogy as a radical critique that displaces the philosophical discourse of modernity vis-à-vis metaphysics. By critically examining Foucault's reading of Kant and Nietzsche, I propose to show that critique and genealogy meet at the very locus where a methodological displacement of metaphysics has been operated, in particular in the critical region that was assigned by modernity to the conception of human nature. Both Kant's critique of dogmatic, speculative metaphysics and Nietzsche's genealogical overcoming of metaphysical morality were directed against foundationalist attempts to articulate a philosophical discourse on God, human nature, and the world. To be sure, only Kant's transcendental criticism meant to displace --and replace-- traditional metaphysics on a methodological level. However, as I propose to show in the second chapter, Nietzsche's perspectivism and aesthetic experimentalism fulfill a similar task in

---

[2] "Why Study Power: The Question of the Subject" was originally written in English by Foucault, and incorporated into the after-word on "The Subject and Power," in BHS 208-226.

the very attack on metaphysics and its transcendental foundations --as proposed by Kant and later German idealists. Foucault has succeeded in showing how Nietzschean genealogy has contributed to consolidate a historicized conception of human nature, in particular, of human agency, through the critique of metaphysical subjectivity.

The book is divided into five chapters. The first chapter presents a reconstruction of Kant's critique of metaphysics as the setting of truth on new epistemological grounds. This analysis is preceded by a discussion of the Foucauldian articulation of critique and archaelogy, and followed by a study of criticism and the fate of human nature in modern philosophy. It is then shown how Kant's critique of metaphysics made possible the birth of "modern man," based upon a conception of morality that follows the practical use of pure reason. As a being endowed with reason which ought to be rational, man is to fulfill in history (empirical sociability) his moral destination (transcendental freedom) -- hence, what Foucault terms the empirico-transcendental doublet. Kant's dualism in anthropology and morality is bridged only by means of a teleology which betrays the historical constitution of its subjectivity. Hence the Kantian articulation of problems of theoretical and practical reason will be explored only insofar as they will help us understand the paradigm of modern metaphysics, where human nature ceases to be a given representation (e.g., *imago dei*) and becomes a self-constituted, self-active being. The correlated problems of the unity of practical philosophy, the presupposition of autonomy (or positive freedom), pure practical reason (moral autonomy), the relation of aesthetics and ethics in light of the unity of the three *Critiques*, and the teleological conception of history will be briefly outlined.

The second chapter offers an excursus on Hegel's critique of Kant that will serve as a transition to the third chapter, where the question of how Nietzsche's critique of power undermines the metaphysical foundations of transcendental idealism and its claims to truth is examined. I attempt to highlight the aestheticist dimension of Foucault's strategic post-Hegelian return to Kant, so as to introduce the radicalization operated by Nietzsche's critique of German idealism.

The third chapter takes up Nietzsche's critique of Kant, precisely where the limits of representation led to a moral world view, transforming the critical impetus of pure reason into a humanist dogma of practical reason. Nietzsche's attack upon Kant will be thus articulated in terms of the former's threefold critique of religion, morals, and philosophy. The will to power and the eternal return, nihilism and the genealogy of morals, will be focused on with a view to elucidating the problematization of the critique of metaphysics originally undertaken by Kant, at the very foundational level of subjectivity. Nietzsche's critique of Kant's teleology is thus evoked in order to show that genealogy unmasks the truth of modern man in a radical, self-overcoming critique of morality. The knowing subject of Kant's critique is unmasked as the moral subject of a metaphysics that remains bound to the morality of *ressentiment*, as its will to truth betrays a reactive will to power. The birth of modern man ultimately signals the death of God, and the latter entails man's self-overcoming and his own death.

In the fourth chapter, an excursus on Nietzsche's aestheticist critique of Christianity will lead us to the genealogy of modern ethics thematized by Foucault. It is thus demonstrated that the death of God and the correlated theme of the death of man paved the way for the kind of rationalization *qua* moralization of human life required by the very disciplinary society that would come under attack in Foucault's genealogy of modernity. Secularized humanism becomes now the target of an anti-humanism that takes nihilism seriously --what one may call a "sober nihilism" that resists both modernist and postmodern blackmailing.

In the fifth chapter, I reexamine Foucault's genealogical account of modern ethics, so as to respond to Jürgen Habermas's critique of Foucault expounded in *Der philosophische Diskurs der Moderne* (1985).[3] I will argue that Foucault's reading of Kant and Nietzsche are decisive for an understanding of his critique of rationalism and historicism, insofar as the genealogical project is concerned, for the teleological, universalizable conception of subjectivity is precisely what must be unmasked in modern humanist claims to world liberation. In particular, Nietzsche's genealogical critique of Kant is shown to have been appropriated by Foucault in his aestheticist articulation of truth, power, and ethics, with the important difference that Kant's ontology of the present is also invoked by Foucault's permanent critique of normalization and disciplinary power. I will conclude with a Foucauldian account of what may be called a non-universalizable, noncognitivist "ethics of self-care," to contrast with messianic and utopian ethics of liberation.[4] The fifth chapter will be supplemented, in the conclusion, with a brief account of the reception of Foucault's social philosophy among French cultural historians and sociologists of culture, such as Michelle Perrot, Roger Chartier, Jacques Le Goff, Paul Veyne, Michel Maffesoli, and Pierre Bourdieu. It will be shown how, by marking himself off from *l'histoire des mentalités* and

---

[3] Cf. Chapters IX and X: "The Critique of Reason as an Unmasking of the Human Sciences" and "Some Questions Concerning the Theory of Power".
[4] Cf. Chapter Three, Section 4 infra. Foucault remarked once that "recent liberation movements suffer from the fact that they cannot find any principle on which to base the elaboration of a new ethics." (FR 343) As we will see, Foucault's ethics is not an alternative set of moral beliefs, but a philosophical ethos that seeks to address the main problems of our age.

l'histoire des idées, on the one hand, and the *Annales* school and Marxist structuralism, on the other, Foucault has contributed to the emergent *histoire nouvelle* (and the *nouvelle histoire*) that gave rise to new forms of cultural history in contemporary France. Foucault's lasting contribution to social philosophy is shown to parallel his revolutionary approach to theory of history, precisely by historicizing the former and rescuing the sociocultural thrust of the latter.

2. KANT, NIETZSCHE, AND THE FOUCAULT-HABERMAS DEBATE

Michel Foucault is credited with welcoming the concept of power into the contemporary philosophical landscape. Jürgen Habermas is critical of Foucault for doing so, not because power is incongruous in that landscape, but because Foucault's conception of it inflicts environmental damage for which he can be held philosophically accountable. (CP 1)

The so-called "Foucault-Habermas debate" was definitely institutionalized with the publication of an anthology, edited by Michael Kelly, in a serious attempt to address the critique of power in relation to the ethical, political, and social theory of the past two decades.[5] Foucault's untimely death in June 1984 did not allow for the debate to actually take place, as arrangements had been made for an American meeting to discuss Kant's essay "What is Enlightenment?" in November, according to Habermas's own recollections.[6] It is beyond the scope of the present study to re-evaluate the philosophical problems that have been raised in connection to Habermas's critique of Foucault, since the debate has been recast by Kelly and other thinkers. My principal interest in alluding to this debate is rather to situate Foucault's genealogical thesis in the contemporary scenario of ongoing discussions on ethics and politics. As I will argue throughout this study on the genealogy of modernity, the Nietzschean-Foucauldian paradigm of the critique of power is not doomed to irrationalism, quietism or indifference vis-à-vis the role and nature of human agency in our *fin-de-siècle* societies, though it is theoretically opposed to a universalizable conception of ethics, power, and truth. Now, there are of course serious problems to be dealt with, when one embarks on this kind of genealogical critique, among them, the questions of rationality and

---

[5] Michael Kelly (ed.), *Critique and Power: Recasting the Foucault/ Habermas Debate*, Cambridge, Mass.: MIT Press, 1994. (Abbreviated CP)

[6] Cf. J. Habermas, "Taking Aim at the Heart of the Present: On Foucault's Lecture on Kant's *What is Enlightenment?*" CP 149-154.

historicism, highlighted in the two lectures Habermas devotes to Foucault in his *Philosophical Discourse of Modernity*.

Because of Habermas's continuous interest in the question of history and its social-philosophical implications, his discussion of Foucault in that book should not be dismissed as just another "sin of youth." In effect, that Habermas places his own *Diskurs* vis-à-vis other seminal studies in French post-structuralism and the critique of power[7] only confirms --perhaps *malgré lui*-- the philosophical magnitude of these lectures. It is instructive to compare, for instance, Habermas's reading of Kant and Hegel with Foucault's, since Habermas uses both against Nietzsche's critique of modernity. In effect, Habermas invokes Hegel's critique of Kant so as to reconstruct a "dialectic of the Enlightenment" that takes into account the historical unification of the institutionally differentiated realms of science, morality, and art. I will attempt to show that Foucault's reading of Kant's criticism is consistent with his appropriation of Nietzsche's genealogy, and this is precisely what accounts for an original, philosophical style of his own. Although dealing with hermeneutical *questions de fond* such as "What is Foucauldian?" and "How should one read *Surveiller et punir*?," I will deliberately avoid aestheticist and eclecticist responses to neo-Kantian misreadings of Nietzsche, Heidegger, and Foucault. I am particularly interested in reformulating a Foucauldian "genealogy of modernity" that avoids the modernist and postmodernist aporias opposing "critique" and "power," on the one hand, and the "transcendental" and "empirical" bases for the methodology of social and behavioral sciences on the other. It is not so much a question of going beyond modernity or post-modernism as to make sense of the practical and discursive implications of modern social thought, in particular, of Kant's criticism and Nietzsche's radical critique of it.

It is precisely in order to problematize such facile plays of opposites that I will attempt to show that, while breaking away from the transcendental grounds of traditional metaphysics, Foucault's genealogical method does not depart from philosophical critique --as might be expected, given that "critique" and "genealogy" remain perspectival, strategic undertakings-- but it rather seeks to undermine its rationalist and historicist claims. In effect, modern social theory has emerged in reaction to both rationalism and historicism, as witness Durkheim's and Weber's critique of positivism. However, following the Marxian reversal and the Nietzschean unmasking of the Hegelian *Wissen*, both the "dialectic of the enlightenment" of the early Frankfurt School and Foucault's "unmasking of the

---

[7] Cf. Manfred Frank, *Was heißt Neostrukturalismus?*, (Frankfurt: Suhrkamp, 1984); Albrecht Wellmer, *Zur Dialektik von Moderne und Postmoderne*, (Frankfurt: Suhrkamp, 1985); Axel Honneth, *Kritik der Macht*, (Frankfurt: Suhrkamp, 1985) [ET: *The Critique of Power*, trans. Kenneth Baynes, (Cambridge, Mass.: MIT 1991)].

human sciences" arrived at the same conclusion that modern social criticism has not been radical enough, insofar as it has exhausted the paradigm of consciousness without fulfilling the revolutionary promises of its practical intent. Although Habermas convincingly shows that the fate of Western rationality was to be decided in the *après-Hegel* since "Hegel inaugurated the discourse of modernity" (PDM 51), his contention that an irrational, postmodernist aestheticism was the only alternative left for those who followed neither Left nor Right Hegelians remains far from doing justice to the Nietzschean critique of rationalism and historicism. On the contrary, as Nietzsche's greatest epigones criticized by Habermas --Heidegger, Foucault, and Derrida -- have all shown, there was much more to the "genealogy of morals" than a mere reversal of values, in the very Hegelian terms of the *Geschehen* of the *Sittlichkeit*. To be sure, both Habermas and Foucault subscribe to the Hegelian rule that modernity must create its "normativity out of itself" (PDM 7). And yet, while for Habermas this is precisely what maintains the discourse of modernity in its communicative rationality vis-à-vis the lifeworld and its material life processes (PDM 294-326), Foucault will seek to avoid this "methodological dualism" (between *Lebenswelt* and systems)[8] by conceiving of the historically constituted experience as "the correlation between fields of knowledge, types of normativity, and forms of subjectivity in a particular culture." (HS2 4) Although it is beyond the scope of this book to explore Hegel's philosophy and compare it with Nietzsche's agonistic, nondialectical "revaluation of values," the problem of modernity and historicity lies at the heart of the Foucault-Habermas debate. Both Foucault's and Habermas's indebtedness to Hegel's *Phänomenologie* require thus that it not be overlooked in this study, especially if we are reminded that the French reception of Nietzsche takes place in the aftermath of a Hegelian renaissance orchestrated, in great part, by one of Foucault's mentors, Jean Hyppolite. By exploring Foucault's critical appropriation and displacement of "epistemological,"[9] historical-critical, and hermeneutical methods, and his articulation of, respectively, the methods of archaeology, genealogy, and interpretive-analytics, I

---

[8] Cf. PDM 357: "...system imperatives and lifeworld imperatives form new frictional surfaces that spark new conflicts which cannot be dealt with in the existing compromise structures. The question posed today is whether a new compromise can be arranged in accord with the rules of system-oriented politics --or whether the crisis management attuned to crises that are systematically caused and perceived as systemic will be undermined by social movements no longer oriented to be the system's steering needs, but to the *processes at the boundaries between system and lifeworld*."

[9] I am thinking here of the French term "épistémologie," as it was used by Bachelard and Canguilhem, as a historical philosophy of sciences, between a *Wissenschaftslehre* and a "history of sciences."

will attempt to arrive at a broader understanding of Foucault's overall conception of critique, archaelogy, and genealogy. I am thus proposing to read the Foucauldian corpus in its discursive coherence, within the three-axial grid that articulates the discourses on knowledge, power, and subjectivation. In order to deal with questions such as "What is critique?" and "How is critique possible in modern society?" I shall attempt to reconstitute the Foucauldian shift from a "critique of the (Kantian) critique" towards a "(Nietzschean) genealogy of modernity." Because I am confined to the genealogical critique of power within the Foucauldian threefold (*savoir*, *pouvoir*, *subjectivation*), I am placing the topic of this book at the methodological intersection of political philosophy, ethics, and social theory, against the background of other general questions such as:

(i) How can philosophy contribute to the conception of a critical theory of society without compromising the latter with a transcendental foundationalism that would betray its empirical claims to scientific objectivity?

(ii) Does political philosophy, after all, in its classical conception from Plato and Aristotle to Machiavelli and Hobbes, still have a say in the self-understanding of the social order and its ever-changing configurations of power relations?

(iii) In the last analysis, what is the philosophical meaning and relevance of a social theory for modern society, in which rationalization has effected highly complex levels of relations between state and society, legal structures and individual rights, political power and the subjectivation of citizens?

(iv) How can Foucault's genealogical critique of power contribute to historical, social analyses of third world societies that still resist North Atlantic colonization and neoliberal globalization, so as to avoid the shortcomings and contradictions of both liberal and socialist models of democratic organization? In particular, how can a critique of modernity contribute to the sociocultural process of democratization and modernization of developing countries?

(v) How can Foucault's microphysics of power contribute to crosscultural discourses and practices of resistance vis-à-vis sexism, racism, and neocolonialism?

3. SEVEN THESES ON TRUTH, POWER, AND ETHICS

L'oeuvre est seule, désormais. Elle parlera encore; d'autres la feront parler, et parleront sur elle. (Michel Foucault, *Annuaire du Collège de France* 1980)

Foucault's words on the legacy of Barthes's oeuvre, following the death of the author, apply to his own work as well. In effect, Foucault draws an important distinction between the authorship of certain works (e.g., Marx's *Das Kapital* or Freud's *Traumdeutung*) and the "discursivity" that allows for endless analogical and differential interplays with reference to their works (Marxism and psychoanalysis). (FR 114)[10] To be sure, one cannot claim to be a "Foucauldian" or a "Nietzschean" in the same way that one may be clearly identified with a Marxist, Freudian or Kantian school of thought --precisely because of the former's critique of truth and method in the very formulation of theories and systems. As I speak of an ensemble of theses supposedly inspired by my readings of Kant, Nietzsche, and Foucault, I thus explicitly commit myself to what I assume to be a Foucauldian principle of hermeneutics, namely, that discursivity not only transcends the author's intention (as both Schleiermacher and Ricoeur pointed out), but also unveils the very function of the author as such ("the subject as a variable and complex function of discourse," FR 118). Although I have carefully sought to do justice to these three authors, I have also structured this book in accordance with what I have interpreted to be a Foucauldian major thesis ("on the genealogy of modernity"), resulting from his readings of Kant and Nietzsche. The subject-matter of this book can thus be summarized through the following main theses:

(1) *"Zur Genealogie der Moderne"*--to borrow Nietzsche's vernacular-- can be said to constitute Foucault's major thesis, the Foucauldian problematic par excellence, based upon his reading of Kant's critique and Nietzsche's genealogy. The genealogy of modernity is made possible by the articulation of three axes, namely, truth, power, and ethics, that determine the historical a priori of our modern ethos, i.e., the modern condition of who we are, the self-formation of modernity with its regimes of veridiction and jurisdiction, modes of subjectivation, and practices of freedom.

(2) Kant's critique of metaphysics has made possible the birth of "modern man," based upon a modern conception of morality, following the

---

[10] Cf. M. Foucault, "What Is an Author?" [1969], in FR 101-120.

practical use of pure reason. Kant's metaphysics of morals thus runs parallel to the metaphysics of nature, and its practical intent must not be confused with the theoretical use of reason, since its foundations are no longer placed in the natural order of beings or human nature (Aristotelian, Stoic, Epicurean ethics) but rather accounts for the very constitution of man as a moral subject and agent. Kant's universalizable ethics of duty signals the emergence of the modern conceptions of freedom, humanity, personality, autonomy, self-consciousness, and self-determination. Therefore, as a being endowed with reason which ought to be rational, it is man's task to fulfill in history (material, empirical sociability) his moral destination (formal, transcendental freedom) --hence, what Foucault terms the empirico-transcendental doublet. This dualism in Kant's anthropology and morality is to be bridged only by means of a teleology-- without lapsing into metaphysical finalism or moral utilitarianism. (GMS; Introductions to KU)

(3) Kant's philosophy cannot fulfill its emancipatory promises precisely because his practical philosophy, although claiming to be grounded in a transcendental, nonempirical conception of morality, turns out to hinge on a teleology of human nature that betrays a historically, socially grounded constitution of the moral subject. Human freedom is, after all, conceived of by Kant as the ultimate *telos* of nature itself. (KU §§ 83-84)

(4) Nietzsche's genealogy can be regarded as the outgrowth of a radical, self-overcoming critique of idealist criticism --similar to Marx's *Kritik der Kritik*, a threefold critique of religion, morals, and philosophy. The knowing self of Kant's critique is unmasked as the same moral subject of a metaphysics which, though claiming to have overcome the dogmatic transgression of theoretical reason, remains faithful to the very onto-theology alluded to in Kant's critique (KrV B 660), subject to the morality of *ressentiment*, as its will to truth betrays a reactive will to power. The birth of modern man signals the imminence of the death of God, as the latter entails the self-overcoming of man.

(5) Nietzsche's will to power seeks to overcome the aestheticism of Schopenhauer's critique of German idealism (and its equation of *Wille* and *Ding an sich*, *Vorstellung* and *Phänomene*). Nietzsche's genealogy of morals can thus be regarded as a prelude to a genealogy of modernity. One may speak of "aestheticism" only insofar as it stresses the aesthetic self-overcoming of ethics, but must also heed its historical and political dimensions, inherent in the correlative conceptions of genealogy and active nihilism, as the will to power always already unveils the self-

legislation of the will and the self-affirmation of power in the subject's historicity. An ethics of self-overcoming stems, after all, from the historicization of truth, power, and subjectivity.

(6) Foucault's genealogy thus combines the Nietzschean three-axial "historical a priori" with the Kantian critique of the present so as to account for political *engagement*. For Foucault, the reversibility of the external spaces of discursive and non-discursive practices is precisely what allows for strategies of resistance to take place on this level of exteriority, where the conditions said to be constitutive of subjectivity will only then unveil their normative thrust, in the particularity of commitments made empirically by the self --both individually and collectively. Such is, indeed, the post-Nietzschean return to Kant operated by Foucault's genealogy of modernity. Foucault's ethics of care for the self as an aesthetics of existence is certainly closer to Nietzsche's *Selbstüberwindung* than to Kant's self-imposed *Ausgang*. But Foucault's strategy seeks to combine both in a permanent critique of normalization and disciplinary power, as the philosophical ethos of modernity denounces the *dispositif* networks that constitute our own subjectivity, drawing a return of morality through practices of freedom which offer no promise of liberation.

(7) Even though he opposed a universalizable conception of truth, power, and ethics, Foucault has decisively contributed to both history and the social sciences with a genealogy of subjectivity that, by combining the Kantian critique and the Nietzschean genealogy, can account for such a complex conception as culture and its political micromeshes. Neither Marxist nor *Annaliste*, his shift from infrastructural analyses of society towards superstructural interpretations of culture was welcomed by the *nouvelle histoire* (Jacques Le Goff, Jacques Revel) and creatively appropriated by cultural historians and social thinkers alike, such as Michelle Perrot, Roger Chartier, Paul Veyne, François Ewald, and Jacques Donzelot.

Chapter One

KANT'S CRITIQUE AND THE TRUTH OF MODERN MAN

INTRODUCTION

> This experience of unreason in which, up to the 18th century, Western man encountered the night of his truth and its absolute challenge was to become, and still remains for us, the mode of access to the natural truth of man... "Psychology" is merely a thin skin on the surface of the ethical world in which modern man seeks his truth. (Michel Foucault, MIP 74)

As John Caputo has shown in a splendid essay on Foucault's "tragic hermeneutics," the latter's Heideggerian-inspired "destruction of the history of psychology" succeeded in unveiling the moralizing internment of madness (*le Grand Renfermement*) that took place in the France of *l'âge classique*, on the threshold of modernity's experience of unreason, as a juridical, institutional legitimation of scientific "truth"--i.e., "the truth about madness" endorsed by psychology and psychiatry.[1] The "night of truth," the truth that there is no "truth of truth" after all, is certainly one of Foucault's felicitous formulas that betray his early indebtedness to Nietzsche. Moreover, as I will argue in this chapter, it also indicates how seriously we must take Nietzsche's critique of Kant's conception of

---

[1] John Caputo, "On not Knowing Who We Are: Madness, Hermeneutics, and the Night of Truth," in John Caputo and Mark Yount (eds.), *Foucault and the Critique of Institutions*, (University Park, PA: The Pennsylvania State University Press, 1993), 233-264. I am indebted to Professor Caputo's lessons and insights into the works of Husserl, Heidegger, and Foucault, while I was a graduate student at Villanova University.

truth in order to grasp the full meaning of our own modern condition. Although inheriting the traditional understanding of truth as *adaequatio intellectus et rei*, Immanuel Kant is best known for the critical revolution that decentered metaphysical truth towards a region defined within the limits of human reason. By the methodic, systematic attacks of the *Kritik* on the pretensions to suprasensible knowledge, Kant set out to establish the true principles that constitute metaphysics as a science that makes possible legitimate knowledge of both nature and freedom. Hence, from the outset, Kant was led to draw the fundamental distinction between the theoretical and practical uses of pure reason, whether constituting or regulating the representations of its objects, respectively directed by the understanding (*Verstand*) applied to the cognition of nature or by reason (*Vernunft*) applied to the realm of freedom. The faculty of judgment (*Urteilskraft*) appears as a third *Erkenntnisvermögen*, following its description in the first *Kritik* as the ability of our understanding to determine whether and how particulars stand under a given law or universal, or, alternatively, whether a universal stands over a given particular and, if so, which universal (KrV A 19, 79; B 105, 132-134; cf. KpV 68, 69; KU 179). The *Kritik* was to Kant's *Metaphysik*, as it were, what the experimental-deductive method was to Newtonian physics.[2] Metaphysics, like all other scientific undertakings, was then to be based on and construed according to certain principles of pure reason without transgressing its theoretical boundaries, so as to avoid the dialectical, empty claims of ancient metaphysics. Kant's conception of *Wahrheit*, strictly speaking, is therefore what makes knowledge possible as objectively adequate *Fürwahrhalten*, in that "only objective validity affords the ground for a necessary universal agreement." (KpV 13; cf. KrV A 820-822; B 848-850) But besides the truth of propositions (such as "the earth is round"), Kant was also categorical about *Wahr-sagen*, truth-telling, in total opposition to lies:

> When the maxim according to which I intend to give testimony is tested by practical reason, I always inquire into what it should be if it were to hold as a universal law of nature. It is obvious that, in this way of looking at it, it would oblige everyone to truthfulness. For it cannot hold as a universal law

---

[2] Cf. KrV A 855f., B 883f. In his 1770 Dissertation (*De mundi sensibilis atque intelligibilis forma et principiis, ᶁ 24)* Kant remarks that "the method of all metaphysics in dealing with the sensitive and the intellectual is reducible in the main to this all-important rule: *carefully prevent the principles proper to sensitive cognition from passing their boundaries and affecting the intellectual."* Such will be the task undertaken by the Critique of Pure Reason.

of nature that an assertion should have the force of evidence and yet be intentionally false. (KpV 44)[3]

As will be shown in this chapter, Kant's greatest innovation in philosophy consists precisely in having distinguished the practical from the theoretical use of reason in his foundation of metaphysics. Just as the theoretical, cognitive truth of the sciences entails the work of a metaphysics of nature, a metaphysics of morals must precede our knowledge of what ought to be done (in opposition to our knowledge of what is the case). And Kant will endorse the thesis of the primacy of practical over theoretical reason, at the same time as he emphasizes their unity:

> ...if pure reason of itself can be and really is practical, as the consciousness of the moral law shows it to be, it is only one and the same reason which judges a priori by principles, whether for theoretical or practical purposes. (KpV 121)

The fact that pure reason is practical, just as the very reality of the categories and things-in-themselves, cannot be approached by theoretical reason--since knowledge of the suprasensible is impossible-- but only through its practical use, by requiring the "practical postulates" of reason. To be sure, as will be shown, Kant presupposes a metaphysical conception of man --insofar as "man" is a citizen of two worlds, the phenomenal and the noumenal-- that allows for the articulation of both faculties (theoretical and practical) with the major thesis that, according to the teleological principle, the final purpose of nature is "humanity" (*Menschheit*), hence the humanization of the human species taken as an ethical, historical collectivity. (KU 298, 434-5; OH 21-23) Gilles Deleuze has pointed out, not without irony, that Foucault's archaeology, which cannot be mistaken for an *histoire des mentalités* or an *histoire des idées*, constitutes indeed "a sort of neo-Kantianism unique to Foucault," as the historical conditions for the epistemic formations, together with their visibilities, form a "receptivity," just as the *énoncés* together with their conditions form a "spontaneity." (F 60) To be sure, Foucault's training in Kantian philosophy and the very task of undertaking an archaeology of the human sciences, where the birth of modern man appears as a guiding motif, will be invoked here to show, to what extent, archaeology can be said to anticipate the methodological need of a genealogy and, in historical, philosophical terms, how Kant's critique of metaphysics, in particular, his

---

[3] Cf. Immanuel Kant, "On a Supposed Right to Lie from Altruistic Motives" (1797), tr. L.W. Beck, in *Immanuel Kant: Critique of Practical Reason and Other Writings in Moral Philosophy*, (Indianapolis: Bobbs-Merrill, 1956), 346-50.

anthropology, anticipates the death of man where also takes place the death of God. Immanuel Kant was --and I cannot overstate it-- one of the most important philosophers of all times, perhaps the greatest thinker of modernity. As opposed to the known allusions to Kant's critique that we often find in analytical thought[4] and in the philosophy of science, Foucault has rescued other aspects of the Kantian critique that had been relegated to second plane, especially his conception of man as citizen of two kingdoms and the philosophy of history that complements and fulfills the practical intent of his metaphysics, and even guides his unwritten political philosophy.

Habermas himself has recognized the merits of Foucault's reading of Kant, in particular, its recovery of a critique of power for today's social theory and ethics, and the relevance of asking ourselves again "What is *Aufklärung?*" And yet, he insists that Foucault's reading of Kant has revealed an aporia at the heart of modernity, namely, that the finite, cognitive subject cannot carry out an emancipatory project that demands infinite power. (CI 153) Of course, it is out of question whether Foucault's reading of Kant does more justice to the philosophical intent of the latter, say, than Habermas's. Monique David-Ménard, for one, has pointed to at least two of Foucault's allusions to Kant that were clearly mistaken, in the *Histoire de la folie*, precisely on the question of unreason (*déraison*), which Foucault himself had translated and transposed from the German text of Kant's *Anthropologie*.[5] Along the same lines of Habermas's criticism, James Schmidt and Thomas E. Wartenberg remark that the Foucauldian Kant of the essay "Qu'est-ce que les Lumières?" "differs markedly from the thinker Foucault confronted two decades earlier in *The Order of Things*." (CP 283)[6] Contrasting with the Kantian "anthropological slumber"[7] that reduces all questions of philosophy to the humanist quest "*Was ist der Mensch?*," the Kant of the *Aufklärung* essay is the one who offers us "the possibility of no longer being,

---

[4] To be sure, analytical philosophers such as Rawls, O'Neill and others have written extensively on Kant's practical philosophy in a creative way.

[5] Cf. Monique David-Ménard, "Le laboratoire de l'œuvre," in Luce Giard (ed.), *Michel Foucault: Lire l'œuvre*, (Grenoble: Jérôme Millon, 1992), 27-36. Commenting on Foucault's allusion to Kant in HF (p. 139 and 258), David-Ménard refers us to, respectively, Kant's "Versuch über die Krankheiten des Kopfes" (1764) and "Träume eines Geistersehers erklärt durch Träume der Metaphysik" (1766), where is drawn a distinction between daydreaming, delirium, and madness.

[6] "Foucault's Enlightenment: Critique, Revolution, and the Fashioning of the Self." CP 283-314.

[7] "Le sommeil anthropologique," in French (*Les mots et les choses*, 351), is obviously a parody on Kant's "dogmatic slumber" (*Prolegomena* 260). Cf. Hugh Silverman, "Foucault and the Anthropological Sleep," in *Inscriptions: Between Phenomenology and Structuralism*, (New York: Routledge & Kegan Paul, 1987).

doing, or thinking what we are, do, or think," precisely because of this shift from a transcendental to an empirical standpoint that now takes into account "the contingency that has made us what we are." I will argue in this chapter that the modernist aporia and the theoretical-practical dichotomy are at the heart of Kant's critical project, and that they will motivate both Nietzsche's and Foucault's genealogical proposals.

The main purpose of this chapter is to examine, thus, Foucault's reading of Kant, in particular, the latter's critique of metaphysics, his proposal of a non-theological foundation of ethics, and how the problem of method in his conception of human nature will contribute, indirectly, to a genealogy of modernity. It is certainly not a matter of exploring all the technicalities and difficulties inherent to Kant's critical project, but rather highlighting three specific problems that interested Foucault's early analyses, namely, critique, human nature, and truth. These three taken together seem to constitute, along with the correlated fields of discourse and knowledge, a major problematic for Foucault's elaboration of a method for the human sciences. It is my contention here --to be developed in the fifth chapter-- that Foucault's reading of Kant is very instructive for understanding how he proceeds to shift from archaeology to genealogy, and why he finds in Nietzsche not simply the counter-paradigm for the former but its conceptual counterpart, as it were, in the history of the systems of thought that lead to an understanding of what is termed "modernity."

1. CRITIQUE, ARCHAEOLOGY, AND HUMAN NATURE

> ... [pour] affranchir l'histoire de la pensée de sa sujétion transcendantale (...) il fallait montrer que l'histoire de la pensée ne pouvait avoir ce rôle révélateur du moment transcendantal que la mécanique rationnelle n'a plus depuis Kant... (*L'archéologie du savoir* 265)

It is precisely because neither phenomenology nor structuralism had overcome the crisis which accompanies transcendental philosophy since Kant, that Michel Foucault undertook an archaeological history of thought in a radical attempt to analyze the philosophical discourse of modernity. The crisis which Husserl dealt with in the 1930s, when asked to comment on "the mission of philosophy in our time," translated more than the renewal of a practical, theoretical problem on the eve of the Nazi genocide.[8] For Husserl's transcendental phenomenology, grounded in his critique of Kantian psychologism and neo-Kantian logicism, struggled with the same foundational problems which, according to Foucault, were taken up by structuralists in their attempt to formalize what had been left out, the "unthought" of founding acts --especially, language and the unconscious. At the heart of this crisis of transcendental reflection, Foucault spots the anthropological quest, the humanist ideologies, and the status of the subject.[9] Merleau-Ponty --together with Lévinas and Ricoeur one of the main introducers of phenomenology in France-- has been rightly regarded as the major influence on Foucault's attempt to go beyond phenomenology having also contributed to foster Foucault's reservations about structuralism. (BSH 33f, 166f)[10] As Foucault remarked in an interview, "the transition from phenomenology to structuralism [in France] occurred and focused basically on the problem of language."[11] Foucault regarded the problem of language, in both hermeneutical and semiological traditions, as inseparable from subjectivity. Hence the early interest in the methodological question applied to history and psychiatry was essentially related to the epistemological problem raised by Bachelard and Canguilhem, as a philosophical question to be systematically pursued --in opposition to both *épistémologie* and the history of ideas. What is at stake for Foucault, as it was for Kant, is the question of method (critique) in philosophy, and in particular when philosophers are asked how special sciences are to be taken as legitimate means to express knowledge. Of course, while for Kant it was a transcendental logic that assured the success of scientific knowledge, Foucault grounds his logic of self-constitution upon the historical a priori of epistemic formations. That will not prevent him from the charges of a "transcendental historicism" --as will be seen in Habermas's *Philosophical Discourse of Modernity*. Furthermore, Foucault appropriates Kant's critique in an aesthetic, non-normative sense that radically differs from Habermas's neo-Kantian use of the same term. As we will see, Foucault's critique, together with genealogy, is at work in the very practices of self-constitution that, beyond epistemological claims, translate an ethics of thought and an aesthetics of existence.

---

[8] Cf. Edmund Husserl, *The Crisis of European Sciences and Transcendental Phenomenology*, trans. David Carr, (Evanston: Northwestern University Press, 1970). The main themes of the *Krisis* were worked out from 1934 through 1937.
[9] Cf. M. Foucault, *L'archéologie du savoir*, (Paris:Gallimard, 1969), 266
[10] Cf. Gérard Lebrun, "Note sur la phénoménologie dans *Les mots et les choses*, in MFP.
[11] "How Much Does it Cost for Reason to Tell the Truth?," in *Foucault Live*, ed. Sylvère Lotringer, (New York: Semiotext(e), 1989), 236. On Foucault's relationship to Merleau-Ponty and Sartre, cf. "Foucault Responds to Sartre," ibid., 35-43.

What has been called the archaeological method was elaborated in Foucault's first writings --notably, in *Naissance de la clinique* (1963), *Les mots et les choses* (1966), and *L'archéologie du savoir* (1969)-- and has been opposed to the genealogy and hermeneutical analytics of the later works on power and subjectivation. The first two works bear, in effect, the word *"archéologie"* in the subtitle (respectively, *Une archéologie du regard médical* and *Une archéologie des sciences humaines*), although the term had already been used as early as 1954 in *Maladie mentale et personnalité*, a term that Foucault deliberately borrows from Kant's *Fortschritte* address to the 1791 *Preisfrage*.[12] As Foucault would observe later on, both archaeology and genealogy were already at work in an early writing such as his doctoral thesis (*Folie et déraison*, 1961), together with the hermeneutics of subjectivity although none of the three axes were then explicitly delimited as objects of investigation. In fact, the analysis of discursive, epistemic formations in the archaeological investigations does not exclude but rather presupposes the co-originary spaces generated by the other two --i.e., nondiscursive formations of institutions and power networks, as well as the formations of subjects and techniques of the self. The historical a priori can be thus understood as a fourfold, nonhomogeneous "spacetime," as it were, where *savoir*, *pouvoir*, and *subjectivation* define a threefold space and historical time appears as the fourth variable. Of special interest for Foucault is the critique of "épistémologie" and "science," particularly applied to his conception of history as archaeology (from *Les mots et les choses* to *L'archéologie du savoir*).[13] Foucault's critique of historical consciousness as part of the modern anthropological *épistémé* reveals in effect a much earlier concern with the problem of rationality in its classical and modern formulations, as attested by his translation of Kant's *Anthropology* into French (Paris: Vrin, 1962), also reflected in his doctoral thesis, and in the Collège course on the Enlightenment.[14] To be sure, Foucault's interest in Kant dates back to the École Normale courses he took

---

[12] I. Kant, *Über die von der Königl. Akademie der Wissenschaften zu Berlin* ed. W. Weischedel, Band VI (Frankfurt: Suhrkamp, 1977).

[13] The best account of Foucault's critique of French *épistémologie* during the archaeological phase remains, thus far, Roberto Machado's doctoral thesis (Louvain), "Science et Savoir," published in Portuguese, *Ciência e Saber*, (Rio de Janeiro: Graal, 1974).

[14] "Introduction à l'*Anthropologie* de Kant," 128 pp., complementary thesis for the "doctorat ès lettres," Faculté de Paris (typed; Bibliothèque de la Sorbonne)-- this text, together with his translation of Kant's *Anthropology* and his main thesis, *Folie et déraison: Histoire de le folie à l'âge classique*, (Paris: Plon, 1961), fulfilled the formal requirements that allowed Foucault to defend his doctoral dissertation on May 20, 1961, before the committee formed by Georges Canguilhem, Henri Gouhier, Daniel Lagache. The other text on Kant, "Qu'est-ce

with Jean Beaufret, the addressee of Heidegger's "Letter on Humanism." According to Didier Eribon, Beaufret commented and lectured on Kant's *Kritik der Urteilskraft* at the École of rue d'Ulm, with frequent allusions to Heidegger.[15]

The Foucauldian three-axial account of his genealogical enterprise (knowledge, power, subjectivation), in its very radicalization of archaeology, can to a certain extent be regarded as stemming from a historicizing critique of Kant's threefold questioning of the *Critiques* (What can I know? What ought I do? What may I hope?)[16] While the first question is "merely speculative" and constitutes the object of the first *Kritik*, the second is "purely practical" and the third "at once practical and theoretical," and both are dealt with in the *Critique of Practical Reason* and in the *Critique of Judgment*. To these questions Kant later adds a fourth question, in the Introduction to his course on *Logic*, namely, "What is man? [*Was ist der Mensch?*]," and makes the intriguing remark that all the other three questions may well be brought back to *anthropology* insofar as they all relate to the last question.[17] For Foucault, it is this modern, anthropocentric revolution that consolidates the humanistic fate of Western philosophy and its subsequent disintegration and self-overcoming in the aftermath of the death of God. As in Heidegger's reading of Kant, it is the anthropocentric gesture that translates and betrays the Kantian project not so much in its attempt to elaborate a "philosophical anthropology" but rather as the idea of a new metaphysics, a "fundamental ontology."[18] Foucault's reading of Kant thus takes Heidegger's destruction of the onto-theo-logic into account, but also remains attentive to Kant's classification of his "pragmatic anthropology" between an "empirical psychology" (or "theoretical anthropology") and a "moral anthropology." Thus the *Aufklärung* metaphor of growing up, coming of age (*Mündigkeit*), translates for Foucault an *ethos*, "a philosophical life in which the critique of what we are is at one and the same time the historical analysis of the limits that are imposed on us and an experiment with the possibility of going beyond them." (FR 50) Now,

---

que les lumières?" was first published in the *Magazine littéraire* 207 (May 1984); English translation in FR 32-50.

[15] Cf. Didier Eribon, *Michel Foucault (1926-1984)*, (Paris: Flammarion, 1989), 49.

[16] Cf. Immanuel Kant, *Critique of Pure Reason*, trans. Norman K. Smith, (New York: Saint Martin's Press, 1965), 635ff.; *Les mots et les choses*, p. 352.

[17] Immanuel Kant, *Logique* [1800], tr. L. Guillemit, (Paris: Vrin, 1966), 23-25.

[18] Cf. M. Heidegger, *Kant et le problème de la métaphysique*, tr. A. de Waehlens and W. Biemel, (Paris: Gallimard, 1981), p. 170: "Kant, certes, ramène les trois questions de la métaphysique proprement dite à une quatrième question sur l'essence de l'homme; mais il serait prématuré de considérer pour cela cette question comme anthropologique et de confier l'instauration du fondement de la métaphysique à une anthropologie philosophique. L'anthropologie ne suffit pas, du seul fait qu'elle est anthropologie, à fonder la métaphysique."

how does Foucault depart from a (negative) critique of Kant's anthropology towards a (positive) critique of who we are? I think the only plausible way to approach this question is by means of what can be termed a "critique of modernity," characterized by an historical awareness that philosophy articulates with its own constitution as a body of knowledge and truth. Although Kant was one of the precursors of this self-conscious, self-determined attitude toward one's own time, Hegel has been often regarded as the epitome of modernity in the making, thus conceived. It will be seen, throughout this book, why modernity must be viewed rather as an aesthetic, deteleologized *ethos* and as a philosophical attitude towards one's history of the present.

Both Husserl (in the *Krisis*) and Heidegger (in *Die Frage nach dem Ding*) had already explored the constitutive implications of Kant's critique for the phenomenology of human Dasein qua being-in-the-world, its historicity, and *Lebenswelt*.[19] These themes also permeate Foucault's narrative of epistemic formations that lead from the Renaissance system of similitudes to the great breaks of the Classical Age (17th century) and Modernity (18th century). It is important to remark *en passant* that, as Herman Lebovics observes, "Foucault's adaptation of Bachelard's idea, also fruitfully employed by Thomas Kuhn in his notion of a scientific paradigm, should not be so narrowly understood as to allow for only one episteme in any epoch."[20] With this proviso, we can spot the birth of man at the modern epistemological rupture, that signals the transition from a system of representations towards a new unifying paradigm, "man," this "strange empirico-transcendental doublet":

> Whereas Hume made the problem of causality one case in the general interrogation of resemblances, Kant, by isolating causality, reverses the question; whereas before it was a question of establishing relations of identity or difference against the continuous background of similitudes, Kant brings into prominence the inverse problem of the synthesis of the diverse. (OT 162)

---

[19] It is very interesting to undertake a comparative reading of these two works with Foucault's *Les mots et les choses*, and remark how the three works attempt at a critical "reconstruction" of an intellectual history leading to the birth of modernity by undermining traditional conceptions in the history of philosophy. There must be indeed some way of relating Husserl's conception of *Überlieferungsgeschichte* and Heidegger's *Destruktion der Geschichte der Metaphysik* to Foucault's *archéologie des sciences humaines*.
[20] Herman Lebovics, *True France: The Wars Over Cultural Identity 1900-1945*, (Ithaca, NY: Cornell University Press, 1992), 190 n.

Man is also the bearer of being and historicity, a "recent invention" on "the threshold of a modernity that we have not left behind." (OT xxiv) For Foucault, "the threshold of our modernity is situated not by the attempt to apply objective methods to the study of man, but rather by the constitution of an empirico-transcendental doublet which was called *man*." (OT 319) Hence follow the two kinds of analyses proposed by Kant: the transcendental aesthetic and the transcendental dialectic, in that there is a nature of human knowledge that determines its forms and that can at the same time be made manifest to it in its own empirical contents, and that there was a *history* of human knowledge which could both be given to empirical knowledge and prescribe its forms. Kant's discovery of a transcendental field where man figures as the "being such that knowledge will be attained in him of what renders all knowledge possible" (OT 318), is precisely what questions representation, not in accordance with the endless movement that proceeds from the simple element to all its possible combinations, but on the basis of its rightful limits. The critique sanctions for the first time that event in European culture which coincides with the end of eighteenth century: the withdrawal of knowledge and thought outside the space of representation. That space is brought into question in its foundation, its origin, and its limits: and by this very fact, the unlimited field of representation, which Classical thought had established, which Ideology had attempted to scan in accordance with a step-by-step, discursive, scientific method, now appears as a metaphysics. But as a metaphysics that had never stepped out of itself, that had posited itself in an uninformed dogmatism, and that had never brought out into the light the question of its right. (OT 242-3) Foucault goes on to assert that criticism also opens up the possibility of a different sort of metaphysics, making possible the philosophies of Spirit, Life and the Will --indeed Kant is the legitimate precursor of Hegel, Schopenhauer, and Nietzsche, and of contemporary phenomenology as well. Modernity is thus regarded as the age of subjectivity, insofar as the emergence of self-consciousness, self-determination, and historicity reveals the temporal grounds of human finitude. As Deleuze points out, Foucault's indebtedness to Heidegger's reading of Kant is also manifest here:

> According to Kant, time was the form in which the mind affected itself, just as space was the form in which the mind was affected by something else: time was therefore 'auto-affection' and made up the essential structure of subjectivity. But time as subject, or rather subjectivation, is called memory. (F 107)

The Foucauldian "conversion of phenomenology into epistemology" --as Deleuze termed it-- will be dealt with in the fifth chapter. It is sufficient for the purposes of the present study to signal, *en passant*, that the Foucauldian theme of "man and his doubles" (*pli, doublure*, the fold, doubling, etc.) is related to Merleau-Ponty's view of the body qua chiasmus (*le chiasme*) and the reversibility of the inside and outside of space, in a phenomenological attempt to overcome the subject-object opposition.[21] As Deleuze put it, "the double is never a projection of the interior; on the contrary, it is an interiorization of the outside."[22] Because of man's chiasmatic dimension, Foucault goes on to assert that there has been a displacement in relation to the Kantian paradigm in that contemporary thought (phenomenology, from Husserl to Heidegger and Merleau-Ponty) no longer asks "How can experience of nature give rise to necessary judgements?" but rather "How can man think what he does not think, inhabit as though by a mute occupation something that eludes him, animate with a kind of frozen movement that figure of himself that takes the form of a stubborn exteriority?" (OT 323) Thus truth gives way to being, nature to man, the possibility of understanding to the possibility of a primary misunderstanding, and the unaccountable nature of philosophical theories as opposed to science gives way to "a clear philosophical awareness of that whole realm of unaccounted-for experiences in which man does not recognize himself." This fourfold displacement of transcendental philosophy revives, according to Foucault, the theme of the *cogito* --no longer the Cartesian concern with the most general form of thought, but the "I think" that traverses, duplicates, and reactivates "the articulation of thought on everything within it, around it, and beneath it which is not thought, yet which is not foreign to thought, in the sense of an irreducible, an insuperable exteriority" (OT 324). Foucault's quest for who we are is thus situated between the Kantian critique of the representational thought of the Same and the irruption of the Other in the exteriority of thought (OT 325):

> What is man's being, and how can it be that that being, which could so easily be characterized by the fact that 'it has thoughts' and is possibly alone in having them, has an ineradicable and fundamental relation to the unthought?

The archaeological method draws close to Kantian criticism as it seeks to establish the regularities of statements (*énoncés*) preceding propositions that will bind words and things, articulations and visibilities. Just as Kant sought to establish the a priori conditions of the possibility for knowledge, Foucault's archaeology is concerned with a priori conditions (statements and visibilities) that

---

[21] Cf. Maurice Merleau-Ponty, *Le visible et l'invisible*, (Paris: Gallimard, 1964), 172-204: "L'entrelacs: le chiasme;" OT 322-328: "The Cogito and the Unthought."
[22] G. Deleuze, op. cit., 98.

rule over the discursive, epistemic production at a given time, for a given society. Henry Allison has defined Kantian epistemic condition as "one that is necessary for the representation of an object or an objective state of affairs," to be distinguished from the "logical conditions of thought."[23] Foucault does not confuse the two --as many critics of Kant have done-- nor does he use the word *epistémé* in the way Kant does, since he follows Nietzsche in his refusal to embark on a transcendental philosophy of sorts. To focus on the Kantian problem of representation can help us understand the unity of subjectivity, in particular the faculties of human rationality. Foucault recognizes that it was with Kant that the limits of representational thinking reached their ends, at the same time that the articulation of the phenomenal and the noumenal made possible, for the first time in the history of Western thought, the conditions for a "presentation" (*Vorstellung*)[24] of man that broke away from essentialist analogy and play of similitudes. Ironically enough, *Les mots et les choses* was rendered in English as *The Order of Things*, translating thus a Kantian formula, "*Die Ordnung der Dinge*," as applied to the *übersinnliche* as opposed to *Ordnung der Erscheinungen* (GMS III BA 104 ff; Rel III, i, 7 Anm.). While the former is structured according to the laws of freedom, the latter is ruled by the laws of understanding that bind together our representations. It is, therefore, on the level of a transcendental unity of subjectivity and thought, that the conditions of the possibility for all knowledge must precede the interplay of representations. This is the very problematic which allows for the Kantian equation of subject and thinking "I," on a transcendental level that Foucault calls into question throughout his works.

2. KANT AND THE LIMITS OF REPRESENTATION

After Descartes, we have a subject of knowledge which poses for Kant the problem of knowing the relationship between the subject of ethics and that of knowledge. There was much debate in the Enlightenment as to whether these two subjects were completely different or not. Kant's solution was to find a universal subject, which, to the extent that it was universal, could be the subject of knowledge, but which demanded, nonetheless, an ethical attitude--

---

[23] Cf. H.E. Allison, *Kant's Transcendental Idealism: An Interpretation and Defense*, (New Haven: Yale University Press, 1983), 10.
[24] As Pluhar remarks, Kant's usage of *Vorstellung*, even if translated as *repraesentatio*, should not mislead us into reading Kant as a representational thinker which he is not. *Vorstellung* simply refers to objects of awareness such as sensations, intuitions, perceptions, concepts, ideas, schemata. Cf. KrV A 320, B 376; A 140, B 179.

precisely the relationship to the self which Kant proposes in *The Critique of Practical Reason*. (FR 372)

The archaeology elaborated in Foucault's *Order of Things* sought to describe the formation of *connaissances*, in particular, the constitution of the human sciences in light of the formation of interrelated *savoirs*, in their building of conceptual structures. Archaeology was not yet articulated with the genealogical interest in social practices, but remained confined to the discursive practices of epistemic formations. The emergence of the modern human sciences and social, behavioral sciences --history, sociology, psychology, ethnology-- was only made possible with the raise of the empirical sciences --biology, economy, philology-- and modern, critical philosophy in the 19th century, as "man" replaced "similitudes" (Renaissance) and "representations" (Classical Age) as the epistemic paradigm, at once subject and object of knowledge. To represent "man" means something altogether different from the classifying system that ordered things and objects of thought in the Classical Age, up to Destutt de Tracy and the *idéologues* at the turn of the eighteenth century. Although Ideology and Kantian criticism had the same point of application --the relation of representations to each other--, Foucault remarks that Kant does not seek what gives this relation its foundation and justification on the same level of representations, but on a transcendental a priori that make representations themselves possible. (OT 241-143) A new metaphysics had to emerge, as "a system of pure rational concepts independent of any conditions of intuition" (MS 375), so that philosophical knowledge could deal with representations. The birth of transcendental philosophy, moreover, is what accounts for the new positivity of the sciences of life, language and economics. For the transcendental field reveals a nonempirical, finite subject that "determines in its relation to an object = x all the formal conditions of experience in general," making possible the synthesis between representations. Furthermore, as Foucault remarks,

> ...the conditions of possibility of experience are being sought in the conditions of possibility of the object and its existence, whereas in transcendental reflection the conditions of possibility of the objects of experience are identified with the conditions of possibility of experience itself. (OT 244)

Foucault mentions then how pre-critical metaphysics (although post-Kantian in their chronology) and positivism will follow on the objectivation of transcendentals (like a posteriori syntheses), along with the emergence of those empirical fields. This irony in the history of transcendental philosophy is, according to Foucault, what links Hegelian phenomenology ("the totality of the empirical domain was taken back into the interior of consciousness revealing itself to itself as Spirit") to Husserl's phenomenology ("to anchor the rights and limitations of a formal logic in a reflection of the transcendental type, and also to link transcendental subjectivity to the implicit horizon of empirical contents").[25] And he adds:

> It is probably impossible to give empirical contents transcendental value, or to displace them in the direction of a constituent subjectivity, without giving rise, at least silently, to an anthropology --that is, to a mode of thought in which the rightful limitations of acquired knowledge (and consequently of all empirical knowledge) are at the same time the concrete forms of existence, precisely as they are given in that same empirical knowledge. (OT 248)

Since Foucault's critique of transcendental subjectivity will be only fully explored in the fifth chapter, we must turn now to the anthropological question proper, such as it was pursued by Kant in his articulation of practical and theoretical philosophy. To begin with, it must be recalled that for Kant, the object of anthropology is defined in terms of a knowledge of human rationality, where man is understood, at once, as the being endowed with reason that he is (*animal rationabile*) and as the rational being he ought to be (*animal rationale*)(Anth B IV, 673).[26] It is very instructive that Kant's conception of man's *Sollen* is found in an earlier writing such as "Idee zu einer allgemeinen Geschichte in weltbürgerlicher Absicht" (1784) and in later writings such as the *Metaphysik der Sitten* (1797) and the *Anthropologie* (1798). In those texts human nature is articulated in terms of rationality and historicity in such a manner that his political philosophy is made dependent on moral philosophy. According to Kant, history is concerned with narrating the appearances of freedom of the will, or human actions, which like other natural events are determined by universal laws. (OH 11) Kant proceeds then to formulate nine theses on the idea of such a universal history, stating *inter alia*, some of the teleological principles that will recur in the third *Critique*, such as "all natural capacities of a creature are destined to evolve completely to their natural end" and that, because he is the only rational creature on earth, man's "natural capacities which are directed to the use of his reason are to be fully developed only in the race, not in the individual." (Theses 1 and 2)

---

[25] Cf. also Jean-François Lyotard, *La phénoménologie*, (Paris: PUF, 1954), 40-44.
[26] Cf. Foucault's translation into French, *Anthropologie du point de vue pragmatique*, 2e.éd., (Paris: Vrin, 1970), 161.

These are in full agreement with the conceptions of the *sensus communis* and intersubjectivity that Kant will articulate in the KU, when dealing with the problem of obtaining a transcendental deduction of judgments of taste. Of particular importance for a study of Kant's philosophy of history are theses 5, 8, and 9 (OH 23):

5. The greatest problem for the human race, to the solution of which Nature drives man, is the achievement of a universal civic society which administers law among men.
8. The history of mankind can be seen, in the large, as the realization of Nature's secret plan to bring forth a perfectly constituted state as the only condition in which the capacities of mankind can be fully developed, and also bring forth that external relation among states which is perfectly adequate to this end.
9. A philosophical attempt to work out a universal history according to a natural plan directed to achieving the civic union of the human race must be regarded as possible and, indeed, as contributing to this end of Nature.

Since Kant anticipates Hegel's dialectics by assigning to human "antagonism in society" the means employed by Nature to bring about the development of all capacities of men, it is possible to assert, with Yirmiahu Yovel, that the major purpose of the human race is to realize in history the highest good, namely, the good will (GMS 396; KpV 110), "as the worthiness to be happy." By "antagonism" Kant means "the unsocial sociability of men, i.e., their propensity to enter into society, bound together with a mutual opposition which constantly threatens to break up the society." (OH 15) Thus Kant goes on to observe that the question "How is the highest good practically possible?" remains "an unsolved problem in spite all previous attempts at conciliation," due to the fact that happiness and morality belong to two different realms, so that the *summum bonum* is indeed a "synthesis of concepts," namely, of nature and freedom. (KpV 112-113) Such is in effect the messianic, eschatological dimension of Kant's philosophy of history, as the meaning of the "kingdom of ends" lies in the ethical community and its moral universality. (Rel 101-2, passim)[27]

We can now approach the Kantian articulation of representations in his first *Critique* without reducing his overall project to a theory of knowledge, on the one hand, nor to a disguised theory of morals, on the other. In effect, as Denis

---

[27] Cf. Yirmiahu Yovel, *Kant and the Philosophy of History*, (Princeton, NJ: Princeton University Press, 1980).

Rosenfield has shown in his seminal study on evil,[28] Kant's moral philosophy is indeed to be regarded as a reflection on the *humanum*, a philosophical anthropology *lato sensu*, as the study of "what man as a free agent makes or can and should make of himself" (Anth 119; DM 45). That allows for the new metaphysics to draw the fundamental distinction between the phenomenal and noumenal realms:

> The formal distinction between man's sensible and rational nature would be confirmed by the process through which reason builds its rules for knowing, thinking, and acting, which, on their turn, validate this presupposition. (DM 54)

Foucault himself recognizes that Kant's practical philosophy appears as the solution to the two ethical traditions that the West has known thus far:

> The old one (in the form of Stoicism or Epicureanism), which was articulated upon the order of the world, and by discovering the law of that order it could deduce from it the code of a principle, a code of wisdom or a conception of the city; even the political thought of the eighteenth century still belongs to this general form. The modern one, on the other hand, formulates no morality, since any imperative is lodged within thought and its movement towards the apprehension of the unthought. (OT 328)

And he remarks, in a footnote: "The Kantian moment is the link between the two: it is the discovery that the subject, in so far as he is reasonable, applies to himself his own law, which is the universal law." (OT 343) Indeed, with the formulation of the categorical imperative (GMS 422, 429) --in its three versions stressing respectively the principle of universalizability, the teleology of human nature, and the realm of ends-- what "is represented as necessary by the imperative" (*den Imperativ eigentlich als notwendig vorstellt*) is the conformity of the maxim of action to the universality of the moral law. Theoretical reason, as it was critically examined in the KrV, was proved incapable of knowing through intelligible intuition, and that is why *Verstand* occupied the central role in the staging of a knowledge that brought together *Anschauungen* and *Begriffe*, *erkennen* and *denken*. Kant set out to write the second *Critique* in order to examine the self-active character of the same thinking being staged in the first

---

[28] Denis L. Rosenfield, *On Evil: Introducing the Concept of Evil in Philosophy*, (French translation: *Du Mal*, Aubier, 1990). I am relying on the Brazilian edition, *Do mal: Para introduzir em filosofia o conceito de mal*, trans. Marco Antonio Zingano, (Porto Alegre: L&PM, 1988). Hereafter, DM.

Critique (KrV §§ 16-25). The pure practical *Vernunft* is therefore what defines man as an essentially practical being, where the Idea of Freedom appears as the only knowable idea, as the very condition of the moral law that makes us free, rational beings. And yet, the questions: How do representations relate to our being?, How is human nature to be represented?, remain to be systematized beyond the boundaries (i.e., opposing theoretical to practical reason) established by what has been known as transcendental idealism. Before I proceed to examine the Kantian conception of practical reason vis-à-vis his metaphysics of human nature, a few remarks must be made on the use of *Vorstellungen* in the first *Critique*. The entire *Critique* is, to a large extent, devoted to the criticism of phenomenalistic idealism, according to which representations would be reduced to mere "appearances." When Kant sets out to investigate how a priori synthetic knowledge is made possible, he is embarking on a long journey that will bring both analytic and synthetic judgments together in the task of unifying representations in one single consciousness. For while sensible intuitions rest on affections, concepts rest on functions. "By function," says Kant, "I mean the unity of the act of bringing various representations under one common representation." (KrV A 68, B 93) And he goes on to define judgment as "the mediate knowledge of an object, that is, the representation of a representation of it." In his refusal of psychological idealism, Kant refers to the end of the first chapter of the Transcendental Dialectic, where he alters the passage as follows:

> ...all grounds of determination of my existence which are to be met with in me are representations; and as representations themselves require a permanent something distinct from them, in relation to which their change, and so my existence in the time wherein they change, may be determined. (KrV B xl Rem.)

And he says in the next page,

> The representation of something *permanent* in existence is not the same as *permanent representation*. For though the representation of [something permanent] may be very transitory and variable like all our other representations...it yet refers to something permanent. This latter must therefore be an external thing distinct from all may representations, and its existence must be included in the *determination* of my own existence, constituting with it but a single experience such as would not take place even inwardly if it were not also at the same time, in part, outer. (B xli)

Insofar as they are determinations of the mind, all representations belong to our inner state, which ultimately belongs to time (KrV B 50, A 34). Hence all representations have a necessary relation to a possible empirical consciousness (A 118), since it must be possible for the "I think" to accompany all my representations (B 131). On the other hand, Kant defines intuition as "the representation which can be given prior to all thought." In this sense, the representation "I think" cannot be accompanied by any further representation, since it refers not to an empirical apperception, but to a pure apperception, whose unity is also called "the transcendental unity of self-consciousness." (B 132) In brief, representations in general designate the genus, under which are subordinate both intuitions and concepts, through the immediate or mediated objective perception of an object. (A 320, B 377) Foucault sought to show, in *Les mots et les choses*, that Kant's philosophy maintained the "limits of representations" in the very articulation of the empirico-transcendental doublet. It is only after having reached the limits of representations in the first *Critique* that we may venture now to explore the bounds of a "practical" metaphysics of human nature.

3. THE CRITIQUE OF METAPHYSICAL REASON

Ich frug mich nemlich selbst: auf welchem Grunde beruhet die Beziehung desienigen, was man in uns Vorstellung nennt, auf den Gegenstand? *Brief an Markus Herz*, 21. Feb. 1772

Kant's itinerary from the 1770 dissertation through the composition of the three *Critiques* is visibly marked by a constant preoccupation with the relations between representations, between the knowing subject and the object represented, and the grounds for establishing such relations. Since our understanding is not the cause of objects --either by passive representations (*intellectus ectypus*) or by active representations (*intellectus archetypus*),-- Kant sought the source of their concepts in "the nature of the soul" (*in der Natur der Seele*), more specifically, in the faculties of the mind (*Gemütsvermögen*). In a pre-critical writing of 1764, "Enquiry Concerning the Clarity of the Principles of Natural Theology and Ethics" (Second Reflection), Kant defined metaphysics as "nothing other than a philosophy of the first principles of our knowledge [*Die Metaphysik ist nichts anders als eine Philosophie über die ersten Gründe unseres Erkenntnisses*]." (A 79) In the preface to GMS, metaphysics is defined, in opposition to the merely formal approach of logic, as the science that deals with "definite objects of understanding" (GMS 388) and their laws (such as the laws of nature and moral laws). Moreover, Kant draws an opposition, within the field of ethics, between practical anthropology and the a priori part of the theory of morality, dealing respectively with empirical and pure moral sciences. A metaphysics of morals is supposed to furnish the grounds or foundations of obligation, which are "not to be sought in the nature of man or in the circumstances in which he is placed, but sought a priori solely in the concepts of pure reason." (GMS 389) Therefore, Kant is simply asserting that morality precedes anthropology, and not the other way round. In sum, according to Kant's morality, there must be universalizable rules that can be adopted by every rational being and human beings, on their turn, are such beings endowed with reason, who ought to act, therefore, in accordance with these universalizable rules. Now, that human beings are endowed with reason -- hence ought to act as rational beings-- remains an anthropological presupposition that Kant tacitly assimilates into his teleology of human nature. However misleading it may sound, to speak of a "metaphysics of human nature" refers, in this context, to the limit-thoughts on human nature, in light of Kant's own taxonomies. In a revealing footnote to the third version of the categorical imperative, Kant remarks:

> Teleology considers nature as a realm of ends; morals regards a possible realm of ends as a realm of nature. In the former the realm of ends is a theoretical Idea for the explanation of what actually is. In the latter it is a practical Idea for bringing about that which does not exist but which can become actual through our conduct and for making it conform with this Idea. (GMS 437)

And he proceeds to define the specificity of this teleology of human nature "in that it proposes an end to itself." Although there is no such a thing as "natural morality," Kant maintains that man has indeed a disposition to morality by nature. Just as Aristotle maintained that, *kata physin*, man is a "political" animal and the only animal in possession of *logos* (Politics I.i. 9-10), Kant's theory of teleology is what accounts, in the last analysis, for mankind's potential progress towards the partial fulfillment of the highest good and the establishment of a moral commonwealth, by bringing about a reconciliation of practical and theoretical philosophy. To be sure, Kant's ethics cannot be identified with the teleological naturalism that characterizes the Aristotelian eudaimonism, being rather described as a deontological or duty-based ethics (in opposition to an areteic or virtue-based ethics, though socially acquired by habituation). For Kant, human beings should rationally explore their natural resources so as to achieve a socially just world order. Thus, the classical problematic of opposing freedom to nature finds its solution in the very understanding of human nature. In the Preface to the *Anthropologie*, Kant draws the distinction between Physiological Anthropology -- which deals with nature's work on man-- and Pragmatic Anthropology --which deals with man qua "citizen of the world" (*Weltbürger*), a pragmatic knowledge (*Erkenntnis*) that regards man as a free being. It is certainly the case that, as Hannah Arendt has shown, the aesthetic field of Kant's *Critique of Judgment* must be brought into this discussion in order to fully understand the articulation of practical and theoretical reason.[29] The third *Kritik* will be examined in the fourth section, as it will lead us to the problem of Nietzsche's reading of Kant and Foucault's aestheticism --to be dealt with in the fifth chapter.

For now, what really interests us here is the problem raised by Kant's opposition of man's dispositions (technical, pragmatic, and moral) qua progressive characterizations of the species to their negation in radical evil, in a will that deliberately transgresses all the maxims that ground moral law: "Dieses Böse ist *radikal*, weil es den Grund aller Maximen verdirbt" (Rel I 3) Evil is precisely what accounts for man's natural and paradoxical "unsocial sociability" mentioned above. As Rosenfield has argued, "the Kantian concept of action does not refer exclusively to the moral domain, but to *action in general*, to the very concept of human action. The universality and the formal character of moral propositions have an ontological reach regarding a questioning on the essence of man." (DM 43) Thus, in order to understand Kant's practical philosophy one must examine the relationship between nature and human nature so as to fully grasp the metaphysical structure of man, at once a sensible and intelligible being. (DM 43) Kant's "anthropological problem," as Rosenfield remarks, "is that of a formal universality, of a creative power of reason whose essentially moral trait is its distinctive sign." (DM 38) This is certainly the most important feature of Kant's anthropology, that it should not be mistaken for an analysis of human, empirical behavior but rather in the sense of that which makes human beings human. For moral propositions are to be derived from the concept of practical reason, in their process of elaboration, presupposing an anthropological ground, a veritable "metaphysics of man." (DM 38) True humanity, accordingly, is not the bearer of evil, since morality is the true mark of humanness.

It is well known how the second *Critique* (1788) came out as a systematic attempt to provide the transcendental foundations that were only announced in the simplified introduction to Kant's moral philosophy, the *Grundlegung zur Metaphysik der Sitte* of 1785. According to Foucault, the Kantian problematic of

---

[29] Cf. H. Arendt, *Lectures on Kant's Political Philosophy*, (Chicago: University of Chicago Press, 1982).

opposing the theoretical cognition of the KrV to the practical cognition of the KpV, i.e., of what is the case to what ought to be done, is better understood in the very articulation of the empirico-transcendental double that was already introduced in the first *Critique*. In effect, if the KrV had shown the possibility of a suprasensible order of things it is in the KpV that we come to the cognition of the freedom of the will and the moral law --the fact of reason--, that constitute together the practical knowledge (*Wissen*), i.e., objectively adequate assent. As we have seen, the KrV set out to examine the scope and limits of our cognitive faculties by undertaking a rigorous critique of dogmatic metaphysics, in particular, rationalism and empiricism, to conclude that we can know only the natural, phenomenal world, as we experience it, in opposition to the noumenal realm of freedom and of the things in themselves (the suprasensible). Foucault has pointed to the limits of representations in the formulation of a transcendental ego, in the KrV, where self-consciousness was on the boundaries of the practical reason, where the moral law was given to us a priori, as a fact of reason, that we have a moral consciousness. A question that is raised at the boundaries of consciousness and its self-constituted representations that reveal a subjectivity, is how "the consciousness of the fundamental moral law," the so-called "fact of reason," constitutes its practical object? How, for one, does freedom arise in the horizon of human experience? (KpV § 8)

In KpV 162-3 we are reminded that, if on the one hand, the principle of autonomy proves to be foundational only in the practical use of reason, on the other hand, the fundamental interest of reason is eminently practical. Contrasting with the Kantian analysis that distinguishes the uses of reason, the Hegelian synthesis will seek to reconcile the theoretical and the practical interests in the speculative unity of dialectical reason. That is why we must verify how such an ideal principle of rational autonomy is justified in the practical-ethical field. Even before delving into a rereading of Hegel's critique of Kant in Excursus One, I must remark that the idea of a rational self-determination of ethics appears as the first commonplace between Kant and Hegel, in opposition to traditional conceptions that privilege the ends of action, taken empirically or materially conceived in the proposal of moral foundation. According to Kant, the critical philosopher cannot appeal to "empirical principles" in order to found his or her moral doctrine (*Sittenlehre*) nor can even "lay as foundation any intuition (of the pure noumenon)," but can legitimately add to the "will empirically affected" the "moral law". (KpV 165) At any rate, the Kantian distinction between *Verstand* and *Vernunft* as superior faculties of knowledge, invoked in the KrV in the theoretical field of the former (nature), should also be presupposed in the practical field of freedom, through which is articulated the practical use of pure reason. As much can be said of the Kantian distinction between *Recht* and *Moral*. As Kenneth Baynes has argued in his meticulous study of Kant's theory of justice,

> ...Kant not only drew a sharp distinction between the realm of legality and the realm of morality, he also claimed that progress in the former does not insure any improvement in the latter. Moral improvement consists in greater conformity of the agent's maxims to the categorical imperative, but no amount of coercive legislation can create a good will. Moreover, Kant believed that the task of creating a just political order could be solved by a "race of devils" as long as they possessed understanding, that is, *Verstand* in contrast to *Vernunft*. (NGC 12)[30]

The pure moral law appears, therefore, as the genuine motive of pure practical reason. Far from being a mere formula that "illustrates" the principle of autonomy, the categorical imperative is in fact "the fundamental law of the pure practical reason [*Grundgesetz der reinen praktischen Vernunft*]":

> The practical rule is, therefore, unconditional and thus is thought of a priori as a categorically practical proposition. The practical rule, which is thus here a law, absolutely and directly determines the will objectively, for pure reason, practical in itself, is here directly legislative. The will is thought of as independent of empirical conditions and consequently as pure will, determined by the pure form of the law, and this ground of determination is regarded as the supreme condition of all maxims. (KpV 55)

It is thus necessary to recognize such a fundamental law as "synthetic a priori proposition," whose consciousness Kant calls the "fact of reason" (*Faktum der Vernunft*), anterior to the very consciousness of freedom, and whose universality and necessity --required by a law valid for all rational beings, endowed with a will-- constitute it as "principle of morality" (*Prinzip der Sittlichkeit*). Only then Kant proceeds to define the autonomy of the will as the single principle of all the moral laws, in fact, "the only principle of morality [*das alleinige Prinzip der Sittlichkeit*]." (KpV § 8) In order to do full justice to the complexity of Kant's transcendental system, the categorical imperative should be understood in terms of the articulation between the KrV and the KpV, in light of the problematic enunciated in the preface to the KpV (when defining freedom as *ratio cognoscendi* of the moral law, and the latter as *ratio essendi* of the former) and being presupposed the transitions described in the GMS. In this manner, the

---

[30] Kenneth Baynes, *The Normative Grounds of Social Criticism: Kant, Rawls, Habermas*, (Albany, NY: SUNY Press, 1992).

formula of the principle of the autonomy of the will expressed by different versions of the categorical imperative in the Second Section of the *Foundations* (GMS 52-83) would problematize the appearance of a particular case of a conformity to the ends of nature, merely formal, but would also account for the historical empeiria. As Rosenfield remarks,

> The force of the Kantian argumentation resides perhaps in this double conjunction of the formal process of the construction of arguments within which what stems from history is purified from its contingent aspects, acquiring the dimension of a pure synthetic construction. (DM 28)

After all, the philosophy of history in Kant keeps the noumenal-phenomenal duality as a starting point to distinguish the "a priori thread" of a *Weltgeschichte* in opposition to the *Historie* empirically constituted.[31] Although the question of subjectivation in relation to truth and power will be fully articulated in the fifth chapter, I have sought to outline here the Kantian milieu which gives rise to the archaeological field of researches undertaken by Foucault and paves the way for a genealogy of modernity.

4. AESTHETICS AND ETHICS IN THE THIRD *CRITIQUE*

Allein in der Familie der oberen Erkenntnisvermögen gibt es doch noch ein Mittelglied zwischen dem Verstand und der Vernunft. Dieses ist die Urteilskraft, von welcher man Ursache hat, nach der Analogie zu vermuten, daß sie eben sowohl, wenn gleich nicht eine eigene Gesetzgebung, doch ein ihr eigenes Prinzip, nach Gesetzen zu suchen... (KU B XXI)

The problem of articulating the higher faculties[32] of cognition (*Verstand, Vernunft, Urteilskraft*) and the three *Critiques* as a function of Kant's transcendental system as a whole has been the object of different interpretations, from the various formulations of German idealism to our day. Part of the problematic had been delineated by Kant himself, in particular, in the Introduction to the second edition of the third *Critique* (1793). Still in the Preface to the first

---

[31] Cf. the ninth proposition of Kant's "Idee zu einer Allgemeinen Geschichte in Weltbürgerlicher Absicht," quoted above.
[32] Although taking into account Werner Pluhar's English translation of KU, I decided to maintain certain terms translated otherwise, so as to avoid confusion with their English homonyms: "Faculty" translates thus *Vermögen*, to be distinguished from "power" (*Macht* in Nietzsche and *pouvoir* in Foucault). Cf. KU ET 3 n.3.

edition of 1790, Kant defines the twofold concern of investigating whether the faculty of judgment[33] also has a priori principles of its own, whether these are constitutive or merely regulative, and whether this faculty gives the rule a priori to the feeling of pleasure and displeasure, the mediating link between the faculty of cognition (*Erkenntnisvermögen*) in general and the faculty of desire (*Begehrungsvermögen*). (V-VI) According to Kant, the unity of the theoretical and practical uses of pure reason must be assured by "the unity of the suprasensible" (*Einheit des Übersinnlichen*), although the cognition of the latter cannot be possible either from a theoretical or from a practical standpoint. What had been delimited, in a negative sense, in the theoretical use of pure reason is manifest by the practical use of reason, now considered in light of the concept of purposiveness (*Endzweckmäßigkeit*) in nature:

> The understanding, inasmuch as it can give laws to nature a priori, proves that we cognize nature only as appearance [*als Erscheinung*], and hence at the same time points to a super-sensible substrate [*ein übersinnliches Substrat*] of nature; but it leaves this substrate wholly *undetermined* [*unbestimmt*]. Judgment [*Beurteilung*], through its a priori principle of judging nature in terms of possible particular laws of nature, provides nature's suprasensible substrate (within as well outside us) with *determinability* [*Bestimmbarkeit*] by the intellectual faculty. But reason, through its a priori practical law, gives this same substrate *determination* [*Bestimmung*]. Thus the faculty of judgment [*Urteilskraft*] makes possible the transition [*Übergang*] from the domain of the concept of nature to that the concept of freedom. (KU LVI)

According to Gérard Lebrun and Jean-François Lyotard, the KU is to a large extent concerned with the transition (*Übergang*) from the mode of thinking about nature to the mode of thinking about freedom. (B XX)[34] Another thorough study on *Organism and System in Kant*[35], examines the problematic of systematicity in Kant's philosophy, in terms of teleological reflective judgments. These studies are here invoked, together with texts by Gilles Deleuze, Donald Crawford, and Valerio Rohden,[36] with a view to providing the critical-textual background to the

---

[33] I will seek to distingush between *Urteilskraft*, *Beurteilung*, and *Urteil*, respectively translated as "faculty of judgment," "judging," and "judgment."
[34] Cf. G. Lebrun, *Kant et la fin de la métaphysique* (Paris: Armand Collin, 1970); J.-F. Lyotard, *Leçons sur l'analytique du sublime* (Paris: Galilée, 1991).
[35] António Marques, *Organismo e Sistema em Kant: Ensaio sobre o Sistema Crítico Kantiano*. Lisboa: Editorial Presença, 1987.
[36] Gilles Deleuze, *La philosophie critique de Kant*, (Paris: PUF, 1975); Donald Crawford, *Kant's Aesthetic Theory*, (Madison: The University of Wisconsin Press, 1974); Valerio

work of Kant as a whole, in light of which a particular problem will be developed, namely, the relation between aestethics and ethics in the third *Critique*. In particular, I will examine Donald Crawford's work on Kant's aestethics, so as to raise the problem of what would be an "aestheticist" solution to the problem of the unity of the three *Critiques*, and how it relates to Nietzsche's and Foucault's aestheticism. Just as the Marburg Neo-Kantians tended to reduce Kant's philosophy to an *Erkenntnistheorie*, his practical philosophy can be easily turned into a moralism or into an aestheticism, depending on how the conceptions of moral teleology and aesthetic judgments are articulated in relation to reality. In effect, we find in both Schopenhauer and Schiller an aestheticist critique of German idealism --that exerted a decisive influence on Nietzsche-- and that would be revived by the post-modern critique of modernity and the Enlightenment. The question of aestheticism in both Nietzsche and Foucault will be dealt with in Excursus Two and in the last sections of the next chapters.

In his work on Kant's aesthetic theory (hereafter, AT), Crawford starts from the fundamental thesis that cognition is essentially judicative, so as to render possible the articulation of judgments as theoretical, practical, and aesthetic propositional formulations. Both in the first and in the second *Critiques*, understanding and reason presuppose the agreement, by judgment, of the faculties between themselves. Thus as the theoretical judgment expresses the agreement of the faculties in the determination of the object according to understanding, likewise the practical judgment presupposes the agreement of understanding with the reason that presides it, in the determination of actions that are conformed to the moral law. A crucial difference of the third *Critique* in relation to the other two consists precisely in the focus given to the faculty of reflective judgment in the KU, expressing thus the free and indeterminate agreement between the faculties. The question of the deduction of judgments is formulated in a priori terms in the KU by the universal and necessary validity of aesthetic reflective judgments. Thus, as in the KrV it was shown how synthetic judgments are possible a priori and the KpV enunciated the principle of the autonomy of the will as a synthetic a priori proposition (§ 7), the third *Critique* is also concerned with the question of knowing "whether and how aesthetic a priori judgments are possible" (KU § 9), that is, with the a priori grounding of judgments of taste as pure, formal aesthetic judgments:

Rohden, *Interesse da Razão e Liberdade*, (São Paulo: Ática, 1981); Valerio Rohden (ed.), *Colóquio Comemorativo da Terceira Crítica*, (Porto Alegre: Editora da Universidade/UFRGS e Goethe Institut, 1990); Valerio Rohden (ed.), *Racionalidade e Ação*, (Porto Alegre: Editora da Universidade /UFRGS e Goethe Institut, 1992).

It is true that in the *Critique of Practical Reason* we did actually derive a priori from universal moral concepts the feeling of respect (a special and peculiar modification of the feeling of pleasure and displeasure which does seem to differ somehow from the both the pleasure and displeasure we get from empirical objects). (...) Now the situation is similar with the pleasure in an aesthetic judgment, except that here the pleasure is merely contemplative, and does not bring about an interest in the object, whereas in a moral judgment it is practical. (KU § 12/ET 67f.)[37]

It is thus a problem of relating the question "how are possible the judgments of the beautiful?" (first book of the Analytic of Aesthetic *Urteilskraft*) to the question of the subjective universality to be established a priori by the transcendental deduction. It must then be assumed that the judgments of taste be analyzed in terms of the four moments of the table of categories (quality, quantity, relation, and modality),--by analogy with the table of the categories in the Analytic of the Pure Concepts of Understanding (KrV §10) and the table of categories of freedom in the Analytic of Pure Practical Reason (KpV A 101). In the first moment, we see that judgments of taste--contrary to the judgments of cognition-- do not subsume representation to a concept but establish the relation between representation and a disinterested liking (*Wohlgefallen*), i.e., regardless of desire and interest (§§ 1-5). In the second place, although expressed by a particular formulation ("This rose is beautiful") the judgment of taste is object of a universal liking, without demanding the universal agreement at the level of sensible pleasure. It would not be the case, paradoxically, of arguing in order to constrain someone by reason to agree with the judgment of taste. (§§ 6-9, cf. § 33) "The beautiful," as is inferred from the second moment, "is what, without a concept, is liked universally." (KU 32) In the third moment, it is concluded that, despite its purposiveness according to the form, the object of the judgment of taste does not present any finality or purpose--*Zweckmäßigkeit ohne Zweck* (§§ 10-17; cf. § 65 and Introduction). Beauty is deduced as being "the form of the object's form of purposiveness insofar as it is perceived in the object without the presentation of a purpose." (KU 61) Finally, in the fourth moment, the beautiful must be a necessary reference to the aesthetic liking (§ 18); not only when we are led to say that such and such object is beautiful, but when we assert that every other person must have the same liking in such an object. Thus we arrive at the question of the legitimation of the necessity of a subjective universality. What is at work here is a transition from the constative expression "it is beautiful," asserted by all, to the transcendental necessity of being thus judged by every

---

[37] Cf. KpV 71-89; MS 211-213.

rational being. "Beautiful is what without a concept is cognized as the object of a necessary liking" (KU § 22) It is therefore a question of recognizing the transcendental deduction --as it was formulated in relation to nature and freedom by pure reason, both theoretical and practical. (LVIII) As Kant put it in succinct and explicit terms, "this problem of the Critique of the Faculty of Judgment is part of the general problem of transcendental philosophy: how are synthetic judgments possible a priori?" (KU § 36/ ET 153) Without falling into a structuralist systematization of the Kantian architectonic, Crawford tries to rescue the properly transcendental sense of the deduction, through an articulation between aesthetics and ethics. His thesis differs from other interpretations not only as for the role of the KU in relation to the KrV and to the KpV, but also insofar as the harmony of the faculties is concerned, whether it is based on a rational, epistemological requirement (as argues Paul Guyer)[38] or on the universal communicability of representations (sensible, rational or aesthetic), i.e., not so much in the intersubjectivity that prevails over the individual interests, but as it refers us to the transcendental deduction --such is the main thesis defended by Crawford. Accordingly, the transcendental deduction in the KU can be understood through the five distinct stages that culminate with the articulation between aesthetics and morality, as the essential moment in the argumentation of the Kantian thesis that judgments of taste do not relate a representation to a concept (KU § 8) but, as sub-species of aesthetic judgments, refer a particular intuition to the feeling of pleasure in the subject that judges at the same time as it presents universal validity (disinterest). Hence the correlation to be established between the solution of the antinomy and the fifth stage. According to Crawford,

> The complete deduction of the judgments of taste must thus show the basis for having interest in the beautiful and in its judging. This basis must be found precisely in the link between beauty and morality. Since beauty is the symbol of the basis of morality, there is a basis for demanding the agreement with the judgments of taste, for the demand of the moral sensibility on the part of all human beings is justifiable. (AT 28)

Crawford divides the central argument of the KU in 5 stages, each one constituting a fundamental aspect of the transcendental deduction so that it will be valid for every rational being, requiring its agreement, and not only as an expression of a personal liking of the object. As the judgment of taste is regarded as an aesthetic judgment and not only as an expression of sensible pleasure ("this

---

[38] Cf. Paul Guyer, *Kant and the Claims of Taste*, (Cambridge, Mass.: Harvard University Press, 1979), in particular, chapter 11: "Aesthetics and Morality."

song is agreeable to my ears" in opposition to "this song is beautiful"), it is a matter of clarifying how the foundation of pleasure in the beautiful takes place. According to Crawford, we could thus summarily expose the five stages:

At Stage I, the transcendental deduction appears as the positive exposition of what had been negatively exposed in the Analytic of the Beautiful (pleasure in the beautiful cannot be based on interest, on the good, or on whatever is merely agreeable to the senses, emotions or perfections). The deduction envisages therefore explain how, by taking pleasure in the beautiful, it attains the legitimation of the Kantian distinction between judgments of taste and other judgments. The conclusion of the first stage is that pleasure in the beautiful must be based on a universally communicable state of mind (*die allgemeine Mitteilungsfähigkeit des Gemütszustandes*). It would not be the case of giving content to such state of mind before arguing that there is such a state. This must be presupposed, necessarily, so that judgments of taste be made possible. What is at stake is not the discussion whether it is legitimate or even reasonable. (§ 9)

At Stage II, we conclude that such a universally communicable state of mind must be based upon the cognitive faculties --imagination (*Einbildungskraft*) and understanding (*Verstand*)-- which are related in a "free play" that makes it knowable --since, for Kant, only cognition and representations can be said to be "universally communicable." (AT 67) If the judgments of taste must be legitimate, pleasure as the consciousness of the harmony of cognitive faculties must be presented as "the universal communicability of the mental state in the given presentation, which underlies the judgment of taste as its subjective condition, and the pleasure in the object must be its consequence." (KU § 9/ ET 61) In other words, the cognitive faculties must be in harmony, in a free play, however without being determined by concepts so that the merely subjective (aesthetic) judging of the object or of the representation precedes the pleasure in the object and founds it in the harmony of the faculties of cognition.

At Stage III, the focus is the question of the conformity to formal purposiveness. It is then asserted that the harmony of cognitive faculties must be based on the mere conformity to the formal purposiveness of the object, to be differentiated from the fact that such an object has a definite purpose (in the case of conceptual judgment). In the experience of the beautiful, we reflect on the purposiveness (design, regularity that can be regulated) of the internal characteristics and of the relations of the object as it is experienced. It is at this stage that the subjective experience of the one who judges (*beurteilen*) is linked to the formal qualities of the appreciated object. The aesthetic judgment, contrary to logical judgments, "refers the representing [*Vorstellen*], by which an object is given, solely to the subject; it brings to our notice no characteristic of the object, but only the purposive form in the [way] the faculties of representation are determined in their engagement with the object." (KU § 15/ET 75) That is indeed the very reason why it is called an "aesthetic" judgment, as the basis determining it is "not a concept but a feeling of that accordance in the play on the mental faculties [*Gemütsvermögen*] insofar as it can be only sensed."

Stage IV is dedicated to common sense (*Gemeinsinn*). The procedure of the faculty of reflective judgment in the reflection on the beautiful --the harmonious interrelation of the cognitive faculties in a general reflection on the formal purposiveness of the experienced object-- is the procedure that must be exercised in the commonest experience, i.e., whatever be the experience. Pleasure in the beautiful is therefore based on the subjective element that we can presuppose in all human beings, since they are necessary for all possible cognition. Such an element or common principle is the *sensus communis*, not in the vulgar sense of a concept-ruled set of beliefs, but as "ideal norm" that cannot be grounded in experience, but requires the universal assent (*allgemeine Beistimmung*) – "it does not say that everyone *will* agree with my judgment, but that he *ought* to." (KU § 22) Kant is thus very careful to distinguish *sensus communis* from the "common human understanding," which is not relevant to the KU:

> ...we must take *sensus communis* to mean the idea of a sense *shared* [by all of us], i.e., a power to judge that in reflecting takes account (a priori), in our thought, of everyone's way of presenting [something], in order *as it were* to compare our own judgment with human reason in general and thus escape the illusion that arises from the ease of mistaking subjective and private conditions for objective ones, an illusion that would have a prejudicial influence on the judgment. (KU § 40)

Crawford concludes that the subjective principle subjacent to the judgments of taste is analogous to the subjective principle subjacent to all the other judgments, and this must be seen as a necessary assumption for all possible experience. Finally, at Stage V, Crawford proposes the fundamental articulation between aesthetics and morality as a decisive moment in the transcendental deduction, for only here the mere universal communicability of the feeling of pleasure can be imputed to any other person as a duty. The *sensus communis* as a principle that underlies the faculty of judgment is a condition for every experience but does not constitute an argument that completes the deduction of the judgments of taste for it neither explains nor legitimizes the fact that we require pleasure in the beautiful from other persons as necessary. The pleasure that we feel in the judgment of taste is required from everyone, on the contrary, as a duty (*Pflicht*)

(KU § 40), as we require universal agreement (KU § 8) and blame others if they deny the taste. (§ 7) It is necessary that the deduction be thus "completed" with the question of the interest, which in its turn, establishes the link between beauty and morality. Since the beautiful is the symbol of the morally good ("das Schöne ist das Symbol des Sittlichguten," KU § 59) it is thus required the agreement in the judgments of taste, for the demand of moral sensibility in all human beings is justifiable. (AT 143-5) According to Crawford, the stages I through IV of the deduction constitute the deduction of universal communicability, while the stage V constitutes the transitory moment for the realm of morality.

5. CONCLUSION: THE CRITIQUE AND THE END OF MAN

...de cette critique, nous avons reçu le modèle depuis plus d'un démi-siècle. L'entreprise nietzschéenne pourrait être comprise comme un point d'arrêt enfin donnée à la prolifération de l'interrogation sur l'homme. La mort de Dieu n'est-elle pas en effet manisfestée dans un geste doublement meurtrier qui, en mettant un terme à l'absolu, est en même temps l'assassin de l'homme lui-même. Car l'homme, dans sa finitude, n'est pas séparable de l'infini dont il est à la fois la négation et le hérault. C'est dans la mort de l'homme que s'accomplit la mort de Dieu. (*Introduction à l'"Anthropologie" de Kant*, 126f.)

Kant's quest for the truth of man, according to Foucault, finds no response in the system of transcendental idealism and its subsequent criticisms, which will indeed depart from the ideal of personality (second version of the categorical imperative) towards the embodiment of freedom in the historical experiences of national identity. Thus, for Foucault, neither Hegel nor the Young Hegelians -- including Marx-- addressed the challenge posed by Kant's anthropology, insofar as the self-creation of man (Kojève's "anthropogenèse") out of the interstices of social, political existence cannot refer to a level of subjectivity (be it the absolute *Geist* or the proletariat) without resort to another form of metaphysical teleology. On the one hand, humans as self-conscious beings only come of age in the exercise of their ethical, political intersubjectivity as members of the modern State. On the other hand, as we will see in the excursus on Hegel's critique of Kant, even as individual citizens interact to be constituted themselves as such and constitute the State, human nature seems to fall short of a broader teleology that accounts for its destiny, through the very negation of an alien nature and its transformation. It is at this very limit-point, that the question of teleology in Kant's critique seems to prepare the soil for both Hegel's spiritual rupture and

Nietzsche's self-overcoming of human nature. I will conclude this chapter with an alternative reading of the problem of the unity of the three *Critiques*, invoked by Paul Guyer against Donald Crawford.

Starting from the traditional interpretation of Kantian formalism in § 10, Crawford seems to believe that there are certain phenomenal forms that are characteristic of designed objects --hence the postulate of a formal purposiveness-- which would imply that such forms were adequate objects of taste. It is precisely in this point that Guyer criticizes Crawford when the latter affirms that "we can call an object **purposive** on the basis of its formal organization (structure) even when we do not or cannot actually place the cause of this form in a will." (AT 93) In this case, the object's purposiveness is what can be perceived (its form or organization), that which leads us to say that it resulted from a concept. According to Guyer, there is simply nothing about the pure form of the objects involved in Kant's examples (§§10, 15, 64) that requires the idea of purposiveness. It would be impossible to deduce the idea of a will, for instance, that had created the hexagonal form in the cells of a beehive or in a crystal. Starting from chapter 7 ("The Task of the Deduction"), Guyer guides us through a reflection on the universal validity of pleasure. To say that an object would be considered beautiful by all who observe it does not mean that everyone will actually like such an object but only that all must agree with such a judgment and call it beautiful, in harmonious accordance of understanding and imagination. The Kantian argument is that the harmony of the faculties occurs in different people under the same conditions, and that leads us to the deduction of the pure aesthetic judgment. The intersubjective validity of the foundation of the aesthetic judgment is not yet established in § 30, as he introduces the deduction, but only in paragraphs 31 through 37, being formally presented in § 38. Here we find the main point of divergence between Guyer's and Crawford's interpretations as the latter upholds that according to Kant, the presupposition of taste is not limited to an epistemological imputing of pleasure to others, but it also assigns a certain kind of duty or obligation to feel pleasure in certain objects. Besides the demonstration of the harmony of faculties, argues Crawford, it is necessary to prove that there is a moral signification of taste. Guyer criticizes Crawford for confusing the two realms (epistemological and moral), that is, the deduction is essentially epistemological as morality can be regarded in an analogous manner albeit independent of the first.

As he opens the last chapter on "aesthetics and morality" with the question "Completing the Deduction?," Guyer explicitly places his study of the KU in an epistemological perspective (p. 351). The universal validation of the aesthetic judgment is thus justified in epistemological terms. On the other hand, in light of

§ 22 and other passages, we can infer that Kant proposes that the justification be completed with an allusion to practical reason. This is a plausible way to account for formulations in the Third *Critique* such as the assertion that "we require from everyone as a duty, as it were, the feeling [contained] in a judgment of taste." (KU § 40/ET 162) Guyer concedes that it would be impossible to confine the allusion to duty in merely epistemological terms or to the reflective judgment. Hence the procedure adopted by Crawford, as he seeks the foundations in morality. According to Guyer, Crawford would have seen there a transition from the justification by universal intersubjectivity to the moral feeling as the decisive moment required by the transcendental deduction of the judgments of taste. I think that the great merit of Guyer's critique of Crawford lies precisely in having detected the teleological interest that guides the articulation between aesthetics and ethics proposed by the latter. After all, Crawford starts from the problematic that opposes disinterest in the judgment of taste related to pleasure occasioned by the object that is declared beautiful to the interest that can be linked to pleasure in the beautiful. (§ 41) As he concludes Stage IV with the postulate of the common sense, Crawford resorts thus to Stage V so as to raise the question "Why should we require, after all, the agreement of others when judging the beautiful?," "why do we say, with Kant, that everyone must find such an object beautiful?" (AT 143) To simply assume the communicable universality does not seem for him to be a sufficient argument to have completed the deduction. It is necessary to relate the judgment of taste to interest, in an indirect manner, just as interest in the good in itself, the morally good, is linked to intellectual interest. (KU § 42) According to Kant, the sociability peculiar to human beings is what moves one to cultivate and communicate to others his or her taste. But the empirical interest in the beautiful would not be, in this case, relevant to our discussion. We must examine therefore if there is an actual transition from the pleasure of aesthetic experience to the moral feeling. There must be a connection, however indirect it might be, between the moral virtue and the contemplation of the beautiful and the sublime. Pleasure in the beautiful, contrary to the pleasure in the good (including moral good) and pleasure in sensation, is not the interested pleasure. Kant asserts that "a judgment of taste, by which we declare something to be beautiful must not have an interest *as its determining basis*." (§ 41/ET 163) Already in the title of § 2, we find the formulation of a central thesis, namely, "The liking that determines a judgment of taste is devoid of all interest." As we saw above, Kant establishes an analogy between the KpV and the KU (§ 12), as for the transcendental foundations of the critique of both faculties. In order to corroborate his thesis, Crawford resorts to a teleological analogy: the intellect would have an interest in any indication or natural vestige of a correspondence (harmony, fairness) displayed between what was naturally produced and our faculties, insofar as morality --as a human legislation of universal laws-- presupposes the possibility of exerting causal influence over the natural, phenomenal world. (AT 148) According to Kant,

> [R]eason must take an interest in any manifestation in nature of a harmony that resembles the mentioned [kind of] harmony, and hence the mind [*Gemüt*] cannot meditate about the beauty of *nature* without at the same time finding its interest aroused. But in terms of its kinship this interest is moral, and whoever takes such an interest in the beautiful in nature can do so only to the extent that he has beforehand already solidly established an interest in the morally good. Hence if someone is directly interested in the beauty of nature, we have cause to suppose that he has at least a predisposition to a good moral attitude. (KU § 42 / ET 167)

For Crawford, the analogy between our moral destination (final purpose of our existence) and the "purposiveness without purpose" that grounds the judgment of taste, that is, the analogy between the moral judgment and the judgment of pure taste, would converge thus to establish "the foundation of the unity of the supra-sensible," announced in the Introduction to the Second Edition (KU II, B XX). According to Crawford, this foundation, which is the basis for morality, is symbolized by the beautiful and by the sublime. (AT 157) Beauty is therefore the symbol of the basis for morality, argues Crawford, insofar as the experience of the beautiful results from ourselves suprasensibly legislating the principle that determines the world as we know it by experience.

The articulation between aesthetics and ethics in the Third *Critique* problematizes the transcendental grounding of the System as a whole, as Crawford has shown, but can be approached only by analogy, even as one starts from the notion of purposiveness. In effect, it is the concept of purposiveness in nature that allows for the link between the sensible and the intelligible, according to the articulation between the three *Critiques*, delineated by Kant himself. More precisely, it is in the Kantian conception of an anthropology from a pragmatic point of view that we find an entire articulation of the three faculties within the "human nature," simultaneously conceived as noumenal and phenomenal. Through a conception of man as ultimate purpose of nature (*lezter Zweck*) and final purpose (*Endzweck*) of creation under moral laws, thus teleologically conceived, we may reformulate the Kantian problem of understanding freedom as the suprasensible intervenes in the phenomenal course of the natural world. We see also that we may draw an analogy between the regulative use of the reason in the KrV and the teleological argument in the KU: far from concluding in favor of the existence of a transcendent causality, above the course of nature, it has simply reaffirmed the autonomy of practical reason. Now, does this mean that morality is implied in a teleological reflection, or that ethics is presupposed in a formulation of the deduction of aesthetic judgments? All we conclude is that there is indeed an agreement between the faculties and their a priori principles (*Gesetzmäßigkeit, Zweckmäßigkeit, Endzweck*). As Lebrun remarks,

> Agreement [*Zusammenstimmung*] is one of the key words of the *Critique [of the Faculty] of Judgment*. While the first *Critique* makes intelligible the agreement between the form of nature and our understanding, the faculty of judgment places us in the presence of contingent agreements, and yet, too marvelous to be assigned to chance... It is this formal purposiveness that the judgment of taste allows to analyze: when I say that one thing is beautiful, I mean that its representation seems destined to place my imagination in unison with my understanding; I appreciate the spontaneous agreement between the representation of a natural thing and my faculties of knowledge, and the feeling of pleasure that then I experience is nothing else than the recognition of such an agreement. But the faculty of judgment, by itself, cannot go beyond this recognition. That final forms have been actually laid with a view to their exercise and that this is the end of nature, the faculty of judgment cannot affirm.[39]

As Lebrun shows in the same essay, the agreement between the aesthetic *Urteilskraft* and the practical *Vernunft* reveals the propaedeutic function of teleology for a moral theology and for a philosophy of history. But this is not exactly a subtle return to metaphysical finalism, for Kant keeps the distinction between the theoretical and practical uses of reason in a systematic manner, throughout the three *Critiques*. It is in this particular point, that Nietzsche--following Schopenhauer--develops a reading of Kant so as to attack the latter's teleology of human nature that, although was not intended by Kant as a metaphysical device, seems to betray his critique of metaphysics.

---

[39] G. Lebrun, "A Razão Prática na Crítica do Juízo". In *Sobre Kant*, (São Paulo: Edusp, 1993), pp. 103-4.

Chapter Two

HEGEL'S CRITIQUE OF KANT

INTRODUCTION

> Mais échapper réellement à Hegel suppose d'apprécier exactement ce qu'il en coûte de se détacher de lui... cela suppose de savoir, dans ce qui nous permet de penser contre Hegel, ce qui est encore hégélien; et de mesurer en quoi notre recours contre lui est encore peut-être une ruse qu'il nous oppose et au terme de laquelle il nous attend, immobile et ailleurs.
> (M. Foucault, *L'ordre du discours*, 74f.)

Foucault's reading of Hegel has shown the continuities in the midst of all discontinuities that characterize the latter's indebtedness towards Kant. Of particular interest, following Foucault's archaeology of the modern human sciences in OT, is the fate of the foundational role of Kantian ethics from Fichte to Hegel and Marx. As both Foucault and Habermas contended, the Young Hegelians signalled the end of an era of metaphysical foundationalism as the problems of ethics came to be discussed on empirical rather than transcendental grounds. And yet, just as the young Marx's *Kritik der Kritik* remained inscribed within the critical tradition of German idealism, I will examine how Hegel's critique of Kant's criticism remained within the bounds of an ethical, foundational problematic delineated by the latter. In effect, although Hegel himself claimed to be breaking away from Kant's conception of the foundation of ethics, the principle of rational autonomy was indeed common to both. The problem of the foundation of ethics will be, therefore, elaborated here out of the semantic displacements operated within the movement known as "German idealism," so as to establish the continuities and discontinuities that link Kant to Hegel. By examining this problematic, I hope to have covered some important aspects that complement the historical, philosophical background to Nietzsche's critique of Kant and German idealism. Also of particular interest is to provide some *Materialen* for a comparative understanding of Foucault's and Habermas's reading of Hegel and how they differ. Much of the ongoing debate in ethics between neo-Kantian universalists and neo-Hegelian contextualists point to the problems of foundations, universalizability, and effectiveness that characterized Hegel's critique of Kant. The question "what is morality / ethics?" can be, therefore, reformulated nowadays with reference to its original formulation in both Kant and Hegel. Starting from the formulation of morality in Kant, grounded in a conception of practical reason that makes possible and is distinguished from the theoretical use of reason, I will seek to problematize the dialectical solution proposed by Hegel's *Sittlichkeit*[1] in his attempt to rescue the unity between the subject and the object, supposedly lost in Kant's opposition between the theoretical and practical uses of the *Vernunft*, between the transcendental-logical foundation and the practical-ethical justification. It is thus a matter of examining two different conceptions --albeit akin-- of the rationality of human acting.

The problem of the rational foundation of ethics, such as it was formulated by Kant and Hegel, and in particular, their conceptions of *Moralität* and *Sittlichkeit*, have been re-examined by different philosophers of our day, such as Dieter Henrich, Jürgen Habermas, and Ernst Tugendhat, with the same preoccupation of articulating the foundation of practical propositions with today's ethical problems.[2] I will be profiting from the reading of an essay by Jean-François Kervegan on the foundation of ethics in Kant and Hegel,[3] where is shown that Hegel's critique of Kant, while drawing the crucial distinction between *Moralität* and *Sittlichkeit*, does not preclude the adhesion of the former to the latter's principle of the autonomy of the will. In effect, Hegel's practical philosophy turns out to be "the true expression of the rational foundation of ethics undertaken by Kant." (PFE 33)

Hegel's critique of Kant does betray an important feature of German idealism, besides the role assigned to reason in the historical conquest of human freedom, and that is the principle of autonomy of the rational will, on the very level of the

---

[1] I will systematically maintain the term in German (*Sittlichkeit*) and avoid other objectionable translations (ethical life) or neologisms (ethicity).
[2] Cf. D. Henrich, *Kant oder Hegel?* (Stuttgart: Reclam, 1983); J. Habermas, "Moralität und Sittlichkeit: Treffen Hegels Einwände gegen Kant auch auf die Diskursethik zu?" *Revue Internationale de Philosophie*, vol. 46, n. 166 (1988): p. 320-340; E. Tugendhat, *Probleme der Ethik*, (Stuttgart: Reclam, 1984).
[3] I wish to thank Professor Jean-François Kervegan, of the École Normale of St. Cloud, for his valuable insights. Cf. "Le problème de la fondation de l'éthique: Kant, Hegel," (hereafter, PFE) in *Revue de Métaphysique et de Morale* 95/1 (1990) 33-55.

determination of action and its justification. As Kervegan shows, there is an affinity between the transcendental foundation of Kant's practical philosophy and the Hegelian dialectic that seeks to overcome it (*aufheben*) through the historical objectivation of moral action. For Kervegan, Hegel's "anti-Kantianism" unveils, by the very negativity of his philosophy, the essentially "Kantian" character of his "objective idealism"[4] --the free act of self-foundation. Without denying the merits of his reading of Hegel's critique of Kant, I will attempt to show that the problematic enunciated by Kervegan fails to address the ethico-philosophical problem of foundation it promises to explore. More specifically, Kervegan seems to appropriate Hegel's critique of Kant without exploring the philosophical presuppositions that distinguish the two projects of foundation, notably in what regards the usage of transcendental-logical tools that Hegel appropriates from Kant.[5] This is, to my mind, a similar tendency we find in Habermas, in his attempt to obtain a deteleologized, post-metaphysical *Grundlegung* for ethics, by resorting to Hegel's critique of Kant.[6]

Undoubtedly, it is only with Hegel and his critics that the modern conceptions of self-consciousness and self-determination can be concretely formulated, being historically and politically conceived in the objectivation and sedimentation of moral values through social institutions.[7] But it was only thanks to the anthropocentric revolution operated by Kant's practical philosophy that the Hegelian anthropogenesis came to consolidate a conception of the modern ethos based on human freedom and not on the mere individual quest for happiness. Thus as German idealism turned the concept of freedom into "the central idea of all philosophy," as Denis Rosenfield remarks, it was Hegel who elaborated on a conception of history qua "locus of the effectiveness of the Spirit," (DM 114) both for the triumph of the figurations of freedom and for the "process of the negative

---

[4] Of course Hegel's "idealism" deserves a more careful qualification than the one provided by Kervegan's reading. Cf. Kenneth Westphal, "The basic context and structure of Hegel's *Philosophy of Right,*" in F.C. Beiser (ed.), *The Cambridge Companion to Hegel*, (New York: Cambridge University Press, 1993), 234-269. I am grateful to Allegra de Laurentiis for her critical remarks and insights into a Hegelian reading of Hegel.

[5] Cf., for instance, *Science de la Logique* (French edition I, 49) where Hegel writes: "*Kant a, de nos jours, créé, à côté de ce qu'on appelle couramment Logique, une Logique transcendantale. Ce que nous appelons ici Logique objective correspondrait en partie à cette Logique transcendantale...*"

[6] Cf. Jürgen Habermas, *Moral Consciousness and Communicative Action,* tr. C. Lenhardt and S.W. Nicholsen, (Cambridge, Mass.: MIT Press, 1990); *Postmetaphysical Thinking*, (Cambridge, Mass.: MIT Press, 1992).

[7] Cf. PDM ch. on Hegel; Ernst Tugendhat, *Self-Consciousness and Self-Determination,* (Cambridge, Mass.: MIT Press, 1980).

figuration of freedom, itself constitutive of the Geist." (DM 117)[8] As we read in one of Ganz's Additions to Hegel's *Philosophy of Right*, "the principle of the modern world is freedom of the subjectivity, the principle that all the essential factors present in the intellectual whole [*geistigen Totalität*] are now coming into their right in the course of their development." (RPh § 273)[9] I will seek to show in this chapter that the conception of a *Sittlichkeit* that proves to be objective by the effectiveness of the principle of subjectivity in the constitution of the modern State, must presuppose, before anything, that the Kantian logic of foundation be effectively "actualizable," in the sense of its *Wirklichkeit*. Thus, the major problem of a formalism that enunciates the categorical imperative does not reside so much in its formulation (*énoncé*) as in its formal universalizability, that is, that its propositional formulation claims to be foundational for any rational conception of morals. This will be, in effect, the central thesis of this chapter, which is divided in three sections dealing with Kant's morality, Hegel's *Sittlichkeit*, and the latter's foundation of ethics.

1. KANT'S CONCEPTION OF *MORALITÄT*

> Freiheit ist aber auch die einzige unter allem Ideen der spekulativen Vernunft, wovon wir die Möglichkeit a priori *wissen*, ohne sie doch einzusehen, weil sie die Bedingung des moralischen Gesetzes ist, welches wir wissen. (KpV 6)

When he wrote, in the preface to the second edition of the KrV, that it was "necessary to deny *knowledge* [of supersensible reality] in order to make room for *faith*," Kant was preparing the second *Critique* that would provide us with the synthetic arguments presupposed by the common moral judgments expounded in the *Foundations of the Metaphysics of Morals*. In particular, the conception of a rational will needed to be justified, hence "deduced" in transcendental-critical terms, by elucidating its meaning qua practical reason, in the exercise of freedom and in accordance with the moral law. Just as the KrV had assigned the cognition

---

[8] Denis Rosenfield, *Du Mal: Pour introduire en philosophie le concept du mal*, (Paris: Aubier, 1982), 18 (hereafter, DM); *Politique et Liberté* (Paris: Aubier, 1982), 51-59 (hereafter, PL).

[9] G.W.F. Hegel, *Grundlinien der Philosophie des Rechts*, Suhrkamp Taschenbuch, (Frankfurt am Main: Suhrkamp, 1970)(hereafter, RPh). Although following T.M. Knox's translation of the RPh, I had to take some liberty whenever necessary so as to avoid terms such as "mind" for *Geist*. *Bestimmtheit, Bestimmung* and *Beschaffenheit* have been rendered "determinateness", "determination," and "disposition," respectively, following the French translation of Hegel's *Logic*, by P.-J. Labarrière and G. Jarczyk, *Science de la Logique*, (Paris: Aubier-Montaigne, 1972 and 1976).

of natural causation to the empirical sciences, the KpV sets out to prove that there can be initiated a new causal chain in nature through what he names a "causality of freedom." Freedom is therefore a real component that allows for the very understanding and cognition of nature and human nature, and yet cannot be empirically approached under the principles of causal necessity that account for the latter but requires an objective, rational belief in the "practical postulates" of pure reason --corresponding to the ideas of God, freedom, and immortality in the KrV. Only freedom, however, can be proved as it implies and is implied by the moral law, given as a "fact of pure reason." (§ 7) Kant's conceptions of freedom and morality depart, as we have seen, from both eudaimonist and utilitarian moral systems. However, as Kervegan shows, Hegel refuses, in a more radical gesture than Kant, the "technical finalism," that once applied to the moral domain, would lead to the "sacrifice of right/law." (*le sacrifice du droit*, PFE 35) Kant distinguishes, to be sure, "technico-practical rules" (such as the prescriptions of prudence and happiness) from "moral-practical rules" (such as the moral laws of the will, referring to the principles of a "theory of morals," *Sittenlehre*). (Introduction to the Second Edition of 1793, KU XII). And Hegel would recognize this, when he ironically remarks that every conception of human acting guided by "good intention" or "benevolence" (*guten Herzens*) stems from the "pre-Kantian philosophers and constitutes, e.g., the quintessence of well-known dramatic productions." (RPh § 126) In brief, both Kant and Hegel resort to pure practical reason so as to confirm the objective reality of freedom. But while for Kant reason (*Vernunft*) cannot constitute but only regulate the object of cognition, Hegel extends to its jurisdiction the former role assigned to the *Verstand*.

It can be said thus that the gulf that separates Hegel from Kant lies precisely in the ethical domain, where a major opposition between the two takes place. First, we must notice the differences in terminology. Kant uses the terms *Ethik* and *Moral*--and likewise *Sittlichkeit* and *Moralität* -- to designate, respectively, the science that studies the "laws of freedom" and its "rational part" (in opposition to the "empirical part" of ethics). (cf. Preface to the GMS) In fact, we observe in this text that *Ethik* and *Sittenlehre* are equivalent, just as *Moral* and *Moralphilosophie*. (e.g., GMS III-IX) What is undoubtedly more important in these terms, besides the semantic affinity by classical etymology (moralitas, Ἠθική), is the Kantian innovation of having opposed the a priori, "pure" employment to the a posteriori, empirical usage of the terms. In effect, in the second part of his *Metaphysik der Sitten*, as he approaches the "doctrine of virtues," Kant distinguishes between the legality of an action from its *Moralität* or *Sittlichkeit* (MS 219), and in MS 225 he employs *Sittlichkeit* as synonym of *moralitas*. In MS 239, Kant makes allusion to the metaphysic of morals --to both parts (that is, both the *Rechtslehre* and the *Tugendlehre*)-- as *Sittenlehre* or *Moral* to designate the "doctrine of morals" or of duties in general (*überhaupt*).

We see thus that the Kantian distinction between law/right (*Recht*) and ethics only makes sense if we take into account the formal principle of morality, interchangeably *Moralität* or *Sittlichkeit*. We can now distinguish ethics as the "doctrine of ends that are duties" and whose legislation is internal to the subject, from law as the "doctrine of external values." (MS 219) It is precisely this abstract opposition that Hegel seeks to overcome in his *Philosophy of Right*:

> *Moralität* and *Sittlichkeit*, which perhaps usually pass current as synonyms, are taken here in essentially different senses (...) Kant generally prefers to use the word *Moralität* and, since the principles of action in his philosophy are always limited to this conception, they make the standpoint of *Sittlichkeit* completely impossible, in fact they explicitly nullify and spurn it. But even if "moral" and "ethical" (*sittlich*) meant the same thing by derivation, that would in no way hinder them, once they had become different words, from being used for different conceptions. (RPh § 33 Rem.)

For Hegel, *Sittlichkeit*, "objective morality" or "ethical life," translates "the unity and truth of these two abstract moments" that are law and morality --dealt with, respectively, in the first and second parts of the RPh. Hegel's dialectical philosophy operates, thus, the conceptual displacement of the ethical, on the very level of its foundation, as indicated by the rational effectivity (*Wirklichkeit*) of its self-determination, seen that moral subjectivity is an "empty principle" that "determines nothing." (RPh § 134, 148 Rem.) Kervegan affirms that the remarkable terminological change undertaken by Hegel aims at resolving what was for him a "deficiency of conceptuality" in Kant. (PFE 35) Kervegan omits, however, the criteria that would legitimate Hegel's reasoning against Kant, which he tacitly endorsed from then on. Before dealing with the Hegelian conception of *Sittlichkeit* and relating it to the ethical-political concept of the State in the next section, it is important to examine here the "three vices of Kantian morality," following Kervegan's reading of Hegel's critique of Kant.

The first --and most known-- charge that Hegel addresses against Kantian morality is that its empty, sterile formalism would be incapable of effectively actualizing determinations of concepts. After all, this was the criticism outlined by Hegel in the Preface to his *Phenomenology of the Spirit* of 1807. (PhG 48/ET § 50)[10] Now, Kant systematically rejects the possibility of basing the rational

---

[10] G.W.F. Hegel, *Phänomenologie des Geistes* (hereafter, PhG). I am using A.V. Miller's translation, *Hegel's Phenomenology of Spirit*, (New York: Oxford University Press, 1977). The numbers refer to the paragraph of this edition. I am also using the German "Suhrkamp

grounds for ethics on material principles (Theorems I and II of the KpV). As he concludes in § 8,

> Since it was shown that all material principles were wholly unfit to be the supreme moral law, it follows that the formal practical principle of pure reason --according to which the mere form of a universal legislation, which is possible through our maxims, must constitute the supreme and direct determining ground [*Bestimmungsgrund*] of the will --is the only principle which can possibly furnish categorical imperatives, i.e. practical laws which enjoin actions as dutiful.Only a so-defined principle can serve as a principle of morality [*Sittlichkeit*], whether in judging conduct or in application to the human will in determining it. (KpV 71)

Hegel rejects the Kantian formalism insofar as it proves incapable of promoting a concrete, speculative universality, and remains on the abstract level, separate from the particular. In effect, such is the crux of Hegel's critique of Kantian idealism in the first writings, in particular, in the *Differenz* and *Glauben und Wissen* essays, where the Schellingian notion of a "transcendental intuition" comes to fulfill the speculative demands of the *Vernunft* before the reflective antitheses of the *Verstand*. (Cf. Diff A. VI; GW A. II and III)[11] The dialectical movement of *Aufhebung*, which produces its self-differentiation in the determinations of singularity, particularity, and universality, reconciling a conceptual logic with an historical genesis of becoming, permeates Hegel's works of maturity and, notably in the PhG and RPh, characterizes the great rupture that his idealist, absolute system intends to operate in relation to Kant, Fichte, and Schelling. However, we would commit a *petitio principii* if by resorting to Hegel's logic to criticize Kant's we claimed to have found a more "concrete" rationality to ground our ethics. After all, both are representative of an idealist philosophizing and both refer us to a universalist ideal of rational foundationalism. It is true that the foundation proposed by Kant seems to favor the principle of pure universalization that has been appropriated by universalists and liberals in contemporary debates, while contextualists and communitarians

---

Taschenbuch" edition (stw 603; Frankfurt am Main: Suhrkamp, 1986). I am following Mary Rawlinson in her critical use of Miller's translation. Therefore, I shall translate *Begriff* as "concept," *Einzelheit* as "particularity," and so forth, and/or leave the term as it appears in the original so as to avoid misunderstandings.

[11] Cf. *Difference* 103: "...[I]n its highest synthesis of the conscious and the non-conscious, speculation also demands the nullification of consciousness itself. Reason thus drowns itself and its knowledge and its reflection of the absolute identity, in its own abyss: in this night of mere reflection and of the calculating intellect, in this night which is the noonday of life, common sense and speculation can meet one another."

rather resort to Hegel as they emphasize the socio-cultural context of moral institutions.[12] At any rate, Kervegan omits the fact that Hegel borrowed terms from the table of judgments of Kant's transcendental logic (KrV A 70/B 95, Analytic of Concepts § 9), which he appropriated in a reversal (*Verkehrung*) of meaning--precisely following the intellectual-intuitive, anti-Kantian understanding, going from the "synthetical-universal to the particular, i.e., from the whole to the parts." (KU § 77) The very Hegelian conception of *Wirklichkeit* refers us to such a practical-conceptual reversal. (PhG §§ 328-9) I limit myself to signalling here the contrast between the positive signification of Kant's formalism ("the self-determination of reason") and its negative signification, namely, "the reduction of the universal to the abstract non-contradiction," the same principle of identity that the *Science of Logic* dissolves in contradiction. (cf. RPh §§ 31, 135) Kervegan finds inspiration in Hegel's reading of the Kantian concept of internal purposiveness to affirm that Kant had the philosophical resources to overcome his formalism and keep the principle of the autonomy of the will, had he developed the hypothesis of an "intuitive understanding" --equivalent to speculative reason in Hegel. (cf. KU § 77; PFE 39) Although he does not explicitly touch on the question of the systematic unity of the three *Critiques*, Kervegan seems to share some "teleological solution" in his reading of the §§ 76 and 77 of the third *Critique* (PFE 38-40), failing to realize that Kant's formalism indeed postulates the employment of a substantive morality.

A second criticism regards the Kantian impotence (*ineffectivité* or *Unwirklichkeit*), resulting from the opposition between *Sein* and *Sollen* in Kant's philosophy. What is envisaged here is the lack of determination in Kant's doctrines of the sovereign "Good" --that Hegel discovers as the "universal abstract essentiality of the will, i.e. as duty." (RPh § 133) As actions demand for themselves particular contents, a definite goal, and duty remains the abstract universal, Hegel praises Kant for having introduced such a universal principle on a purely rational level of the will --above passions, desires, and inclinations -- but criticizes, in the same paragraph (RPh §135), its abstract indetermination. Hegel would have seen a double defect in Kant's *Sollen*, namely, the logical flaw of making infinity finite and the practical flaw of creating the insurmountable abyss

---

[12] Cf. the special issue of *Philosophy & Social Criticism* 14:3/4 (1988) dedicated to "Universalism versus Communitarianism: Contemporary Debates in Ethics." Habermas and Rawls are placed among the most remarkable representatives of the first group (*procedural universalism*) while Taylor, Walzer, and MacIntyre figure in the second (*contextualist communitarianism*).

between the rational, universalizable will and the empirical, particular will.[13] We would be thus before a mere interpretation of the practical philosophy of "as if" (*als ob*) --at least this is the reading obtained by Kervegan's comparison of the KU § 76 to PhG 435. (PFE 40-41) There remains, however, a positive lesson that Hegel managed to draw from Kant's moral view, namely, that moral subjectivity is to be overcome and elevated to a stage beyond, as objective, universal, and concrete *Sittlichkeit* that will carry out the "ethical promotion of morality."

Finally, we arrive at the final judgment of Kant's transcendental system, precisely in his dualism of the "moral view of the world," characteristic of "philosophies of understanding." Hegel contributed, thus, in a decisive way to vulgarize the caricature of Kantian dualisms, supposedly enchained in a logic as systematic as naive: thing-in-itself and phenomenon, infinity and finiteness, reason and understanding, freedom and necessity, spontaneity and receptivity, in brief, everything is reducible to the binomial being and ought --"nothing else than contradiction eternally posited." (Enz § 60) Kervegan concludes, provisionally:

> In order to meet [Kantian ethics'] main requirement (the absolute self-determination of reason), one needs to replace subjective reason, maintained by Kant, which is a "reason of understanding," by a rationality at once subjective and objective that unveils the truth bore by the former as it reveals the objective conditions of the historical, political order of effectiveness. Morality is actualized in ethics. (PFE 43)

2. HEGEL'S CONCEPTION OF *SITTLICHKEIT*

--eine Ethik. Da die ganze Metaphysik künftig in die Moral fällt --wovon Kant mit seinen beiden praktischen Postulaten nur ein Beispiel gegeben, nichts erschöpft hat-- so wird diese Ethik nichts anderes als ein vollständiges System aller Ideen oder, was dasselbe ist, aller praktischen Postulate sein. (Das älteste Systemprogramm des deutschen Idealismus, 1796/7, *Frühe Schriften* 234)

We see that for Hegel, as it was for Kant, idealist ethics is contrary to ethical doctrines of the determination of ends, intentions, virtues, eudaimonisms, in a word, to every attempt at an empirico-material foundation. In § 27 of his *Philosophy of Right*, Hegel affirms that the absolute determination of the Spirit consists in making its freedom its own object, *um für sich*, "to be explicitly, as

---

[13] Cf. G.W.F. Hegel, *Des manières de traiter scientifiquement du Droit Naturel*, tr. Bernard Bourgeois, (Paris: Vrin, 1972), 35-46.

Idea, what the will is implicitly," for "the definition of the concept of the will in abstraction from the Idea of the will is 'the free will which wills the free will'.[*der abstrakte Begriff der Idee des Willens ist überhaupt der freie Wille, der den freien Willen will*]." Although he appropriates Kant's principle of the autonomy of the will, Hegel elaborates on a conception of the will that differs from the former's rational will. Like Kant, Hegel links the philosophy of law to the study of the "will" and "freedom":

> The basis of right is, in general, the spiritual [*das Geistige*];its precise place and point of origin is the will, which is free [*der Wille, welcher frei ist*], so that freedom [*die Freiheit*] is both the substance of right and its determination [*seine Substanz und Bestimmung ausmacht*], while the system of right is the realm of freedom made actual [*das Reich der verwirklichten Freiheit*], the world of the Spirit brought forth out of itself as a second nature [*als eine zweite Natur*]. (RPh § 4)

As over against interpretations that make of Hegel the Machiavellian *Realpolitiker* of the modern *Machtstaat* and the precursor of the *Staatsethik* of contemporary totalitarian bureaucrats, Kervegan seeks to rescue the "truth of morality" that lies at the roots of Hegel's critique of Kant. Responding to Kant's assertion that "true politics can never take a step without rendering homage to morality,"[14] Hegel affirms that "the ethical substance [*die sittliche Substanz*], the State, has its determinate being [*Dasein*], i.e. its right, directly embodied in something existent, something not abstract but concrete [*in einer nicht abstrakten, sondern in konkreter Existenz*]" (RPh § 337 Rem.) and "can only be this concrete existent," adds Hegel, "and not one of the many universal thoughts supposed to be moral commands [*moralische Gebote*]." Although rejecting the Kantian subordination of politics to law and morals, on the one hand, and the foundation of the ethics in happiness, on the other hand, Hegel follows Kant in the formulation of a morality that is distinguished from legality but which is its correlate:

> The good is the Idea as the unity of the concept of the will with the particular will. In this unity, abstract right, welfare [*Wohl*], the subjectivity of knowing and the contingency of external fact [*Dasein*], have their independent self-subsistence superseded [*für sich selbständig aufgehoben*], though at the same time they are still contained and retained within it in their essence. The good is thus freedom realized, the absolute end [*Endzweck*] and aim of the world. (RPh § 129)

---

[14] Immanuel Kant, *Zum Ewigen Frieden* 380. OH 128.

The abstract, subjective morality not only is presupposed by the *Sittlichkeit*, but as it is united with the objectivity of abstract law, allows for the effective actualization (*Verwirklichkeit*) of the self-conscious, self-determining movement of human freedom, through the history of its figurations. Knowledge (*Wissen*) and the willing (*Wollen*) are effectively generated in the very self-consciousness (*Selbstbewußtsein*) that will unveil, in the last analysis, the substantiality of true freedom, that is, the figure of the abstract good (determined by morality) that is finally, concretely actualized in ethics (in the concrete concept of *Sittlichkeit*). As Hegel defined it in the famous § 142 of his *Rechtsphilosophie*,

> *Sittlichkeit* is the Idea of freedom [*die Idee der Freiheit*] in that on the one hand it is the good become alive --the good endowed in self-consciousness [*Selbstbewußtsein*] with knowing and willing and actualized by self-conscious action [*Handeln*]-- while on the other hand self-consciousness has in the ethical realm its absolute foundation and the end which actuates its effort [*an dem sittlichen Sein seine an und für sich seiende Grundlage und bewegenden Zweck hat*]. Thus *Sittlichkeit* is the concept of freedom developed into the existing world and the nature of self-consciousness.

Thus, Hegel articulates ethics with politics in order to reject moralism and the Kantian position of the "political moralist,"[15] although he does not reject subjective morality as a necessary moment for the effective actualization of objective ethics. Politics is thus distinguished from ethics precisely because of its particular character, that envisages empirical cases and determined interests of particular communities. "A distinction between ethics and morality," as remarks Kervegan, "implies a relativization or delimitation of the moral standpoint but not its rejection." (PFE 44) One can then distinguish two standpoints, the "historical" and the "logical," so as to elucidate the Hegelian opposition between morality and *Sittlichkeit* --Kervegan avoids the equivocal translation of "moralité objective" and the neologism "éthicité." Within an historical perspective, "freedom, objectified according to the institutional figure of the State is the condition for morality." Alluding to §§ 124 and 260 of the RPh, Kervegan upholds that the principle of the moral autonomy of the subject, by itself, would not be sufficient to universally ground an ethics that assures the rights of the subjective will. Historically, only with the emergence of the modern State, can morality "cease to be an abstract revindication of subjectivity" and make effective the principle of autonomy in the individual, as citizen and member of civil society. On the other

---

[15] Kant too rejects this position in favor of the "moral politician." Cf. OH 121-128.

hand, from a logical perspective, "morality is the presupposition of ethics for the subjective reflection on the objective Spirit is in itself the mediation or negativity thanks to which is overcome the abstraction of this objectivity." (PFE 45) Kervegan concludes, thus, that *Sittlichkeit* is the *Aufhebung* of *Moralität*, in the threefold sense of preservation, negation, and suppression, proper to the Hegelian dialectic, which finds in the French word "relève" one of its best translations.[16] The dialectical movement of objectivation, translating in concrete reality the externalization (*Entäußerung*) of the concept, from its externation (*Äußerung*) in diremption and placed outside of itself, without loss in alienation (*Entfremdung*), effects the self-determination of the autonomy of the will in its transition from moral subjectivity to objective *Sittlichkeit*. Both in the PhG and in the RPh, Hegel articulates his logic of the Concept with the historical genesis of the objective Spirit's figurations --in the case of *Sittlichkeit*, in the moments determined by the family (*der unmittelbare oder natürliche sittliche Geist*), by civil society (*eine Verbindung der Glieder als selbständiger Einzelner in einer somit formellen Allgemeinheit*), and by the constitution of the State (*den Zweck und die Wirklichkeit des substantiellen Allgemeinen und des demselben gewidmeten öffentlichen Lebens*). (RPh § 157) It is important to place here the Objective Spirit according to the general classification of the Logic-Nature-Spirit structure and according to the particular classification of the Philosophy of Spirit (*subjective-objective-absolute*), in order to fully grasp the locus assigned to the philosophy of law in the second division. In the threefold division of the *Enzyklopädie der philosophischen Wissenschaften*, we find the different spheres of the Science of the Idea:

1. *Logic*: the science of the Idea in and for itself.
2. *The Philosophy of Nature*: the science of the Idea in its otherness.
3. *The Philosophy of the Spirit*: the science of the Idea come back to itself out of that otherness. (§ 18)

We see that *Logik* and the two philosophical sciences (*die beiden realen Wissenschaften der Philosophie, die Philosophie der Natur und die Philosophie des Geistes*), according to an 1831 note that Hegel himself wrote for the preface to the *Science of Logic*, constitute the exhaustive project that comprises the entire reality of human experience and existence. Ironically enough, we can also notice that *Phenomenology* does not figure in this division, for it appears as subdivision

---

[16] Both Paul Ricoeur and Jacques Derrida have been using this felicitous translation for *Aufhebung* (*relève*).

of the first part of three movements of the development of the Spirit.[17] The Philosophy of the Spirit is divided as follows:

1. *Subjective Spirit*: the Spirit's relation to itself, an only ideal totality of the Idea. This is Being-near-to-itself in the form of only internal freedom.
2. *Objective spirit*, as a world to produce and produced in the form of reality not only ideality. Freedom here becomes an existing, present necessity [*vorhandene Notwendigkeit*].
3. *Absolute Spirit*: the unity, that is *in itself and for itself*, of the objectivity of the Spirit and of its ideality or its concept, the unity producing itself eternally, Spirit in its absolute truth --*Absolute Spirit* (§ 385)

The tension between the historical genesis and the conceptual genesis is dialectically resolved by *Aufhebung* precisely in the transitions from one moment to the other, passing and exhausting the contradictions inherent to the movements of the Spirit. Although one may speak of a "process" to describe such movements, keeping thus a theological, intra-Trinitarian connotation, this may well be avoided, if we take into account the secularizing thrust of Hegel's later writings.[18] After all, for Hegel, the spirituality of the Concept cannot be dissociated from its cultural, historical representations --including theology and religious institutions. As Rosenfield remarks, the modern State is, for Hegel, "the 'natural' element in which are developed artistic, religious, and philosophical activities." (PL 275) Kervegan succeeds in showing, however, that the objectivity of institutions does not preclude but rather integrates the subjectivity of the members that constitute it, in the case of *Sittlichkeit*, by an ethical disposition (*sittliche Gesinnung*) or by a political virtue, insofar as they make possible "the adaptation of the individual to duty." (RPh § 150; PFE 46) Kervegan goes on to show how ethical disposition as the "true moral consciousness" operates, within civil society and the State, the effectiveness of *Sittlichkeit*, at once subjective and objective. The corporation, following the family the "second ethical root of the State" (RPh § 255), plays an ethical, regulative role as it links the subjective will to the objective universal in

---

[17] Namely, (a) *in itself or immediate*, this is the *soul* or *natural-spirit* (*Natur-Geist*), the object of the *anthropology* that studies man in nature; (b) *for itself or mediate*, as an identical reflection in itself and in the other, spirit in relation or particularization (*im Verhältnis oder Besonderung*), consciousness, the object of the phenomenology of the spirit; (c) *spirit determining itself in itself*, as a subject for itself, the object of psychology. (*Encyclopaedia* 387)

[18] Cf. Charles Taylor, *Hegel*. Cambridge University Press, 1975, p. 55 n. 1. Kervegan employs this term very often, even when referring to the movements of the Spirit in the world.

the organization of modern civil society. The political disposition, on its turn, designates the state of mind of the citizen of the rational State (RPh §§ 167-8), as the subjective, individual consciousness recognizes the objectivation of its own freedom in the political institution of the State. If the civil society already offered to the individual the possibility of overcoming his/her selfish interest it is only in the State that is concretely actualized the "shape of freedom" (RPh § 266) This is how the individual can adhere to the ethical conditions of his/her social existence. By these ethical and political dispositions, exemplified in the corporate honor and everyday patriotism, moral individuality is thus elevated to the level of mediation, internal to the objective Spirit of *Sittlichkeit*. It is precisely here that we find the most original point of Kervegan's essay, as he shows that Hegel's *Sittlichkeit* preserves Kant's moral subjectivity in the rational effectiveness that reconciles moral and political abstractions. In effect, this will be the conclusion drawn from his analyses of the self-determination of the subjective will in Hegel and the Hegelian category of "action" (*Handlung*). (PFE 48-54)

Kervegan quotes § 107 of the RPh to emphasize the continuity between the determination of the will as concept in its relation with itself (subjective) and its right (objective) expressed in morality, that is objectified by the principle of subjective autonomy --a right in the Hegelian terminology. Morality is, in effect, included in the doctrine of the objective Spirit, where is dialectically operated the displacement of morality towards legality. Kervegan observes that moral subjectivity appears, in Hegel's text, as the most concrete, real moment of abstract law, hence the closest moment towards the fulfillment of freedom. (RPh § 106 Rem.; PFE 50) In this regard Hegel is clearly following Kant, in subordinating law to morals. Since the will is essentially ethical substance, Hegel succeeds in maintaining within the same logical structure the moral subjectivity (starting from the principle of autonomy) and the ethical objectivity. Thus, we read in § 147, regarding ethical authority, that laws and institutions "are not alien [*ein Fremdes*] to the subject," but "his Spirit bears witness to them as to its own essence, the essence in which he has a feeling of his selfhood." And in the Remark to § 148, that "the ethical doctrine of duties [*Die ethische Pflichtenlehre*]," objectively understood, cannot be reduced to "the empty principle moral subjectivity [*der moralischen Subjektivität*]" but is "the systematic development of the circle of ethical necessity [*der sittlichen Notwendigkeit*]." Action is thus defined as "the externation of the subjective or moral will [*Die Äußerung des Willens als subjektiven oder moralischen ist Handlung*]" (RPh § 113), applied to the normative act of the subject. "The law is no agent," writes Hegel, "it is only the actual human being who acts," so that his/her actions are judged by law. (RPh § 140 Rem.) It is the objective contents of *Sittlichkeit* that, by replacing the abstract good, through subjectivity, assures the right in the preservation of "laws and institutions existing in themselves and for themselves [*an und für sich seienden Gesetze und Einrichtungen*]." (RPh § 144) Moral action is the practical solution to the contradiction inherent to the Kantian *Sollen*, which Hegel judges incapable, by moral consciousness, to will its duty. In order for the subject's action to honor the three rights (of his/ her subjective will, of the world as it is, and of the universal norm of the good) intrinsic to the Idea of the free will (RPh § 33), it is necessary that moral action works out the "practical mediation of the subject's autonomy with the two universal terms that confronted it, the norm of the good and the real." (PFE 53)

3. KANT, HEGEL, AND THE FOUNDATION OF ETHICS

Chronologiquement, Hegel vient après Kant; mais nous, lecteurs tardifs, nous allons of l'un à l'autre; en nous quelque chose de Hegel a vaincu quelque chose de Kant; mais quelque chose de Kant a vaincu Hegel, parce que nous sommes aussi radicalement post-hégéliens que nous sommes post-kantiens... C'est pourquoi la tâche est de les penser toujours mieux, en les pensant ensemble, l'un contre l'autre, et l'un par l'autre. Même si nous commençons à penser autre chose, ce "mieux penser Kant et Hegel" appartient, d'une manière ou de l'autre, à ce "penser autrement que Kant et Hegel."[19]

Kervegan concludes his essay with a brief analysis of the teleological problem already mentioned above. To our surprise --and to the general wonder of many Hegelians -- Kervegan omits the relevance of the modern State for Hegel's critique of Kant on this specific question of teleology. Kervegan invokes, on the contrary, the teleological conception of history, perhaps so as to emphasize the affinity between the two thinkers and minimize some political interpretations that turn Hegel into a theoretician of State ideologies. I will shortly reexamine the *Phenomenology* so as to address some foundational problems in Hegel's articulation of *Sittlichkeit* and the State .

Although Kervegan does not state it explicitly, he seems to structure the foundation of ethics as a semiology of acting (*une sémiologie de l'agir*). After all, according to Hegel, the logic and the ethical are mutually grounded. Thus, the dialectic of the *Wissen*, the *Wollen*, and the *Handeln* appears as Hegel's response to Kant's idealism, in its critical limitations that hinders the transition from the a

---

[19] Paul Ricoeur, paraphrasing Eric Weil, in *Le conflit des interprétations. Essais d'herméneutique*, (Paris: Seuil, 1969), 403.

priori to the a posteriori. As Kervegan points out, "in action is already operated the transition to ethics." (PFE 53) It is a matter of an *Aufhebung*, where the opposition between the sensible and the intelligible is overcome (*aufgehoben*) by the Representation (*Vorstellung*) that mediates between both. Because this concrete movement cannot dissociate what is rational from its effective reality, the task of philosophy, for Hegel, consists in apprehending its own time in thought: "*so ist auch die Philosophie ihre Zeit in Gedanken erfaßt.*" (RPh 26) As a child of his time, heir of the French Revolution and of the constitutional reforms in Europe, Hegel is not concerned with what the State ought to be (*sein soll*), but rather with what the State is (*das was ist zu begreifen*). Thus an inadequate representation of the moral subject, as the one proposed by Kant's formalism, must be replaced by a philosophy that, as "thought of the world, it appears only when actuality is already there cut and dried after its process of formation has been completed." (RPh 28) Hegel's critique of the abstract moralism of German *Aufklärung* ultimately seeks to reconcile the subjectivity of the moral will with the objectivity of the social, political world (*Sittlichkeit*), so that freedom is concretely effected in human history. Hegel extols thus political virtue, to avoid all subordination of politics to morality. As Hegel himself had already anticipated in the Preface to his *Philosophy of Law*, it is a matter of reformulating the nature of the State qua political reality resulting from the historical shapes of freedom. Both the State and World History (*Die Weltgeschichte*) figure at the summit of *Sittlichkeit*'s effectiveness:

> The State is the effective actuality of the ethical Idea [*die Wirklichkeit der sittliche Idee*]. It is ethical Spirit qua the substantial will manifest and revealed [*offenbare*] to itself, knowing and thinking itself, accomplishing what it knows and in so far as it knows it. (RPh § 257)

> The State is absolutely rational inasmuch as it is the effective actuality of the substantial will which it possesses in the particular self-consciousness once that consciousness has been raised to consciousness of its universality. This substantial unity is an absolute unmoved end in itself [*absoluter unbewegter Selbstzweck*], in which freedom comes into its supreme right. On the other hand, this final end [*Endzweck*] has supreme right against the individual [*Einzelnen*], whose supreme duty is to be a member of the State [*Mitglieder des Staats zu sein*]. (§ 258)

> World history [*Die Weltgeschichte*] is the necessary development, out of the concept of the Spirit's freedom alone, of the moments of reason [*Momente der Vernunft*] and so of the self-consciousness and freedom of the Spirit. This

development is the interpretation and the actualization of the Universal Spirit [*die Auslegung und Verwirklichung des allgemeinen Geistes*]. (RPh § 342)

These remarkable citations reveal the imposing logical-structural cohesion that characterizes Hegel's System. If compared with the last paragraph of the PhG (§ 808 of Miller's ET) where history is described as "Spirit externalized in time" (*an die Zeit entäußerte Geist*) and history's becoming as a *Galerie von Bildern*, the unity of the synthesis of subjectivity and objectivity envisaged by Hegel comes full circle. In the Introduction the 1822 *Vorlesungen* on the *Philosophy of History*, Hegel writes that "History [*Geschichte*] unites the objective [*objektive*] with the subjective [*subjektive*] side, and denotes quite as much the *historia rerum gestarum*, as the *res gestæ* themselves."[20] Hegel unites thus historical narrations to the happening of historical deeds and events. And yet, because he problematizes Aristotle's conception of natural history (e.g., αι περι τα ζωα ιστοριαι, "animal history" --in contrast with περι ζωων γενεσεως, "animal theory") in the dramatic opposition of *Natur* and *Geschichte*, Hegel's conception of the self-mediating becoming of the absolute *Geist* itself points to what history is all about, namely, to reveal the τελος of human, concrete existence (*Dasein*), *hic et nunc*, "the revelation of the depth of the Spirit [*die Offenbarung der Tiefe*]," nothing less than "the absolute *Begriff*." (PhG § 808) It is in their active relation to nature that human beings consciously posit themselves as historical beings, whose ethical, political, and rational relations distinguish them from other animals.

The problem of a necessitarian logic of reconciliation between what *dē jure* constitutes the object of history and what *de facto* constitutes the historicity of past events that historians can investigate in the present, translates what has been termed "historicism." This terminology is, to say the least, misleading and ambiguous, especially when applied to Hegel's philosophy of history, as opposed to other logical conceptions of becoming (such as the biological, anthropological, and meteorological ones, i.e. based upon observations of nature). To be sure, as it has been already suggested, Hegel's conception of history cannot be separated from his view of becoming, since it is precisely in its becoming that history appears as a distinct, reflective feature of consciousness, distinguishing itself from nature. In effect, for Hegel,"organic nature has no history." (PhG § 295) And yet, to merely equate rational or logical necessity with the effective becoming of reality would betray the very *historical meaning* of Hegel's most famous aphorism, "*was vernünftig ist, das ist wirklich; und was wirklich ist, das ist*

---

[20] Georg W.F. Hegel, *The Philosophy of History*, trans. J. Sibree, (Buffalo, NY: Prometheus, 1991), 60.

vernünftig." (RPh 36) After all, what is "rational" and what is "effective" in Hegel's System apart from their historical becoming? How is the historical becoming to be differentiated from the natural becoming of things and beings? How does consciousness (and self-consciousness) emerge out of animal life? How does the dialectic of self-consciousness repeat the dialectic of consciousness "at a higher level"? The very *dénouement* of the *Phenomenology* points to the central place ascribed to the Spirit, which is indeed the only concrete reality in Hegel's *Phänomenologie*, with consciousness, self-consciousness, and reason coming on the scene as abstractions of the *Geist*. Hegel sums this up in his discussion of the rational actualization (*Verwirklichung*) of self-consciousness through its own activity:

> Just as Reason, in the role of observer, repeated, in the element of the category, the movement of consciousness, viz. sense-certainty, perception, and the Understanding, so will Reason again run through the double movement [*die doppelte Bewegung*] of self-consciousness, and pass over from independence into its freedom. (PhG § 348)

As they move from the abstract to the concrete, the *mises en scène* of successive and overlapping triads in the *Phenomenology* provide us with a conceptual account of knowing in the development of consciousness (sense-certainty, perception, and understanding, PhG §§ 90-165), an historical account of the rise of empirical consciousness to absolute knowing (PhG §§ 166-671), and a phenomenological account of religion qua universal expression of the Absolute (natural religion, religion in the form of art, and revealed religion, PhG §§ 672-787). Of course the specific shapes (*bestimmten Gestalten*) constituting the different moments of those movements of the Spirit (its *begreifen, geschehen*, and *vollenden*) can be related to--and are actually said to "belong to" (PhG §§ 680)--the particular moments (*einzelnen Momente*) of the Spirit, viz. *Bewußtsein, Selbstbewußtsein*, and *Vernunft*, in its march leading to the pure self-consciousness that crowns the *Phenomenology* with *das absolute Wissen*, "Spirit that knows itself in the shape of Spirit." (PhG § 798) Whether such discursive accounts can be (or should be) reduced to necessarily thus differentiated parts in a *pars toto* structure of meaning, whether there is a universal subject-matter proper to the Science of History, that remains a major problematic for both neo-Hegelian (e.g., Collingwood and Croce) and post-Hegelian (e.g., Betti and Gadamer) critics of historicism.[21] The problem lies, therefore, in the very articulation of the

---

[21] Cf. Benedetto Croce, *La storia come pensiero e come azione* (1938), R.G. Collingwood, *The Idea of History* (1946, translated into German as *Philosophie der Geschichte*), Emilio Betti,

movement of becoming of the Spirit through the moments of the difference between knowledge and truth (*Phänomenologie*) and the *Aufhebung* of the latter in manifesting the Spirit as Science (*Wissenschaft*). (PhG §§ 803-5) Hegel's dense conclusion is worth being quoted here (PhG § 807):

> The self-knowing Spirit knows not only itself but also the negative of itself, or its limit: to know one's limit is to know how to sacrifice oneself. This sacrifice is the externalization in which Spirit displays its becoming Spirit in the form of *free contingent happening*, intuiting its pure Self as Time outside of it, and equally its Being as Space. This last becoming of Spirit, *Nature*, is its living immediate Becoming; Nature, the externalized Spirit, is in its existence nothing but this eternal externalization of its *continuing existence* and the movement which reinstates the *Subject*.

The problem of the Self, Being, and Becoming is thus situated at the intersection of phenomenology and history, as the *Geist* attains to supreme freedom in the immediate identity to itself, as its dialectical movement comes full circle. Hegel's opposing of the *Geschichte* to *Phänomenologie* (as *die Wissenschaft des erscheinenden Wissens*) points again to a subtle *coincidentia oppositorum* effected by the logic of *Aufhebung*. Indeed, Hegel's conception of history as a logical becoming remains the stumbling block for historians and philosophers alike who may rightly accuse Hegel of falling back into the onto-theo-logical view of a predetermined plan for God's creation. There is nothing further from the truth, if one takes into account that Hegel not only deliberately avoids Kant's reduction of history to empirical events, but he also flattens out any vertical appeals to a higher, transcendent court. Consequently, Hegel's philosophical, critical conception of history operates --perhaps *malgré lui*-- a veritable displacement of the *humanum* vis-à-vis the becoming of the world and its human reappropriation, in the anthropogenesis of self-conscious *Dasein*. Like Spinoza's equation *deus sive natura*, Hegel's dialectical logic of *Aufhebung* calls into question what is really at issue (*die Sache selbst*) in the representation of the Absolute in formulas such as "God is eternal." (PhG § 23) As he writes in the Preface, "[t]he beginning of philosophy presupposes or requires that consciousness should dwell in this element," viz., *pure self-recognition in absolute otherness*. (PhG § 26) The history of God, in which God's death marks also a new beginning for humankind, is in this regard as necessary to theology as the history of geometry has been to the development and breakthrough of

---

Teoria Generale della Interpretazione (2 vols., 1955), and H.-G. Gadamer, "Hermeneutics and Historicism" (supplement to the Eng. trans. of *Truth and Method*).

mathematics. History thus understood operates a return to the concept of the concept, so that contingencies (for the better or for the worse, including political atrocities committed by the State) are relativized by a systematic necessity implicit in the logic of *Sittlichkeit*. Ethics, after all, is logical. The principle of subjectivity which characterizes modernity inaugurates, once and for all, the age of universal freedom, in its triumphal march towards the fulfillment of the liberating ideals of enlightened Reason. It is this dialectic of freedom, subsuming contingency and necessity under the same effective becoming of historical events, that motivates Kervegan's optimism. And yet, as both Nietzsche's and Foucault's critique of modern subjectivity will denounce, there is no teleological assurance that could deliver this all-too-human progress from its tragic detours.

Chapter Three

NIETZSCHE, GENEALOGY, AND THE CRITIQUE OF POWER

INTRODUCTION

Große Dinge verlangen daß man von ihnen schweigt oder groß redet: groß, das heißt, zynisch und mit Unschuld. (WM § 1)

It would be an impossible task to introduce here the thought of a great philosopher as Friedrich Nietzsche, as the subject-matter of his grand *oeuvre* resists the classifications and operations of traditional hermeneutics. Even before Foucault sought to rescue a "critique of power" in the *Sache* of a Nietzschean semiology, Martin Heidegger had remarked, "'Nietzsche' --der Name des Denkers steht als Titel für *die Sache* seines Denkens."[1] The name of the philosopher coincides, in this particular case, with the very subject-matter of the philosophy in question. To assign a "critique of power" to Nietzsche is, to say the least, a risky procedure. It would be thus impossible to relate Nietzsche's thought to Kant's critical philosophy without caricaturing the originality of the former or the systematic rigor of the latter. As shown by many scholarly studies,[2] Kant and Nietzsche have critical projects that radically differ --despite some points of

---

[1] M. Heidegger. *Nietzsche*, vol. 1, Berlin: Neske, 1961, p. 9.
[2] Cf. Bernard Bueb, *Nietzsches Kritik der praktischen Vernunft*, (Stuttgart: Ernst Klett, 1970); Siegfried Kittman, *Kant und Nietzsche: Darstellung und Vergleich ihrer Ethik und Moral*, (Frankfurt am Main: Peter Lang Verlag, 1984); Olivier Reboul, *Nietzsche critique de Kant*, (Paris: PUF, 1978); Keith Ansell-Pearson, "Nietzsche's Overcoming of Kant and Metaphysics: From Tragedy to Nihilism," *Nietzsche-Studien* 16 (1987) 310-339.

convergence-- not only in their philosophical formulations but in their very presuppositions and concepts, especially in their views of morality and human nature. In order to avoid the simplistic conclusion that Nietzsche did not understand Kant, I decided to articulate Nietzsche's reading of Kant with the former's philosophy as a whole, especially in its radical critique of modernity and the modern conception of human nature (*Menschlichkeit*, the *humanum*). Only in light of a diagnosis of modern man, which Nietzsche undertakes in a quasi-prophetic--albeit non-messianic-- manner, can we understand the true meaning of his critical project, and its implications for our history and culture. What is stake, therefore, is the recasting of what may be termed the Nietzschean problematic of modern subjectivity, to wit, the question of the self-overcoming (*Selbstüberwindung*) of modern man, conjugated with correlative concepts such as the will to power (*der Wille zur Macht*) and the eternal return (*die ewige Wiederkehr*), elaborated in organic, interactive fashion, quasi methodically, within a critical tradition to be overcome by philosophy itself. That the question of human nature steals the scene, as it were, in the staging of a Nietzschean *theatrum philosophicum* does not demean Kant's philosophy, insofar as the critical thrust of the latter is brought to the foreground. Reminiscent of the tripartite division of Kant's "cosmopolitan philosophy," Nietzsche outlined the second book of his unfinished, controversial work on the *Will to Power*[3] (II. Buch: Kritik der höchsten Werte):

1. Kritik der Religion
2. Kritik der Moral
3. Kritik der Philosophie

Such will be the thematic division that will underlie this chapter, as I will seek to elaborate on Nietzsche's genealogical critique of power, starting from his critique of Kant and leading to Foucault's reappropriation of the former. Like Kant's, this threefold criticism is articulated by Nietzsche with a view to rescuing a conception of human nature that avoids the metaphysical impasse of reducing the *humanum* to a reflex of the *divinum*, of a *transcendens*, at the same time as it articulates the historical, immanent presuppositions proper to the human species, qua animal to be distinguished from all the others, by its development and history. If Kant had anticipated Hegel's philosophy of history, it is in the historicizing of human nature that Nietzsche finds one point of rapprochement, in the very

---
[3] According to the Kröners Taschen edition (vol. 78, 1930); I am using the ET by Walter Kaufmann, *The Will to Power*, (New York: Vintage Books, 1968).

conception of an effective historicity, implicit to a genealogy that radicalizes what Hegel called the "science of human experience" (*Wissenschaft der Erfahrung des Geistes*).[4]

"παντες ανθρωποι του ειδεναι ορεγονται φυσει. σημειον δ' η των αισθησεων αγαπησις (...) All men, by nature, aim at knowledge; a sign of this is [our] affection by the senses." The famous words that open Aristotle's *Metaphysics* (I, 1 980a) indicated already the place of the *empeiria* in a classical conception of human nature qua rational being: only the human species (το γενος των ανθρωπων) has the faculty to order its experience (εμπειρια), starting from the sensations and memory, to acquire and develop art (τεχνη) and science (επιστημη). When Nietzsche develops the concept of the "will to know" two millennia later, it is still this same human nature which is to be investigated, starting from experience. Nietzsche's psychological inquiry into the nature of human instincts and drives is indeed very reminiscent of the work undertaken by Kant in the *Anthropologie*. To be sure, it is Kant's refusal to remain on the empirical level of investigation that will prompt Nietzsche's attack upon any future metaphysics of sorts. The question of human nature, the nature in question, "man" as a perennial *remise en question*, has been a major characteristic of philosophy since Heraclitus sought in thought what was common to all human beings, since Protagoras held man to be the measure of all things, and a fortiori since Socrates denied such measure, allowing for Plato and Aristotle to corroborate the shift from a philosophizing on the nature (*physis*) of beings to a philosophizing of their formal essence (*ousia*). It was this teleological, and hence metaphysical, conception of human nature that came under Nietzsche's attack, precisely because of its pretense to know the truth of a human nature, once and for all established. In effect, for Nietzsche --as it was for Heidegger--, the rise of Platonism coincides with the emergence of metaphysics. Although it is beyond the scope of the present study to recapitulate the development of different conceptions of human nature throughout the centuries, it was by deconstructing the history of metaphysics that Nietzsche himself set out to elaborate on a genealogical conception of human nature, beyond good and evil. Therefore, it was in order to recast the modern reformulation of a classical problematic such as "human nature," understood in its Aristotelian correlation between rationality and sociability,[5] that I undertook a brief study of the critical background of Kant's conception of human nature, in its self-constitution within a society of free

---

[4] Subtitle of the original outline for Hegel's *Phänomenologie des Geistes*.
[5] That is, that man is the only animal endowed with the *logos* (speech, discourse, reason) and the *zoon politikon* by nature. Cf. Aristotle's *Politics* I.i.

subjects. The present chapter is confined to Nietzsche's "anthropology" and its relation to the critique of metaphysics and morality, as I seek to highlight the central place it occupies in his overall work and how it anticipates Foucault's genealogy of modernity.

1. CRITIQUE AND GENEALOGY: OF TRUTH AND METHOD

Wahrheitssinn. Ich lobe mir eine jede Skepsis, auf welche mir erlaubt ist zu antworten: "Versuchen wir's!" Aber ich mag von allen Dingen und allen Fragen, welche das Experiment nicht zulassen, nichts mehr hören. Dies ist die Grenze meines "Wahrheitssinn": denn dort hat die Tapferkeit ihr Recht verloren. (FW § 51)

What is philosophy? How is philosophy to be opposed to nonphilosophy? This problematic was announced, from the outset, as constitutive of the methodological analysis that has opposed great thinkers such as Kant and Nietzsche, Habermas and Foucault. As Mary Rawlinson has argued, Foucault's conception of philosophy radically departs from a systematic, scientific undertaking to apprehend reality, such as Kant's and Hegel's *Wissenschaft* or Husserl's *Phänomelogie*. (KPS 371) And yet Foucault --just like Nietzsche-- did not seek to abandon philosophy to the obscure caprices of unreason, but rather refused to have it confined to a purely logical, dogmatic pattern of rationality, supposedly neutral, transcendental or presuppositionless. That question also underlies Nietzsche's writings in its different stages of evolution --*grosso modo*, one may speak of three major phases: the early writings, marked by philology, the artistic passion (in particular, music), and the friendship with Wagner (e.g., *Die Geburt der Tragödie*, 1872, and the four *Unzeitgemäße Betrachtungen*, 1873-76); the second, after the rupture with Wagner (1878), marked by the disillusionment of reason (*Menschliches, Allzumenschliches*, 1878-80, and *Die fröhliche Wissenschaft*, 1882); and the third, marked by the masterpieces *Also sprach Zarathustra* (1883-84, 1885), *Jenseits von Gut und Böse* (1886), *Zur Genealogie der Moral* (1887), *Die Götzen-dämmerung* (1889), and the *Nachlaß*, *Der Antichrist* (1895), *Ecce Homo* (1908), *Der Wille zur Macht* (1901, 1906).[6] In all these works, the question of philosophy is connected to other questions, such as

---

[6] The years refer to the date of publication. Undoubtedly, WM cannot be regarded as a "book" in the same sense as AC and EH are regarded as "nachgelassene Werke". In the present study, I have avoided both extreme positions of either discarding WM as a work rejected by Nietzsche himself (as proposed by Bernd Magnus) or turning it into the *Hauptwerk* containing the quintessential philosophy of Nietzsche (as Heidegger does).

the problems of life, human existence, and truth. And in all these central questions, the Nietzschean experimentalism emerges as the only commonplace that points to a critical, textual pathway, an experimental method of research, at once *Experiment* and *Versuch*, the genealogical perspectivism that characterizes Nietzsche's thought. The problem of truth constitutes the principal frontier between art and science, in the very conception of philosophy as a *tertium quid*, a third genre that resists all systematic classification, for at the same time that it is presented as art (*techne*) in its ends and productions (*poiesis*), it is expressed through the mediation of concepts like a science (*episteme*).[7] For Nietzsche, the philosopher is the man of tomorrow and the day after tomorrow insofar as he always finds himself in contradiction to his today (JGB 212; cf. 211). The philosopher is the physician, the artist, and legislator who says yes (*Ja-sagen*) to the becoming of man through the active, creative overcoming of himself, the self-overcoming of his own moral values and his systems of truth. Therefore, there is no dialectical or transcendental method appropriate to philosophy, since all methods betray always already a certain will to truth. (JGB §§ 35, 36) One can only speak of "methods" in an immanent, practical sense, by turning the very pathways (*hodoi*) that take one beyond (*meta*) their safe origins and destination into an effective undergoing of life. To paraphrase Heidegger, human beings are always already *unterwegs*, *en route*, in their pre-given relations of appropriation vis-à-vis their being, thinking, and speaking. Thus, Nietzsche places the question of truth on the same level of problematization as the question of method, in particular, the subjectivity that betrays the impartial, impersonal ideal of methodical quests:

> The will to truth which will still tempt us to many a venture, that famous truthfulness of which all philosophers so far have spoken with respect --what questions has this will to truth not laid before us! (...) *Who* is it really that puts questions to us here? *What* in us really wants "truth"? (JGB § 1)

In order to show that genealogy can be regarded as a critical principle of interpretation in Nietzsche, it is important to place it first within the broader context of Nietzsche's thought, and then proceed to see to what extent it constitutes the central problematic of his philosophy. This means, before anything, that some unity has been presupposed, not necessarily a systematic one, but a certain coherence of thought in the aphorismatic work of an original thinker

---

[7] Cf. F. Nietzsche, "Le Philosophe. Considérations sur le conflit de l'art et de la connaissance," in *La naissance de la philosophie à l'époque de la tragédie grecque*, (Paris: Gallimard, 1985), 194.

such as Nietzsche. The first great interpreters of Nietzsche, such as Karl Jaspers (*Nietzsche: Einführung in das Verständnis seines Philosophierens*, 1936) and Karl Löwith (*Nietzsches Philosophie der Ewigen Wiederkunft des Gleichen*, 1935), had already to face up to the "contradictions" inherent to the Nietzschean thought, and they offered solutions that strike us today as leaving much to be desired, such as the resort to a "real dialectic" or a primordial return to the Presocratics, respectively. Walter Kaufmann was one of the first to refute such facile solutions, in a book that would become a bestseller, in spite of all its shortcomings -- (*Nietzsche: Philosopher, Psychologist, Antichrist*, 1950).[8] It was then established that in order to fully understand and do justice to the work of Nietzsche one had to take into account not only the exegetical work on the whole of his writings (including *Der Wille zur Macht* and the entire collection of *Nachlaß*), but also its interpretation as Nietzsche himself supposedly expected to be read (a Nietzschean hermeneutics). With the publication of Heidegger's polemic *Vorlesungen* (1936-40) and *Abhandlungen* (1940-46) in 1961, the importance of a self-interpretation of Nietzschean texts --in particular, the *Will to Power*-- was once again emphasized. As in the Talmudic and Lutheran traditions, Nietzsche was to be read in the light of the whole of its own textuality, *scriptura sui ipsius interpres*. It was only following its post-Heideggerian reception in France (with Pierre Klossowski, Gilles Deleuze, Michel Foucault, Sarah Kofman, Jacques Derrida, Eric Blondel, Michel Haar, and others), that a genuine interest in an interpretative "principle" arose. It has become since then insufferable the misreading of existentialist and dialectical features into Nietzsche, and even Heideggerian glosses have become rather dispensable. The "New Nietzsche," as David Allison remarks, "asks the reader to consider the general conditions of life --its prognosis for advance and decline, its strength or weakness, its general etiology --as well as that of its sustaining culture and values." (NN xiii) In order to approach the Nietzschean corpus, the careful reader needs both "a theory of interpretation understood as a general semiotics" and a "genealogical analysis." (NN xvi) As it will be seen throughout the next sections, Foucault was such a reader of Nietzsche, both as a hermeneute of suspicion and as a genealogist of modernity.

To paraphrase Gadamer, it could be said that the hermeneutic problem in Nietzsche could be formulated in terms of truth and method, considering that it was Nietzsche, as Deleuze has pointed out, the first thinker--even before Frege and Husserl, and long before the analytical schools of language-- to have introduced in philosophy and in a correlative manner the concepts of meaning

---

[8] 3rd. revised, augmented ed., (New York: Vintage Books, 1968). Some of Kaufmann's comments and editorial remarks were simply outrageous --e.g., Nietzsche's notes on women and race.

(*Sinn/Bedeutung*) and value (*Wert*).[9] According to Deleuze, it is precisely in Nietzsche's philosophy and not in Kant's that we find the means, both theoretical and practical, to carry out the critique *tout court*.such was the very thesis appropriated and reformulated by Foucault, undoubtedly one of the greatest interpreters of Nietzsche in the last decades. As Gadamer himself has remarked in response to Habermas's charges, our experience of language --including its systematic aspects of rationality-- and our experience in the world --including the *Lebenswelt*--are co-originary and simply cannot be dissociated.[10] As will be shown, that constitutes a fundamental thesis of Nietzsche's philosophy, and failing to understand it may result in misunderstanding his perspectivism and aestheticism. I am following Allan Megill's usage of the term "aestheticism," as applied to both Nietzsche and Foucault, as it refers "not to the condition of being enclosed within the limited territory of the aesthetic, but rather to an attempt to explain the aesthetic to embrace the whole of reality."[11] In light of many passages where Nietzsche spouses this aestheticist view of reality (i.e. GT "Attempt at Self-Criticism" § 5, WP passim), we can better understand Nietzsche's critique of Kant's *désintéressement* in the third *Critique*. (GM III § 6) Long before Heidegger, Foucault, and Derrida, Nietzsche attacked the hypostatizing conceptualization of fictions such as Man, Culture, or History, to account for the bridging of nature and spirit, phenomena and noumena. And yet, I will argue that Nietzsche's aestheticism differs from Heidegger's precisely because of the former's refusal to yield to new forms of mysticism or eschatological expectations. Not even a god can save us, according to Nietzsche, not even the overcoming of metaphysics would deliver us from the completion of nihilism. Heidegger's aestheticism conceives of the will to power as an artwork, so as to

---

[9] To be sure, there were other philosophers who had previously dealt with the problems of meaning and value, without however the modern interest in critically submitting such formulations to a self-criticism of the very method employed. Cf. G. Deleuze, *Nietzsche et la philosophie*, (Paris: PUF, 1962), 1: "Le projet le plus général de Nietzsche consiste en ceci: introduire en philosophie les concepts de sens et de valeur. Il est évident que la philosophie moderne, en grande partie, a vécu et vit encore de Nietzsche...Nietzsche n'a jamais caché que la philosophie du sens et des valeurs dût être une critique. Que Kant n'a pas mené la vraie critique, parce qu'il n'a pas su en poser le problème en termes de valeurs, tel est même un des mobiles principaux de l'oeuvre de Nietzsche."

[10] Cf. Hans-Georg Gadamer, *Truth and Method* [*Wahrheit und Methode*, 1st. ed. 1960; 2nd. ed. 1965], (New York: Crossroad, 1986), p. 495. The debate between Gadamer and Habermas, moderated by Paul Ricoeur (*Hermeneutics and the Human Sciences*, ed. J.B. Thompson, Cambridge University Press, 1981), may to a large extent be regarded as anticipating the Foucault/Habermas "debate."

[11] Cf. A. Megill, *Prophets of Extremity: Nietzsche, Heidegger, Foucault, Derrida*, (Berkeley: University of California Press, 1985), 2.

comprise *all* that Nietzsche understands by truth. I will question this reductionist formulation, insofar as it eclipses other important aspects of the will to truth that Foucault has appropriated in his own genealogy of modernity and, in particular, in an aesthetic conception of the relationship between ethics and politics.

As opposed to Kant's reduction of truth to a propositional correspondence of the categories to the cognitive faculty of understanding, Nietzsche sought to rescue a pre-theoretical, nontranscendental aesthetics that allows for the appearing of beings to remain on the surface of being, without any resort to a suprasensible, noumenal realm that accounts for the possibility of their cognition. In JGB § 11, Nietzsche recognizes the tremendous influence that Kant exerted on German philosophy --tainted with the comical *niaiserie allemande*-- by the very introduction of the cognitive faculties of the mind. Above all, it was the suprasensible --which, as Nietzsche rightly remarked, inspired Schelling's "intellectual intuition" (and Hegel's critique of Kant)-- that betrayed the veritable *virtus dormitiva* ("sleepy faculty") of Kant's attempt to base truth on transcendental grounds--"*Vermöge eines Vermögens*" ("by virtue of some virtue"). In order to awake the senses once again, and anticipating Foucault's overcoming of Kant's "anthropological slumber," Nietzsche calls for new philosophers to create, with the hammer, new values and new truths: "*Genuine philosophers, however, are commanders and legislators:* they say, '*thus it shall be!*'" And he adds, "Their 'knowing' is *creating*, their creating is a legislation, their will to truth is --*will to power*." (JGB § 212) Nietzsche's antidote is their remedy, just as the real and the true are the appearing of what is always a shadow, a false reverse. Nietzsche had already addressed the question "what is truth?," in an oft-quoted paragraph from an 1873 *Nachlaß*, *Über Wahrheit und Lüge im aussermoralischen Sinne*, that unmasks the perspectivism of every knowledge:

> What, then, is truth? A mobile army of metaphors, metonyms, and anthropomorphisms --in short, a sum of human relations, which have been enhanced, transposed, and embellished poetically and rhetorically, and which after long use seems firm, canonical, and obligatory to a people: truths are illusions about which one has forgotten that this is what they are...

Commenting on this passage and comparing it with classical definitions of rhetoric, Derrida has shown how Nietzsche sought to take his distances from philosophical interpretations of the concept of truth and conceptual philosophizing --as metaphor subverts the generative role of philosophical concept.[12] As over

---

[12] J. Derrida, "La mythologie blanche: La métaphore dans le texte philosophique", in *Marges de la philosophie*, Paris: Minuit, 1972.

against the rule of the Aristotelian-Hegelian metaphor of the intelligible (*ousia, geistig*) over the sensible (*phainomena, sinnlich*), according to which certain philosophemes conquer a conceptual privilege, Derrida finds inspiration in Nietzsche to propound metaphoricity as nonconcept --an effect of *différance*-- expressing thus "what is proper to man," in this perpetual *metaphorein* (transposing, transferring, transforming, "la relève de la métaphore") of appropriating and expropriating what is his own--language, rationality, thinking. Hermeneutics is thus radicalized into "deconstruction," so that every meaning is always already (*toujours déjà, immer schon*) an effect of interpretations. Although I do not intend to examine how Derrida's reading of Nietzsche (and Heidegger) leads us to the *Abbau* of metaphysical traditions to be re-interpreted, I must signal the relevance of the metaphor and the correlation between semiology (or semiotics) and ontology for a full understanding of Foucault's reading of Nietzsche. That will be fully elaborated in the third chapter, by invoking Foucault's essay on "Nietzsche, Freud, Marx," at the threshold of the era of the hermeneutics of suspicion in post-existential France, in the 60's and 70's.

In the above-mentioned essay on truth, Nietzsche articulates also the "drive to truth" in terms of the instinctive need that makes possible for human beings to survive as social beings, out of "the obligation to lie according to a fixed convention, to lie herd-like in a style obligatory for all." However conventionalist and relativist, this Nietzschean formulation, very reminiscent of the Hobbesian *pactum*, should not be taken *prima facie*, as some sort of irrationalist creed but as an expression of his philosophical perspectivism, thoroughly consistent with his view of the world as human interpretation. That modern, European man, after thousands of years has reached a certain state of self-consciousness, in which his existence makes sense, according to Nietzsche, proves nothing else than the all-too human wish that such a sense is true and founded. After all, nothing can assure us that the human species will be preserved forever --that the fate of humans will be different, say, from that of the dinosaurs or other extinguished species. If rationality --and sociability, for that matter-- distinguishes us from other species, that remains all the same an effect and not a cause, "a means for the preservation of the individual" (§ 1) and not an end in itself. In effect, Nietzsche does not advocate any promise of "improving" humankind (EH Preface § 1), for in this consists what has been called thus far morals (cf. *Twilight of Idols* "The 'Improvers' of Humankind" § 2). The taming, breeding, weakening, sickening, and catechizing of the human beast, which Christianity so arrogantly acclaims as a civilizing "improvement" of humanity, anticipates in Nietzsche what Foucault would later develop as the practices of subjectivation that, through normalizing and disciplinary techniques, consolidates the formation of modern subjects. The

Nietzschean genealogy, as a radical critique that problematizes the epistemological delimitations of a method and of a system of universal truths, stems thus from a calling into question (*remise en question*), historically and culturally situated --decadent Europe of *fin de siècle*--, philosophically formulated around the old question: "Who are we?" Even a superficial reading of Nietzsche's major texts brings to the fore the theme of the human condition and humankind, in its relation to all the other themes of his works, even if such a thematization takes on a grave timbre, that is, as a theme to be unmasked, demythologized, and overcome. Not without reason, Nietzsche has been more known for the metaphor of the "Overman" (*Übermensch*) than any other concept. In effect, the transvaluation of values, nihilism, the death of God, the eternal return, and the will to power are all thematically related with the problem of the self-overcoming of man (*die Selbstüberwindung des Menschen*). Thus, the anti-humanism of Nietzsche's critique of religion, morals, and metaphysics is rooted in a philosophy directed towards the future, without delineating, however, any utopian, eschatological, or messianic horizons. "Who, then, amidst these dangers besetting our age, will pledge his services as sentinel and champion of *humankind* [*Menschlichkeit*]?,"

> asks Nietzsche, "Who will raise the *image of man* [*das Bild des Menschen*] when everyone feels in himself the worm of selfishness and a jackal terror, and has fallen from that image into bestiality and even robot automatism?" (Third *Unmodern Observation*, "Schopenhauer As Educator" § 4) Nietzsche seems to be thus engaged in a prophetic mission, with the conviction of a Daniel or a Jeremiah, predestined to announce the tragic fate that is about to assail nations and tribes. However apocalyptic it may sound, like many other of his texts, Nietzsche's atonality forbids any stylistic harmonization in function of a determinate literary genre or philosopheme. Hence the apparent oppositions (e.g., the Apollinean vs. the Dionysian, the Socratic vs. the tragic) which will only be overcome by the affirmation of the *amor fati*, the Nietzschean formula for greatness in a human being: "that one wants nothing to be different, not forward, not backward, not in all eternity. Not merely bear what is necessary...but love it." (EH "Why I am so clever" § 10) Such is, without doubt, the only *sollen* of human nature, which Nietzsche translates in autobiographical manner in the *Ecce Homo*: "How to become what one is." The aphorisms of the *Nachlaß* "Die Unschuld des Werdens," dedicated to the composition of *Zarathustra*[13] reveal the "anthropological" character of the will to power, conceived as that which makes both cosmology and ontology possible, correlate to the eternal return of the Same.

---

[13] In Kröner's edition, vol. 83, §§ 1208-1415.

It is important to add that, in this Nietzschean context, "anthropology" cannot be mistaken for a metaphysical, philosophical conception of human nature, for the place of the *anthropos* vis-à-vis the *kosmos* is not that of a cognitive opposition between subject and object (Kant's *Gegenstand*), since human-being is always displaced by its becoming-in-the-world. For the world itself, according to Nietzsche, "the world viewed from the inside, the world defined and determined according to its 'intelligible character'" --to parody Kant-- is "'the will to power' and nothing else." (JGB §36) If one discounts the dangerous rigor of formulas of proportionality, one may say that the will to power is for being what the eternal return is for the becoming of the same. Being human is to become in the world what one should be in one's self-overcoming. "Der Mensch ist etwas, das überwunden werden soll"-- "man is something that ought to be overcome" --, such is the motto of Nietzsche's magnum opus, *Thus Spake Zarathustra* (see, for instance, Z Vorrede 3, Vom Krieg und Kriegsvolke, passim), and of the Nietzschean *opera* in general (cf. JGB § 257; GM II 10, III 27; EH Z 6, Z 8, IV 5; WM 804, 983, 1001, 1051, 1027, 1060). The will to power itself is decisively introduced as will to overcome oneself (cf. Z Part II, esp. "Von der Selbstüberwindung"), not as the psychological will à la Schopenhauer, but as the cosmological expression of the eternal return (cf. Z Parts III and IV, esp. "Von alten und neuen Tafeln") and from this follows all understanding of Nietzsche's philosophy. Thus, method and truth in the Nietzschean conception of the *humanum* cannot be dissociated from the sense and value assigned to human existence itself, both in ontological and cosmological terms. As we will see, genealogy fulfills the triple task of critique as applied to the analysis of Western European culture, and can thus be seen as a method of cultural, historical diagnosis.

2. HUMAN NATURE AND THE WILL TO POWER

Was es mit unsrer Heiterkeit auf sich hat. Das größte neuere Ereignis --daß "Gott tot ist," daß der Glaube an den christlichen Gott unglaubwürdig geworden ist-- beginnt bereits seine ersten Schatten über Europa zu werfen. (...) In der Hauptsache aber darf man sagen; das Ereignis selbst ist viel zu groß, zu fern, zu abseits vom Fassungsvermögen vieler, als daß auch nur seine Kunde schon angelangt heißen dürfte... (FW § 343)

The death of God is, for Nietzsche, the greatest of all the monumental events of European modernity, the most significant of all, and this is to be taken both in a metaphysical and cultural-historical sense. It must thus call into question a

Heideggerian reading that concludes --for reasons intrinsic to Heidegger's ontological hermeneutics-- that "Nietzsche himself interprets the course of Western history metaphysically and in truth as the ascension and development of nihilism."[14] Now, Heidegger reduces the Nietzschean work to an immanent critique of metaphysics which, precisely because it remains within its historicity, cannot overcome metaphysical thinking, in its very ontotheological, nihilistic constitution. The "will to power," according to Heidegger, must thus figure among the greatest metaphysical motifs of Western philosophy, such as the Platonic *eidos*, the Cartesian *substantia*, and the Kantian *Ding an sich*. Just as Marx could not do away with Hegelian dialectics, Nietzsche would have at most reversed the transcendental epistemology of Kant, without succeeding in thinking its essence in a post-metaphysical gesture. To a large extent, Foucault's work has challenged these blind spots of Heidegger's reading of Nietzsche, ultimately guided by a reduction of the "will to power" to the *Sein des Seienden*. For the purpose of the present study, there is still another aspect that marks off Foucault's reading of Nietzsche from Heidegger's, and that deserves our attention. Commenting on the famous passage on the death of God (FW § 125, *Der tolle Mensch*, complemented by § 343), Heidegger signals the sense of "madness" on the part of the man who proclaims the death of God, to be distinguished from the "foolishness" of denying God as an unbeliever. As for Foucault, he is rather concerned with madness as a broader phenomenon of subjectivation, so that a psychiatric reading of this passage should not exclude a theological one, nor the social analysis minimize its juridical aspects, but the very definitions of madness (*Wahnsinn*) and unreason (*Irrsinn*) are to be called into question, since they were also constituted in the historical process of subject-formations.[15] At any rate, the expression "madman" is used by Nietzsche as a parody to the allusion by the Psalmist to the "fool" who says in his heart: "There is no God" (Psalm 14:1). In the original context --which Nietzsche metaphorically transposes in grand style--,

---

[14] M. Heidegger, "The Word of Nietzsche: 'God is Dead'" [Nietzsches Wort "Gott ist tot", 1943] in *The Question Concerning Technology and Other Essays*, tr. W. Lovitt, (New York: Harper & Row, 1977), p. 54. Heidegger's reading of Nietzsche, insofar as historicity, metaphysics, and nihilism are concerned, has been also elaborated in the essay "Zur Seinsfrage", on the "line" of completion for the fulfilling (*Vollendung*) of nihilism, in response to Ernst Jünger's essay, "Über die Linie," in *Wegmarken*, (Frankfurt: Klostermann, 1967).

[15] Cf. M. Foucault, *Folie et déraison: Histoire de la folie à l'âge classique* (Paris: Plon, 1961; 2ᵉ. ed. Gallimard, 1972); "Nietzsche, Freud, Marx" in *Cahiers de Royaumont* N°. VI, VIIᵉ. Colloque, (4-8 juillet 1964), Paris: Minuit, 1967, pp. 183-200. When he was inquired whether Nietzsche underwent the experience of madness ("que de grands esprits comme Nietzsche puissent avoir l'expérience de la folie"), Foucault replied with a double yea, "oui, oui!"

the word of the Psalmist (in Hebrew, *naval*) refers to the unrighteous and to the unbeliever --whoever does not believe in God, turns out to be a fool, a madman. This is the same sense that will be later transvalued (*umwerten*) by Paul to contrast, in a world of unbelievers, the "folly of God" with the "wisdom of men" (1 Corinthians 1:18-25) and, on the eve of modernity, by Luther and Pascal, in the radical opposition between theology and philosophy ("Le dieu d'Abraham, d'Isaac et de Jacob n'est point le dieu des philosophes"). The madman who in a bright morning lit a lantern and ran to the market place, screaming "I seek God!," cannot be thus identified with Nietzsche himself or even with the character "Zarathustra" --as Heidegger seems to suggest.[16] To be sure, the madman appears as the messenger of an event (the death of God), that he himself interprets as a metaphysical problem:

> **The Madman.** Have you not heard of that madman who lit a lantern in the bright morning hours, ran to the market place, and cried incessantly, "I seek God! I seek God!" As many of those who do not believe in God were standing around just then, he provoked much laughter. Why, did he get lost? said one. Did he lose his way like a child? said another. Or is he hiding? Is he afraid of us? Has he gone on a voyage? or emigrated? Thus they yelled and laughed. The madman jumped into their midst and pierced them with his glances.
> "Whither is God?" he cried. "I shall tell you. **We have killed him** --you and I. All of us are his murderers. But how have we done this? How were we able to drink up the sea? Who gave us the sponge to wipe away the entire horizon? What did we do when we unchained this earth from its sun? Whither is it moving now? Whither are we moving now? Away from all suns? Are we not plunging continually? Backward, sideward, forward, in all directions? Is there any up or down left? Are we not straying as through an infinite nothing? Do we not feel the breath of empty space? Has it not become colder? Is not night and more night coming on all the while? Must not lanterns be lit in the morning? Do we not hear anything yet of the noise of the gravediggers who are burying God? Do we not smell anything yet of God's decomposition? Gods too decompose. God is dead. God remains dead. And we have killed him. (FW § 125)

Madness appears here as a limit-experience of a rationality in crisis, with the secularizing collapse of the belief in a foundation that bestows meaning to human existence, the belief that there must be transcendent grounds for ultimate values. Kant's transcendental criticism, as a true representative of the *aufgeklärte*

---

[16] Cf. M. Heidegger, "The Word of Nietzsche: 'God is Dead'", op. cit., 111-112; id., "Who is Nietzsche's Zarathustra?", in David B. Allison (ed.), *The New Nietzsche*, op. cit., 64-79.

philosophy, was decisive for this event, with its refusal of dogmatic, metaphysical solutions to the antinomies of cosmology, psychology, anthropology, and theology. But Nietzsche also questions Kant's critique of reason precisely at the systematic level that accounts for a practical assurance of pure reason, following the critique of theoretical reason. Even if one cannot prove God's existence or even if God never existed, human reason can always create one and live as if there were such a being. That reason cannot account for its other, that it cannot transgress its theoretical and practical uses, is a clear symptom of its incapacity to judge its own fateful breakdown. It takes a madman to proclaim, however naive it may sound, that God is dead. It takes a madman to proclaim, despite all nonsense, the greatest triumph of modern reason in its endless wars against fear, superstition, and dogma. Nietzsche is certainly using a metaphorical language, but the rather raw description of the putrefaction of a divine corpse signals the proximity and historicity of this tremendous cultural event. After all, we modern men are the ones who killed God. We --the legitimate heirs of the Judaeo-Christian tradition that built up the scenarios of Western civilizations-- are the very ones who submitted ourselves to the yoke of a divine creator and judge. Nietzsche's transvaluation cannot thus be reduced to a mere reversal of values, such as Feuerbach's antitheological manifesto (*homo homini deus est*) or Marx's critique of ideology (*camera obscura*, *Wirklichkeit* versus *Vorstellung*), not even to a Heideggerian *Umkehrung* of metaphysics or self-proclaimed *Überwindung* of Western metaphysics.[17] It is, therefore, an effect of the self-overcoming (*Selbstüberwindung*) of humankind, as the outcome of civilizing processes, with religion appearing as the major expression of this "experience of the history of humanity as a whole" taken individually, above all in the Judaeo-Christian conception of a *Heilsgeschichte* ("history of salvation"). "This godlike feeling," writes Nietzsche, "would then be called --humaneness" ("Dieses göttliche Gefühl hieße dann--Menschlichkeit!" (FW § 337 "Die zukünftige 'Menschlichkeit'"). The modern feeling for one's own participation in universal history, the humanist sense of historical belonging, is what Nietzsche's "history of the present" seeks to unfold in his critique of idealism. The genealogy of Christianity occupies an important place in this radical critique of modernity, although the critique of religion in Nietzsche does not lead to the foundation of a new secular kingdom (Feuerbach) or to a positive critique of politics (Marx), but rather to the self-fulfillment and serenity (*Heiterkeit*), which is the true meaning of the "joie de vivre" of a creative, free spirit and of the *Gay Science*. (cf. §§ 290, 343) For

---

[17] In fact, Heidegger himself problematizes the question of the overcoming (*Überwindung*) of metaphysics in terms of a *Verwindung* (**verwinden, venir à bout de,** to cope with), esp. in the essay "Zur Seinsfrage", op. cit. Cf. supra.

Zaratustra, "God is a conjecture [*Mutmaßung*]," but because it cannot be limited to what is thinkable (*begrenzt sei in der Denkbarkeit*) it deserves to be dealt with as a sickness and vertigo. The *Übermensch*, on the other hand, can be thought and it is within our reach to create it out by willing our self-overcoming. "Willing liberates [*Wollen befreit*]: that is the true teaching of will and liberty." (Z II "Upon the Blessed Isles") Still in the same passage, Zaratustra exclaims: "Away from God and gods this will [to create] has lured me; what could one create if gods existed?" And he adds, "But my fervent will to create impels me ever again toward man; thus is the hammer impelled toward the stone." For Nietzsche, creation, in the broader sense of *poiesis*, is the true vocation of human beings in the full exercise of their freedom, through their will to power, in an active manner, not reactive, without the resentment that characterizes religious man. As will be seen, Foucault's interpretation of Nietzsche does full justice to the latter's aestheticism without reducing it to a *passe-partout* hermeneutics but rather stressing the *poiesis* of "giving style to someone's character" [*seinem Charakter "Stil geben"*], in a self-stylizing, polyphonic aesthetics of existence that multiplies *ad infinitum* the relations of codification and decodification of every experience --taken as fact or human interpretation. The death of God is, therefore, a paradigm of such a critical gesture, at the levelling of facts and interpretations, in the same historical event.

On the other hand, the death of God may be interpreted as the sign of times of modernity, as the triumph of autonomy and the emancipation of human reason announce the imminence of the Great Noon, the fullness of the three great metamorphoses of the camel, the lion, and the child (cf. Z II "Von den drei Verwandlungen" and IV "Das Zeichen"). The collapse of rationality -- understood as "the discipline of their minds [*die Zucht ihres Kopfes*]"-- would be, for Nietzsche, nothing less than "the eruption of madness [*Irrsinn*],... the eruption of arbitrariness [*Belieben*] in feeling, seeing, and hearing, the enjoyment of the mind's lack of discipline [*Zuchtlosigkeit des Kopfes*], the joy in human unreason [*die Freude am Menschen-Unverstande*]." (FW § 76) Humankind up to our days has lived in full agreement, like friends, with the "healthy common sense" (*gesunder Menschen-verstand*)--a question of survival. The man of the future, according to the same paragraph, since he is even more aware of this conventionalism, is led to suspicion and unbelief. Thus, neither truth nor certainty are the opposite of unreason or madness, but "the universality and the universal binding force of a faith [*die Allgemeinheit und Allverbindlichkeit eines Glaubens*]; in sum, the non-arbitrary character of judgments [*das Nicht-Beliebige im Urteilen*]." Therefore, if Nietzsche celebrates madness in the carnival of the death of God, it is because it inaugurates a new dawn of the "de-deification da nature": When will we complete our de-deification of nature? When may we begin to "*naturalize*" humanity in terms of a pure, newly discovered, newly redeemed nature? Wann werden wir die Natur ganz entgöttlicht haben! Wann werden wir anfangen dürfen, uns Menschen mit der reinen, neu gefundenen, neu erlösten Natur zu *vernatürlichen*!" (FW § 109)

The project of reintegrating human nature into cosmological nature -- different, say, from the humanization of nature proposed by the young Marx-- cannot be dissociated from the Nietzschean *motif* of the death of God. The paragraphs 108 through 125 of the *Gay Science* constitute, in effect, the immediate context that culminates with the death of God, namely, the dedeification of nature, whose religious context is clearly articulated in cosmological terms and not exclusively historico-ontological --as would result from a reading that privileges the history of metaphysics in the *Will to Power*. We see thus that the question of rationality and modernity refers to a complex anthropological problematic, where the critique of value and meaning requires a careful exam of different correlative aspects --including the problems of an epistemological, political, and ethical order. I will conclude this section with an allusion to the critique of religion in the *Will to Power*.

After the composition of the *Twilight of Idols* in 1888, in the last year of his literary production prior to his mental collapse, Nietzsche seemed to have abandoned the project of publishing a collection of aphorisms called *Der Wille zur Macht*, and decided to write a book, *Versuch einer Umwertung aller Werte* (subtitle of WM), composed of four essays, of which only one, the *Antichrist* was completed, together with the preface. The final edition of over one thousand notes by Nietzsche (1883-1888) that compose this majestoso *Nachlaß* was carefully undertaken by his friend Peter Gast in 1906. It is interesting to recapitulate the division of the work into four books:

I. European Nihilism
II. Critique of Highest Values Hitherto
III. Principles of a New Valuation
IV. Discipline and Breeding

The first subdivision of the Second Book, "Critique of Religion," as Kaufmann remarked, provided great part of the material for the composition of the *Antichrist*. The Nietzschean critique of religion is itself divided into three parts,

1. Genesis of Religions
2. History of Christianity
3. Christian Ideals

The correlation between power and the formation of subjects (WM § 135), the themes of priestly religiosity, slave morality, pessimistic nihilism (§ 156), *ressentiment* (§ 167), the transition from Judaism to Christianity (§ 181, passim), the herd morality, Paul's psychology (§§ 171, 173), castration (§ 204), self-denial, to sum up, the transvaluation of values, is developed according to the same logic found in *Beyond Good and Evil* and in the *Genealogy of Morals*. It must be noted, however, that the context stresses the social-historical aspects of the evolution of religious phenomena in relation to nihilism. This historical-metaphysical background may thus favor a Heideggerian reading as long as we do not fall prey to a structuralist imposition of a *grille de lecture* to the textual totality of the Nietzschean work, as in a methodical formalization.[18]

No doubt, the clear connection between the death of God and the collapse of the cosmic order (FW § 125) --understood as an interpretation of human nature-- indicates that Nietzsche is invoking here the Judaeo-Christian God the Creator of heavens and earth, the *causa prima*, the metaphysical God of theism --with the transition from the Hebrew to the Greek constituting the cultural background to the transvaluation of religion. (cf. AC §§ 37-45) In another aphorism (FW § 343), opening the Fifth Book ("We Fearless Ones") added to the second edition of the *Gay Science* in 1886, Nietzsche affirms "that God is dead" to mean "that the belief in the Christian god has become unbelievable" --giving sequence to the *incipit tragoedia* of the last paragraph of the Fourth Book, identical to the first chapter of the Prologue of *Zarathustra*. The death of God signals, therefore, the threshold of tragedy, to be rediscovered in the infinite horizon of seas never sailed before --cf. FW §§ 124, 281, 283, 289, 291, with allusions to Columbus and Genoa. Zarathustra, the solitary archaeologist of meaning, begins his ministry under the sign of the death of God as he set out to discover and explore a decodified humanity, in light of past civilizations, leading to its decomposition and whose tragic fate has already been announced in the very negation of tragedy by religious belief. The tragic fate of tragedy in the Western world was, in effect, a theme that Nietzsche had already explored in his GT, and inspired much of Foucault's interest in the cultural diagnosis of civilizations. According to certain

---

[18] Such is in effect the great post-structuralist thesis --and even anti-structuralist-- that Foucault would oppose to the Heideggerian reading of Nietzsche and its fundamental-ontological appropriation of the genealogy.

versions of the death of God, since nihilism itself may be either "active" or "passive" (WM § 22), Nietzschean atheism would likewise be necessary and plausible of being overcome (*überwinden*). In this case, neither theism nor its dialectical negation would suffice to solve the Nietzschean problematic. Thus as the project of an *Umwertung* with reference to the *Geschichte / Geschick* of European nihilism, Nietzsche's sentence "*Gott ist tot*" would point to a quasi-transcendental deconstruction of the "history of God." Hence, among *Hoffnung*, secularization, and liberation theologians, Nietzsche's name is ineptly associated with Feuerbach and Marx in the celebration of a dedeified world, as a cultural, dialectical process.[19]

3. NIETZSCHE'S CRITIQUE OF KANTIAN MORALITY

Die christliche Moralität selbst, der immer strenger genommene Begriff der Wahrhaftigkeit, die Beichväter-Feinheit des christlichen Gewissens, übersetzt und sublimiert zum wissenschaftlichen Gewissen, zur intellektuellen Sauberkeit a jeden Preis. Die Natur ansehn, als ob sie ein Beweis für die Güte und Obhut eines Gottes sei; die Geschichte interpretieren zu Ehren einer göttlichen Vernunft, als beständiges Zeugnis einer sittlichen Weltordnung und sittlicher Schlußabsichten; die eignen Erlebnisse auslegen, wie sie fromme Menschen lange genug ausgelegt haben, wie als ob alles Fügung, alles Wink, alles Heil der Seele zuliebe ausgedacht und geschikt sei: das ist nunmehr *vorbei*, das hat das Gewissen *gegen* sich, das gilt allen feineren Gewissen als unanständig, unehrlich, als Lügnerei, Feminismus, Schwachheit, Feigheit --mit dieser Strenge, wenn irgend womit, sind wir eben *guter Europäer* und Erben von Europas längster und tapferster Selbstüberwindung... (GM III § 27; FW § 357)

The long citation --self-citation of an author that overcomes himself-- is invoked by Nietzsche as he formulates the "law of life" (*das Gesetz des Lebens*) as "a law of *necessary* 'self-overcoming' that is in the essence of life [*das Gesetz der notwendigen "Selbstüberwindung" im Wesen des Lebens*]," to wit, that "[a]ll great things bring about their own destruction through an act self-overcoming [*Alle großen Dinge gehen durch sich selbst zugrunde, durch einen Akt der Selbstaufhebung*]." (GM III § 27) This great Nietzschean thesis is certainly implicit in his doctrines of the will to power and of the transvaluation of all values --as Nietzsche himself saw it in allusion to the "work that he was preparing [*ein Werk, das ich vorbereite: "Der Wille zur Macht." Versuch einer Umwertung aller*

---

[19] Cf. Excursus Two infra.

Werte]." In the three essays explicitly dedicated to the critique of morality --the critique of the morality of *ressentiment* (Christianity), critique of the self-conscious, autonomous morality (Kant), and the critique of the ascetic ideal (nihilism) (cf. EH GM)--, Nietzsche undertakes in a quasi-methodic fashion his project of transvaluation as a new demand for the self-overcoming of "modern man": "we need a *critique* of moral values, *the value of these values themselves must first be called into question.*" (GM Preface § 6) And, in order to accomplish this, one needs a "genealogy," a formulation of the knowledge of the conditions and circumstances of the birth of morality, as a *wirkliche Historie der Moral*, "gray" --as the document, in opposition to the pristine, spiritual "blue" (§ 7)--, in brief, a historical critique and a critical history that are immanent or, in Foucault's words, "a form of history which can account for the constitution of knowledges (*savoirs*), discourses (*discours*), domains of objects, etc., without having to make reference to a subject, which is either transcendental in relation to the field of events, or runs in its empty sameness throughout the course of history." (FR 59). Genealogy is thus presented as the climax of a critique of morals, already outlined and partially elaborated in *Beyond Good and Evil* (1886), though in these two books Kant's morality is approached in a more systematic fashion than in the *Gay Science*. The critique of morals emerges not so much as the logical moment that follows the suppression of religion, but as being adjacent to the very genealogy of modern man. Modernity cannot conceal, therefore, the moral character that constitutes itself as such, in that "'autonomous' and 'moral' are mutually exclusive," according to Nietzsche --contra Kant. (GM II § 2) On the other hand, Nietzsche seeks to rescue a positive conception of modern man in the anticipation of the *Übermensch* that must be celebrated today, in the ought of this innocent becoming that is the self-overcoming of man. Thus, whatever is "moral" is precisely what ought to be overcome in the conception of humanity that culminated with German idealism. The atheist, creative thinking of the modern "free spirit" is to be thus opposed to theistic, metaphysical thought, no longer guided and limited by religious belief. In this Kant and Nietzsche share the same conviction that it is necessary to use one's own understanding, *sapere aude*, so that the spirit of freedom be fulfilled --despite all the divergences as for the meaning of such ideal of freedom, overall in the concepts of "will" and "free will." Rousseau, Voltaire, and French enlightened *philosophes* would have been a common source for both Nietzsche and Kant, in their undertaking of a critical philosophy. Nevertheless, Nietzsche's attitude toward the *Aufklärung* --frequently cited as an example of his supposed irrationalism and anti-modernism-- differs from Kant's not only in its political implications, but also in its historical, philosophical presuppositions. The question of morals is thus decisive for a correct evaluation of these divergences.

In principle, Kant is upheld by Nietzsche as the great champion of the philosophical struggle against the optimism of naïve realism, precisely by having raised phenomena to the status of reality --just as Schopenhauer transvalue them into *Vorstellungen* (cf. GT §§ 18, 19). In 1886, in the preface to the second edition of *Morgenröte*, Nietzsche denounces the seduction of morals in Kant, the belief that cannot be founded upon its own conception of history and nature (M Pref. § 3). In the same book, Nietzsche criticizes Kant for the dichotomy of sensible and non-sensible in the conception of moral man (M §§ 132, 481), but seems to remain faithful to the ideal of *Aufklärung*:

> This Enlightenment we must now carry further forward: let us not worry about the "great revolution" and the "great reaction" against it which have taken place --they are no more than the sporting of waves in comparison with the truly great flood which bears *us* along! (M § 197)

Nietzsche identifies himself, therefore, with the critical thrust of Kant's philosophy, to the extent that it does not fall back into an ascetic ideal, typical of Christian morality (M § 339), which would have been supposedly overcome in Kant's own critique of metaphysics. In effect, it is precisely against the Kantian idea of "progress," reappropriated by Hegel, that Nietzsche undertakes his genealogical critique, already anticipated in the Second Unmodern Observation ("Vom Nutzen und Nachteil der Historie für Leben," 1874). What is at stake, therefore, is the articulation of historicity and humanity so as to avoid the subordination of human development to the logic of progress and the transcendental foundations of morals. As Nietzsche criticizes the utilitarianist conception of Paul Rée (GM Preface § 4, 7), it is not only the evolutionist historicism that he seeks to combat but above all the metaphysical, suprahistorical perspective that subtly guides historiography. Thus, one of the greatest contributions of Nietzsche consists in having denounced a conception of history that presupposes a transcendental unity --typical of the soteriological reading of Christianity. Nietzsche unmasks, therefore, Kantian morality as the return to what had already been overcome by the *Aufklärung*, namely, faith in whatever cannot be thought--for religion itself, according to Kant, does not seek to know God in the same way one claims to know nature. This is outlined in the second part of the Second Book of WM (§§ 253-405, "Critique of Morality"):

1. Origin of Moral Valuations

2. The Herd
3. General Remarks on Morality
4. How Virtue is Made to Dominate
5. The Moral Ideal
6. Further Considerations for a Critique of Morality

The entire question of morality, according to Nietzsche, has been reformulated as a question of faith, as the subtle, dogmatic ideal that remains faithful to the "beyond" --from Plato to Kant and Hegel. Nietzsche's main thesis, following the equivalence between *Leben* and *Wille zur Macht* (WM § 254), is thus enunciated: *"there are no moral phenomena, there is only a moral interpretation of these phenomena. This interpretation itself is of extra-moral origin."* (WM § 258) We are thus transposed into the semiological problem of the metaphor --what may well be discarded as a vicious circle in an ontological hermeneutic, depending on the perspective adopted. I have adopted a critical, textual hermeneutic that simply refers us back to the context of the previous discussion on truth and metaphor: there are no universals in the Nietzschean lexicon. The "extra-moral origin" is only the reversal of morals, the immorality of resentment and of all other *desiderata* of ideals forged for humanity (WM §§ 266, 373, 390), supposedly meant for a "better" humanity. Such is the great *pia fraus* of the Christian religion. The critique of religion and the critique of morals presuppose the conception of sense and value --such as in the formula "good and evil"-- that should not escape the boundaries of critique, as if it were some sort of "immaculate conception."[20] The evacuation of the divine, contrary to a Hegelian *kenosis* that finds its fullness through the positive work of the negative, does not suscitate any hope of reconciliation. The nihilism is a radical, irreversible event:

> What does nihilism mean? *That the highest values devaluate themselves.* The aim is lacking; "why?" finds no answer.
> *Radical nihilism* is the conviction of an absolute untenability of existence when it comes to the highest values one recognizes; plus the realization that we lack the least right to posit a beyond or an in-itself of things that might be "divine" or morality incarnate. This realization is a consequence of the cultivation of "truthfulness" --thus itself a consequence of the faith in morality. (WP § 3)

---

[20] Cf. Jacques Derrida's critique of the Hegelian conception of the concept in *Glas*, (Paris: Galilée, 1974).

The radical critique that Nietzsche undertakes against Christian morality provides us with the methodological clue and the very *Sache* of his experimentalism, still in the "Versuch einer Umwertung aller Werte." Simply by not having nothing (*nihil*) beyond God, once the true, the good, and the beautiful are necessarily transvalued with the death of God. The same fate is, in effect, reserved for the socialist and democratic systems. God is dead, therefore, there is nothing to be grounded in, neither in moral nor in ontological terms. It is not so much the question of having nothing beyond God, but of having no fundamental "beyond" at all. All we have been left with is the immanence of the world, co-originary with the innocent becoming of human nature. Nothing else, nothing beyond, above or underneath us. Nothing is given as principle or end, cause or reason to give meaning to what we are. To the Kantian *Paukenschlag* that opposes "the starry sky above me" to "the moral law within me" (KpV A 288), Nietzsche proposes a *gaya scienza* that transgresses the very boundaries of whatever is "outside" and "inside," by the affirmation of a law without purity or end:

Sternen-Moral

Vorausbestimmt zur Sternenbahn,
Was geht dich, Stern, das Dunkel an?
Roll selig hin durch diese Zeit!
Ihr Elend sei dir fremd und weit!
Der fernsten Welt gehört dein Schein:
Mitleid soll Sünde für dich sein!
Nur *ein* Gebot gilt dir: sein rein![21]

4. NIETZSCHE AND THE CRITIQUE OF SUBJECTIVITY

Es ist, wie man errät, nicht der Gegensatz von Subjekt und Objekt, der mich hier angeht: diese Unterscheidung überlasse ich den Erkenntnistheoretikern, welche in den Schlingen der Grammatik (der Volks-Metaphysik) hängengeblieben sind. Es ist erst recht nicht der Gegensatz von "Ding an sich" und Erscheinung: denn wir "erkennen" bei weitem nicht genung, the auch nur so *scheiden* zu dürfen. Wir haben eben gar kein Organ für das *Erkennen*, für die "Wahrheit": wir "wissen" (oder glauben oder bilden uns ein) gerade so viel,

---

[21] FW Prelude § 63: "Called a star's orbit to pursue,/ What is the darkness, star, to you?/ Roll on in bliss, traverse this age--/ Its misery far from you and strange./ Let farthest world your light secure./ Pity is sin you must abjure./ But one command is yours: be pure!" (Kaufmann' trans.)

als es im Interesse der Menschen-Herde, der Gattung, *nützlich* sein mag... (FW § 354)

The Provençal accent of the "gaya scienza" translates and betrays the "ideal of a free spirit," cultivated by Nietzsche in that year of transition (1882, 1st ed. of FW): the troubadour, dancer, and poet that rediscovers the telluric philosophy, the philosophy of body and surface. *Gaya* is the goddess Earth, the only one to whom fidelity is due. (FW §§ 362-377) Thus, Nietzsche invokes the theme of the Great Navigations (Genoa, Columbus, the seas that defy us to explore infinity). The humanity of the future is doomed to be guided by this new sense of historicity (FW 337, "Die zukünftige 'Menschlichkeit'"), as if we could sense the history of the entire humanity as our own history, "*wer die Geschichte der Menschen insgesamt als eigne Geschichte zu fühlen weiß...*" Historicity, together with "the knowledge of physiology" and "a goal in the future," is placed among the things that are lacking in a philosopher. (WM § 408) The "Critique of Philosophy" outlined in the *Will to Power* (WM §§ 406-465) follows, therefore, the philosophizing with the hammer that characterizes all the work of a critical project of transvaluations: "naturalization of morals"; instead of sociology, "a theory of the forms of domination"; in lieu of society, "the cultural complex"; in lieu of epistemology, "a perspectival theory of affects"; in lieu of metaphysics and religion, "a theory of eternal return." (WM § 462) When Nietzsche wrote the preface to *Jenseits von Gut und Böse* in June 1885, the project of a "philosophy of the future" --explicitly announced in the subtitle--, had already been undertaken forty years earlier by a compatriot, Ludwig Feuerbach. Over une century earlier, Kant had published his *Prolegomena to Any Future Metaphysics* (1783). However, the Nietzschean alternative to Kant's critique and to Right- and Left-Hegelianisms could not be merely reduced to an ambitious overcoming of the philosophy of his time, as if Nietzsche preached just another gospel of "beyond." *Beyond Good and Evil* is, in effect, presented by Nietzsche himself as the aphoristic manifesto of the "good European," comprising the critical typology and social psychology of the *aufgeklärt* man that questions himself as "free spirit," *sehr freien Geister*:

> But we who are neither Jesuits nor democrats, nor even German enough, we *good Europeans* and free, *very* free spirits --we still feel it, the whole need of the spirit and the whole tension of its bow. And perhaps also the arrow, the task, and --who knows?--the goal (JGB Preface)

It seems, therefore, that in spite of all metaphoricity and of dissemination of signifiers, the text offers us the interpretative project of a human existence. The fact that he speaks in the first person of the plural (*wir*), including, "with cynicism and innocence," the very author of this philosophical prelude, already reveals the ethical, political relevance and the polemical character of this collection of thoughts. The enigmatic style of Nietzsche should not obfuscate our understanding of the subject-matter, to wit, whatever constitutes the ultimate object of metaphysics, truth in the apprehension of concepts of the world (cosmology), God (theology), and the self (psychology/anthropology). It is not by chance that Nietzsche introduces in the preface the theme of the book with the enigmatic, phallocentric words: "Supposing truth is a woman..." The metaphor could not be more aestheticist: that philosophers, from Plato through the German idealists --all of them "men" (i.e. males),-- had failed in the art of seducing a woman who never allowed to be conquered --truth as woman-object, *la femme-vérité*. The radicalism of Nietzschean aestheticism does not reside, however, in the reduction of philosophy to an aesthetic relation of appropriation and expropriation of the beautiful and the true, but in the critical immanentism of his perspectivism. If the philosopher is taken for an *artiste manqué*, his failure consists precisely in seeking to transcend the world as artwork, devaluing it as such. The Platonic opposition of sensible to the intelligible, of which the *mimesis-episteme* opposition is the particular case, permeates, according to the Nietzschean diagnosis, all the development of a metaphysics of values that bridge the Aristotelian realism to Kantian idealism:

> Consider any morality [*Moral*] with this in mind: what there is in it of "nature" teaches hatred of the *laisser aller*, of any all-too-great freedom, and implants the need for limited horizons and the nearest tasks --teaching the *narrowing of our perspective* [*Verengerung der Perspektive*], and thus in a certain sense stupidity, as a condition of life and growth. "You should obey --someone and for a long time: *else* you will perish and lose the last respect for yourself" --this appears to me to be the moral imperative of nature which, to be sure, is neither "categorical" as the old Kant would have it (hence the "else") nor addressed to the individual (what do individuals matter to her?), but to people, races, ages, classes --but above all to the whole human animal, to *man*. (JGB § 188)

Thus, in the first chapter, when dealing with the "Prejudices of Philosophers," Nietzsche unmasks the "will to truth" (*der Wille zur Wahrheit*) by calling into question the value (*Wert*) of this will: "The fundamental faith of the metaphysicians is *the faith in opposite values*." (§ 2) The great question for Nietzsche is to determine the motivation, the interest, the value of opposing a "no" to each "yes," the opposition to the innocent becoming of the world, where man is only a vector in a complex field of forces (§ 36, 230, 257). The reason why Nietzsche's conception of agency is here reconstituted, together with its correlative view of subjectivity and power, is to place the valuation of the human being within a whole play of forces (*Gesamtspiel*), where the will to power is defined as *praxis, pathos, physis*, interpretation, self-reflection, and history. And yet the will to power should not be reduced to the very becoming of being just as it cannot be identified with a psychological substratum,[22] as though Nietzsche were falling back into a naïve reformulation of the metaphysical *prima causa*. To be sure, the tension between a modern conception of the domination of nature (Hobbes) and the Romantic conception of the harmonic return to nature (Rousseau) seems to persist in the Nietzschean elaboration of the will to power -- perhaps because of his reading of Heraclitus and Parmenides. A careful reading of JGB §§ 4, 10-12, and 16-19 leads us to the reformulation of the Nietzschean question in the following terms: since the history of metaphysics cannot provide us with a theory of power that isn't itself just another effect of this history, i.e., of the reactive nihilism that underlies Western thought, a critique of power must be placed elsewhere, so as to account for the subjectivity of these theories and practices. Nietzsche proceeds thus to critique the metaphysical conceptions of agency (soul, free will, and will) so as to rescue classical notions of rationality, freedom, and the will in one single, historicized concept of human becoming. In effect, the will to power and genealogy are complementary concepts, insofar as all cultural, historical genesis is effected in human acting. The action-historicity correlation is, in effect, recognized by Nietzsche as the two great legacies of the German *Aufklärung* (WM § 1058):

The two greatest philosophical points of view (devised by Germans):

(a) that of becoming, of development.
(b) that according to the value of existence (but the wretched form of German pessimism must first be overcome!)

To be sure, one does not find in Kant the articulation between religion as a moral, cultural phenomenon, and the historical self-consciousness --as we find it, say, in Hegel, largely due to influence of Kant's writings on history.[23] Once we understand the appropriation and reproduction of historical determinations, action must be deteleologized, evacuated of all metaphysical logic of *progressus* (GM II

---

[22] Such are the readings of Heidegger, *Nietzsche*, op. cit., vol. 1, *The Will to Power as Art*, and Lukács, *The Destruction of Reason*.
[23] Cf. I. Kant, *On History*, ed. Lewis White Beck, (New York: Macmillan, 1973).

§ 12). "let us say that in all willing there is, first, a plurality of sensations, namely, the sensation of the state *"away from which"* [*von dem weg*], the sensation of the state *"towards which,"* [*zu dem hin*] the sensation of this *"from"* and *"towards"* themselves." (JGB § 19) The world is, before anything, given to us through relation and affection, the world is effected through our human existence that acts in the world and through the world. Nietzsche conceives of the will to power, therefore, as the *pathos* of personification, of incorporation, defying the very opposition of "active" and "passive." In the same text (JGB § 19), Nietzsche adds the interpretative aspect of the will to power, and besides the complex of this feeling and thinking, the "affect of command" that unveils the self-reflective character of the will to power. Action is never an end in itself, but the means for the self-experience of agency through the incorporation (*Einverleibung*) and appropriation (*Aneignung*) of experiential, interpretative worlds. Hence the resulting historicity of human practices: the subject is always an historical effect, without presupposing determinism or teleology – "necessity is not a fact but an interpretation." (WM § 552). Acting is always already *temporal*, historicizing, insofar as it is effective (*wirklich*) and not originally efficient (in the Aristotelian sense of causality). If modern metaphysics relates every cause to the third --in the Aristotelian classification of the four causes--, reducing thus the effect to a fact, the Nietzschean transvaluation seeks to rescue the effectivity of the fact in a radical critique that is regarded above all as interpretation.

We arrive thus at the anthropological problem, displaced by the effective history of metaphysics, after the unmasking of the great philosophies that disguised the human phenomenon. As Plato by the mouth of Socrates approached the problem of genre (*genos*) to classify in logical fashion what distinguishes the sophist from the philosopher, and what is just and true, so Nietzsche resorts to a classifying method, without however, arriving at any particular paradigm of classification. The Platonic idea of the Good, according to Nietzsche's reading of metaphysics, would be subsequently disguised as final cause in Aristotle, substance in Descartes, or thing-in-itself in Kant, without ever succeeding in explaining what unites and opposes by analogy human beings vis-à-vis all other beings. Hence the Socratic aporia of knowing that one knows nothing, for the will to know always betrays the belief that there must be meaning for all this endless network of signifiers. Man cannot constitute a superior class, nor his reason a class of classes. All we are left with is the fictionality of our human interpretations. Nietzsche uses thus typologies and comparative observations on peoples, races, and nations of Antiquity, the Renaissance, and Modernity not only to illustrate his doctrine of the will to power but also to account for its historical, immanent grounds, proper to the becoming of the human species. The very imposition of character of being to becoming constitutes, according to Nietzsche, the supreme will to power. (WM § 617) But the character of being is not, as one might expect, stability and permanence; on contrary, "that *everything recurs* is the closest *approximation of a world of becoming to a world of being.*" (WM § 617) In this consists the *amor fati* (WM 1041, EH II, 10), the Dionysian self-affirmation of man that wills all his/her life and the whole world happening exactly as it did happen --the eternal return of the same. "The destination of human nature resides," as runs the Heraclitean fragment, "in its character" --and vice-versa, ηθος ανθρωπω δαιμων (Frag. 119).

5. CONCLUSION: THE CRITIQUE OF MODERNITY

Critique of modern man (his moralistic mendaciousness): --the "good man" corrupted and seduced by bad institutions (tyrants and priests); --reason as authority; --history as overcoming of errors; --the future as progress; --the Christian state ("the Lord of hosts");--the Christian sex impulse (or marriage); --the kingdom of "justice" (the cult of "humanity");--"freedom" (WM § 62) That the man to be overcome is "modern man" can be inferred from the incisive association between the *Übermensch* and the *Zukunft*, the future, the Nietzschean yet-to-come of the becoming. On the other hand, the concept of modernity remains problematic in the study of Nietzsche's thought, insofar as it only serves to envision radical projects --whether futurist or anarchist, nihilist or post-modernist. It is indeed unwarranted, if not impossible, to reconcile Kant's ethics with Nietzsche's radical critique of morals, as shown by the studies by Mark Warren (post-modern political philosophy) and William Connolly (radical liberalism).[24] It was not the intent of the present work to examine the political, social implications of Nietzsche's philosophy and his conception of modern man. All I tried to show is that Nietzsche's genealogy is a continuation of the critical project of modernity, although it breaks away from the philosophical presuppositions of the *Aufklärung*, by radicalizing and suspecting its conceptions of rationality and critique. The rupture with "modernity" may be understood as the inauguration of "post-modernity," but its ethical and political implications remain to be seen. Foucault's contention, in the inaugural address at the Collège de France, that the main difference between genealogy and critique is perspectival and strategic rather than objective or thematic, bring us back to the questions of method that have guided us in our inquiry into the nature of the modern ethos.

---

[24] Mark Warren, *Nietzsche and Political Thought* (Cambridge, Mass.: MIT Press, 1988); William Connolly, *Political Theory and Modernity* (Oxford: Basil Blackwell, 1988).

Genealogy and critique, truth and method, art and science, meaning and valor, ontology and semiology --these are some of the fundamental concepts in Nietzsche's philosophy that proved useful in the formulation of his anthropological problematic. To grasp the Nietzschean "genealogy" as a radical "critique" that defies the metaphysical method adopted by the Kantian *Kritik* in philosophical and historical terms constitutes not only a thesis but also the prelude to a project that articulates the genealogical discourse of modernity. The anarchic, immoral anti-humanism and the anti-democratic aristocracy generally associated with Nietzsche's name--even if we discount here all the unwarranted speculations about an anti-semitic protofascism[25]--, may easily mislead us to the conclusion that the Nietzsche's aestheticism had nothing to contribute to a debate on human nature, let alone to ethics and politics. Nevertheless, it is precisely in this mined field of misunderstandings that we can redirect the Nietzschean critique in a "post-metaphysical" sense that does justice to its original project of the transvaluation of all values through the self-overcoming of human nature. The critique of religion that culminates with the death of God translates, in effect, the historical irreversibility of human advancements in her/his constant search of herself/himself and the meaning of existence, without any resort to grounds that transcend her/him. The impossibility of founding the meaning of existence outside of the human jurisdiction, beyond her/his historical experiences, is what makes Nietzsche's philosophy the paradigm of our modern condition. To be sure, thinkers such as Kant, Hegel and Feuerbach had already unmasked metaphysical conceptions of human nature. The greatest difference between Nietzsche and these philosophers is that he questions the very possibility of formulating a conception of human nature, insofar as there have been and will always be some subjective, power-effected interest behind every search for identity. Whoever asks questions or lies behind them takes part in the codification of moral truths, always bound to power relations. Nietzsche has shown that all philosophical discourses of modernity have to presuppose, in their cultural, historical articulation of ethics and politics, a metaphysics of subjectivity. Nietzsche has thus undermined both the supra-historical and the metaphysical standpoints that have allowed for modern historicism and criticism to proclaim the autonomy of human freedom and reason. It is a matter of rescuing philosophy rather than saving humankind. Hence the philosophical discourse of modernity must unveil its nonphilosophical,

---

[25] Esp. Nietzsche's relationship with Wagner and the speculations about his sister, Elisabeth, married to the leader of an anti-Semitic, German movement, Bernhard Förster. Cf. Walter Kaufmann, *Nietzsche: Philosopher, Psychologist, Antichrist*, 3rd. edition, (New York: Vintage, 1968); Jacques Derrida, *The Ear of the Other*, (Lincoln and London: University of Nebraska Press, 1985).

lowly genesis, where the very creation of modern man is effected by the will to truth and the will to power. In *Beyond Good and Evil* --particularly, in chapters 6 through 9 -- we find out that, besides all the anthropological, psychological, and genealogical analyses --undertaken in chapters 1 through 5--, there is indeed what we may call an "ethnological" dimension to Nietzsche's. To be sure, the word "ethnology" cannot be taken here in the modern sense "cultural anthropology," of a science that studies, from a cultural standpoint, so-called "primitive peoples" and compares them with the social, historical formations of the great Oriental, Mesopotamic, and European civilizations. In fact, as much can be said about anthropology and psychology in Nietzsche, in that they remain on the boundary between the philosophical and the nonphilosophical, as they seek to elucidate our knowledge of human nature without reference to any specific empirical science (*Fachwissenschaft*). Therefore, the Nietzschean discourse on races, civilizations, and cultural values can be examined within the philosophical perspective that characterizes his cultural, historical background of late *Aufklärung*. On the other hand, the originality of Nietzsche's project not only resists the previous classifications of what had been then formulated as anthropology, psychology, and genealogy, but questions all the scientific aspirations of these doctrines that never dissimulated their essentially metaphysical foundations. It is precisely in his antimetaphysical *démarche* that Nietzsche can be considered one of the great precursors of contemporary studies in cultural anthropology, inasmuch as it touches upon the social, historical articulations of civilizing processes with the problem of otherness.[26] It must be noted in passing that the problem of the cultural identity of a given tribe, nation, or people, whatever constitutes them as an *ethnos* or *genos* to be differentiated from others, cannot be thought without referring us back to a certain genealogical analysis of the moral, cultural values (*ethos*) that bind them together as a social group. It is in this articulation of historicity and sociability within one single discourse that resides, in the last analysis, Nietzsche's original contribution to a nonmetaphysical conception of human nature, understood as the indeterminate, plastic becoming constituted by the will to power, in its ontological regionalities and rationalities of self-overcoming. The source of such a discourse is found, as we have seen, in Nietzsche's conception of active and reactive forces at play in the historical effectiveness of the will to power. The ethnological task outlined in JGB can be also elucidated in function of the key concept of the will to power, as opposed to modernist formulations of anthropology.

---

[26] Cf. Tzevan Todorov, *Nous et les autres*, (Paris: Seuil, 1989).

Just as the Kantian project --and the philosophy of the *Aufklärung* in general-- has been fairly characterized by an anthropocentric preoccupation, Nietzsche outlined the true "critique of modern man" (WM § 62, quoted above) and completed it with a "genealogy of modern man." For Nietzsche, however, it is a matter of examining "modernity in the perspective of the metaphor of nourishment and digestion" (WM § 71), i.e., the culture of *fast food* --Nietzsche speaks of "time of influx *prestissimo*"!--, the incapacity to digest, ruminate, meditate, and even think, that characterizes the decadent man of a modernity that totally lost the Renaissance sense of *virtù* and authenticity (WM §§ 74-78). In a nutshell, the advent of the reactive, pessimist nihilism that characterizes our modernity of *fin of siècle* --as Nietzsche's *Zeitgeist*--, only can be overcome in the becoming of its taking place (*geschehen*), interpreted and transvalued in active fashion. Thus, what has become a code of conduct and truth for one epoch can be decodified in the sense of a radical reversal of values, without losses or gains, but in the simple preservation of quanta of forces. For instance, the codification of morals and whatever is assimilated into the culture of a people, is always accompanied by decodifications, hence the interpenetration of the Apollinian and Dionysian principles in the cultural formation of peoples and nations. To the cultural *ethos* of a people, to their *mores* structured by habituation and socialization, correspond instincts of self-preservation, self-affirmation as species, *genos* that generates and reproduces itself in the genesis of a common destiny. It would be, therefore, important to separate, in our reading of Nietzsche and, in particular, in our reading of a genealogical critique, what is relevant to our understanding of a Nietzschean interpretative principle from whatever refers to his idiosyncrasies, in a peculiar context of *fin de siècle* Germany. Whatever suggests anti-Semitism, misogyny, anti-socialism, and even misanthropy in the Nietzschean text can always be decodified in favor of a polyphonic, pluralist, non-exclusive reading --as attested by the diverse appropriations of Nietzsche by anti-racist, feminist, socializing, and liberationist movements. But the great question remains as for the foundation of ethics today, following Nietzsche's critique of Kant's and modernist conceptions of morality. Isn't the post-modern condition, following the Nietzschean radical hermeneutics of modern subjectivity, doomed to sheer ethical relativism? How can a self-overcome conception of human nature be invoked in a concrete situation of ethical crisis? After all, is it possible to found an ethics without metaphysics? Is it possible to have an ethics without a conception of human nature?

I have to conclude this chapter in provisional terms, as I am confined to elaborating on Nietzsche's contribution to the problem of human nature. As Deleuze and Guattari observed, Nietzsche's lasting contribution to the ethnological debate consists in the formulation of a fundamental problem of primitive *socius* in terms of code, inscription, trace: society is inscription-based rather than exchange-based, the trace (on the body, on earth) is what defines culture in its relations of contract and debt.[27] If Kant was the first to have formulated the anthropological problem in a pragmatic perspective --where abound the idiosyncrasies and stereotypical views on gender, sex, ethnicity and social divisions-- Nietzsche had the merits of suspecting and problematizing the Kantian distinction between morals --that can be historically and socially reconstituted-- and the moral law that makes possible, out of a transcendental foundation, the moral actions of human beings. On the other hand, Nietzsche did not seek to reconcile the universal and the particular in one single anthropogenesis, nor did he content himself with a mere reversal of a theological model --as Feuerbach did, in his conception of man as *Gattungswesen*. Nietzsche does not provide us with a social theory, not even a theory of power that may help us reformulate a social critique. And yet his sober nihilism is a living legacy, an aphoristic ensemble of problematizations that enjoins us to revise and rethink our methods of classification and representations of whom we claim to be, at an age of uncertainty and false expectations.

---

[27] Cf. 2nd. essay of the GM; *Anti-Oedipus*, trans. R. Hurley, M. Seem and H. Lane, (New York: Viking, 1977), 234-241.

Chapter Four

AESTHETICISM IN NIETZSCHE AND FOUCAULT

INTRODUCTION

> ...*[L]'herméneutique et la sémiologie sont deux farouches ennemies.* Une herméneutique qui se replie en effet sur une sémiologie croit à l'existence absolue des signes: elle abandonne la violence, l'inachevé, l'infinité des interprétations, pour faire régner la terreur de l'indice, et suspecter le langage. Nous reconnaissons ici le marxisme après Marx. Au contraire, une herméneutique qui s'enveloppe sur elle-même, entre dans le domaine des langages qui ne cessent de s'impliquer eux-mêmes, cette region mitoyenne de la folie et du pur langage. C'est là que nous reconnaissons Nietzsche. (M. Foucault, "Nietzsche, Freud, Marx," 192)

We have seen that, according to Foucault, the Nietzschean motif of the death of God not only implies the self-overcoming of man but proves itself to be an effect of the historicity of finitude brought about by the Kantian critique. To be sure, Kant's critique of dogmatic metaphysics and natural teleology did not seek to overcome the Judaeo-Christian teleology of history which came under attack in the Nietzschean genealogy of morality. We have seen that Nietzsche's genealogical project was guided by a threefold critique of religion, morality, and philosophy, which would ultimately lead to an active conception of nihilism through the supreme configuration of the will to power, hence the aestheticism of the *Übermensch*. As Nietzsche writes at the beginning of the last section of Third Book of the *Wille zur Macht* ("The Will to Power as Art," §§ 794-853), "Our religion, morality, and philosophy are decadent forms of man. The *countermovement: art*." (WP § 794) I will argue in this excursus that Nietzsche's aestheticism --and Foucault's, for that matter-- preserves the political and ethical thrust of a radical critique of values, due to the transvaluation of values intrinsic to his genealogy. And yet, whatever may be taken for a Nietzschean ethical or political motif cannot be invoked as theoretical grounds for collective action. As will be shown in this excursus, this is particularly the case with Nietzsche's genealogy of Christianity. Nietzsche's critique of Christianity, as opposed to Marx's, does not propose any deeper structure of meaning that would allow for a radical political agenda precisely because it does not aim at a new political paradigm to replace the religious --for instance, emancipation in lieu of salvation. Hence there is no room for a liberationist activism in Nietzsche's semiology, contrary to Marxist hermeneutics --as witness liberation theologies in developing countries. In effect, from a Nietzschean perspective, liberation turns out to be a reactive, herd-like movement that betrays a slave morality of *ressentiment*--in the Christian context, nothing less than a *mea culpa* theology.

Without subscribing to any reduction of Foucault's genealogy to a Nietzschean deconstruction and far from reconciling his critique of power with a Marxian-structuralist semiotics, I have sought to recast Foucault's social thought in terms of a "critique of truth" (Kant) and a "critique of power" (Nietzsche) so as to reconstitute his own displacement of the critique vis-à-vis these two masters of suspicion.[1] It has thus been assumed that the young Marx's *Kritik der Kritik* remains inscribed within the critical tradition of German idealism, leading back to Kant's practical philosophy. According to Foucault,

> ...it was Nietzsche who specified the power relation as the general focus, shall we say, of philosophical discourse --whereas for Marx it was the production relation. Nietzsche is the philosopher of power, a philosopher who managed to think power without having to confine himself within a political theory in order to do so. (PK 53)

I have limited myself to focusing on the two breaks that account for the emergence of Kant's criticism and its reversals by Hegel, Marx, and Nietzsche. Since neither Hegel nor Marx breaks away from the Kantian teleological conception of history, Nietzsche is the one who better exhausts modern critique -- even to the point of exploding it, according to Habermas.[2] Insofar as such a

---

[1] To be sure, a third aspect of Foucault's critical displacement would constitute a study of his relation to Freud and Lacan, i.e. the "interpretive-analytics" that radicalizes the "hermeneutics of the subject." As indicated in another endnote, I simply omitted the inclusion of these psycho-analytical and psychological fields in my study, since that would lead me to an entirely different project.

[2] According to Habermas, "Nietzsche wanted to explode the framework of Occidental rationalism within which the competitors of Left and Right Hegelianism still moved. His

radical critique has been identified with nihilism and historicism, as Habermas and others have interpreted it, Nietzsche's critique of morals may as well be regarded as an "aestheticism," in that the overcoming of the Kantian, noumenal rupture is displaced by an aesthetic perspectivism. And yet, nihilism, historicism, and aestheticism in Nietzsche deserve special qualification, since he explicitly marked off his thought from, say, Schopenhauer's, Hegel's and Plato's. Nietzsche's philosophy is in effect so intimately related to his critique of the history of philosophy that it would be misleading to interpret the former without presupposing his own interpretation of the latter. Interpretation in Nietzsche is indeed grounded in his own readings of great philosophers of the past, especially the metaphysical tradition that runs from Plato through German idealism. Nietzsche examined the modern fate of metaphysics in light of the three great movements that, following the Renaissance and the Reformation, characterized the seventeenth, eighteenth, and nineteenth century as the rule of reason (Descartes), feeling (Rousseau), and craving (Schopenhauer) respectively--so that Kant's enlightened critique of metaphysics is placed between the Romanticism of moralists and the fatalism of Hegel's *Geistigkeit*. (WP § 95-97, 101) Thus, the Cartesian contribution to the metaphysical problematic can be summed up in two main assertions: (1) is metaphysically credible (hence true) only that which may be understood with the clarity and the distinctiveness (*clare et distincte*) of mathematical propositions, and (2) whose truthfulness is so intrinsically obvious that it cannot be doubted (as in geometrical postulates) or can be proved with the same rigor as applied to theorems in geometry. To these general assertions that translate, for Nietzsche, the "rule of reason," one must oppose the "sovereignty of the will." (WP § 95) Of course, as both Nietzsche and Foucault have pointed out, Descartes did not suspect that by assigning to the thinking subject a logical certainty (WP § 484), he was assuming a substantial transparency as criterion of truth (WP § 533, 577, 578). Hence the morality of knowledge, inasmuch as our finite cognition was ultimately anchored in God's substance. After Descartes, Spinoza and Leibniz would appropriate in a positive way the project of a foundation of the logic of human knowledge (including the knowledge of God and the immortality of the soul), preserving the rationalist thrust of the Cartesian method, while Locke, Berkeley, and Hume adopted the same project in an empiricist attitude, rather negative (hence skeptical) with respect to the possibility of a certain knowledge without the mediation of our sensations and experiences. Immanuel Kant appears, in this historical context, as the philosopher who

---

antihumanism, continued by Heidegger and Bataille in two variations, is the real challenge for the discourse of modernity." (PDM 74)

revolutionized the fate of metaphysics in modernity. We know that Nietzsche held this rather sympathetic view of Kant during the time he came under the influence of Schopenhauer's critique of Kant.[3] Schopenhauer reduced Kant's dualism to a metaphysical principle that founded the world (*Welt*) as will (noumenal) and as representation (phenomenal).[4] And yet, the honorable place accorded to the Königsberger in Schopenhauer's philosophy will finally give way to Nietzsche's iconoclastic remarks:

> Kant, with his 'practical reason' and his moral fanaticism is wholly eighteenth century; still entirely outside the historical movement; without an eye for the actuality of his time, e.g. Revolution; untouched by Greek philosophy; fanciful visionary of the concept of duty; sensualist with the backdrop of the pampering of dogmatism. (WP § 95)

If one takes into account all the passages in which Nietzsche mentions Kant or some of his ideas --discounting of course Nietzsche's caricatures--, it becomes clear that Kantian philosophy is above all denounced for its claims to overcoming dogmatism, insofar as it remained attached to a Christian morality. However visibly influenced by Schopenhauer, Nietzsche's reading of Kant does not conceal the profound influence that the "Chinese of Königsberg" exerted on the young philologist, e.g. when quoting the § 51 of the Third *Critique* to sustain the Greek conception of "free play" (*das freie Spiel*) in opposition to the Roman conception of the "individual personality" (*die einzelne Persönlichkeit*).[5] We know that Nietzsche's entire work of maturity will reveal the continual movement of overcoming German idealism and, in particular, a radical subversion of Kant's practical philosophy. Thus, Nietzsche's aestheticism culminates in a critique of the teleology that would betray the claims of the overcoming of dogmatic, ontotheological metaphysics, based in the same ideal of truth that prevailed in the history of Western philosophy, from Plato to Kant. It was in order to better evaluate the meaning of aestheticism that I invoked Crawford's reading of the Third *Critique*, in the first chapter, with particular reference to the transcendental deduction in the KU. We have seen that whether or not Kant's system

---

[3] Cf. "Schopenhauer as Educator" in UB; A. Schopenhauer, *On the Fourfold Principle of Sufficient Reason*, trans. E. Payne, (Lasalle, Ill.: Open Court, 1974).

[4] This is the main thesis that structures Arthur Schopenhauer's *Die Welt als Wille und Vorstellung* (1819).ET: *The World as Will and Representation*, trans. E. Payne, (Mineola, NY: Dover, 1969).

[5] F. Nietzsche, "Darstellung der Antiken Rhetorik" (1872-73). In *Friedrich Nietzsche on Rhetoric and Language*, ed. Sander L. Gilman et al., (New York: Oxford University Press, 1989), 2-4.

presupposes a metaphysical conception of finality-- as Nietzsche suspected-- remains a decisive problem for our understanding of a genealogy of modernity. If, in the last analysis, Kant and Nietzsche share radically different conceptions of truth, power, and ethics, the nihilism and historicism associated with the aestheticism of the latter account for much of this convergence. Nietzsche's nihilism, as Arthur Danto has argued, cannot be reduced to the conjunction of "negativity and emptiness."[6] The same can be said about his historicizing of the subject of modernity, which cannot be equated with Hegel's logical historicism or Marx's dialectical historicism. In effect, Nietzsche's active nihilism and his genealogy are to be opposed to both nihilism and historicism, as they have been traditionally understood in philosophy. Thus, if Nietzsche's philosophy has been often characterized as an "aestheticism" that results from the critique of values -- the transvaluation of all values effected by his genealogy of morals--, the interpretative principle that radically conceives of truth as metaphor cannot be reduced to an inflationary primacy of the aesthetic over the ethical. Aestheticism must rather be understood *lato sensu*, as correlative to Nietzsche's perspectivism and experimentalism, inasmuch as all meaning is always already the interpretation of a subject, socially and historically situated, within power relations, and with self-constituted regimes of truth and rights. And this subject is never alone, but emerges within a flock or herd-like framework. It is for this very reason that, as Max Weber would later stress, the critique of religion --and of Christianity in particular-- is of the utmost importance for a full understanding of how modern man has been constituted as a rational, sociable self.

1. GENEALOGY, NIHILISM AND HISTORY

> Perhaps this is where we shall still discover the realm of our *invention*, that realm in which we, too, can still be original, say, as parodists of world history and God's buffoons -- perhaps, even if nothing else today has any future, our *laughter* may yet have a future. (JGB § 223)

As he writes on the genealogy of masquerade in European identity, Nietzsche scorns the possibility of overcoming history and ideology. The revealing expression *Hanswürste Gottes* ("God's buffoons") serves to invoke the aestheticist motif of Nietzsche's nihilism, in that the death of God and the

---

[6] A. Danto, *Nietzsche as Philosopher*, (New York: Macmillan: 1965), 28-35. Danto inadvertently equates Nietzsche's nihilism with a "metaphysics" --as opposed to an "ideology," in his terminology.

revaluation of all values unveil "monumental history" as a parody and genealogy itself, as Foucault observed, as "history in the form of a concerted carnival." (FR 94) If *Beyond Good and Evil* was regarded by Nietzsche himself as a *"critique of modernity"* and a parody on its myths of "objectivity," "pity for all that suffers," and "historical sense" (EH JGB § 2), his *Genealogy of Morals* was meant as its sequel, to "supplement and clarify" its aphorisms. Hence the three essays of the GM will largely focus on the three main topics of modern subjectivity already invoked --namely, the critique of religion (Christianity qua slave morality), the critique of morals (Kant's ethics of duty, autonomy, and conscience), and the critique of philosophy (nihilism and the ascetic ideal). Nietzsche's "psychology of the priest" (EH GM) strikes us as a radical hermeneutics of modern subjectivity, in that hermeneutics --as traditionally understood-- comes under attack and is revalued by Nietzsche's genealogy. In particular, the interpretation and appropriation of classical texts that allowed for the "historical sense" to emerge among modern Europeans, who identified themselves with a universal spirit that evolved from Ancient Greece, Judaism, and Christianity, had to be unmasked precisely because of their moral belief in a solemn origin (*Ursprung*). It is in this sense that, as Foucault points out, Nietzsche's genealogy qua analysis of descent (*Herkunft*) and historical method (GM II § 12) is correlated to a semiology or a radical hermeneutics of suspicion and opposed to a "deep" hermeneutics (Freud, Marx) or to hermeneutics *tout court*--such as the biblical hermeneutics that inspired nineteenth-century historical criticism and historicism. As Foucault remarks in the 1964 essay quoted above, "hermeneutics and semiology are two irreconcilable enemies."[7] I must remark in passing that the postmodern shift from so-called "hermeneutics of suspicion" (Ricoeur) towards "deconstruction" (Derrida) that took place in the sixties finds in Foucault a rather unholy ally, despite the latter's explicit commitment to an aestheticism clearly influenced by Nietzsche and Heidegger. Even though Habermas and others have placed Foucault in the vast field of French post-structuralism, I have argued in this study that, to the extent that Foucault's genealogy remains critical, his aestheticism seeks to avoid both historicism and irrationalism. Hence Foucault's reading of Nietzsche seeks to rescue the ethical, political thrust of the latter's perspectivism. It is under the aegis of a Nietzschean textuality of endless interpretations that Foucault goes on to reaffirm the impossibility of delimiting the subject's closure in history, since every valuation is itself an effect of the will to power. And yet, Foucault denies the primacy of discursivity over nondiscursive practices and

---

[7] M. Foucault, "Nietzsche, Freud, Marx," in *Nietzsche*, Cahiers de Royaumont, VIIe colloque, 4-8 juillet 1964, (Paris: Minuit, 1967), 192: "...l'herméneutique et la sémiologie sont deux farouches ennemies."

institutions, in that they are only different facets of the same historical process of subjectivation. Nietzsche's genealogy of morality allows for a rapprochement with Foucault's genealogy of modernity inasmuch as both unveil the aesthetic unity that binds together the doer (moral subject) and her/his deed (moral action), the governing agent and her/his self-governance. As will be seen in the third chapter, Foucault develops his archaeological studies in the direction of a genealogy, as his early aestheticism is problematized when art, language, or discourse can no longer be said to constitute the primary realm of human experience --as opposed to, say, nondiscursive practices. In effect, Foucault will resort to a co-originary articulation of both discursive and nondiscursive practices, involving both knowledge and power, in the very historical process of our self-constitution as subjects. Aestheticism stands then for a perspectival conception of reality which levels discursivity, historicity, and subjectivity, as over against foundationalist conceptions of a metaphysics of the subject. As Foucault himself said, in response to Sartre:

> ...man as subject of his own consciousnes and of his own freedom is at bottom a sort of theologization of man, the redescent of God on earth which has in some fashion made the man of the nineteenth century theologized. (FL 38)

Both Nietzsche and Foucault endorse an active, aesthetic nihilism as the appropriate attitude for modern existence, the philosophical ethos of modernity. Instead of resenting the meaninglessness of life, they enjoin us to celebrate our innocent becoming in its fullness, by creating our own world and revaluing our most cherished values. This is the kind of nihilism that properly deserves to be qualified as a "sober nihilism," in that it seeks nothing beyond or above the very becoming of human existence to justify its modes of being and yet, contrary to a wild indifference towards the becoming of being, life does affirm itself by becoming what it is. This artistic ideal, which is somewhat reminiscent of Kant's notes on the genius (KU §§ 46-50), is certainly to be regarded as an existential style of self-affirmation and self-assertive subjectivation, rather than as a withdrawal from political existence. Moreover, artistic self-creation also points to the self-overcoming of a de-deified human nature, as human self-creation replaces the divine in the aftermath of the death of God. If "the most extreme form of nihilism" is the view that there is "no *true world*," then everything is "a *perspectival appearance* whose origin lies in us," hence "the necessity of lies." (WP § 15) Since there is no absolute truth, no thing-in-itself, no "intelligible freedom," modern man is alone in this revaluation of all values and "rational faith," like religious and moral beliefs, cannot provide us with an ultimate goal or meaning. (WP § 13, 18-20)

2. Nietzsche's Genealogy of Christianity

> Dionysus versus the Crucified: there you have the antithesis ...One will see that the problem is that of the meaning of suffering: whether a Christian meaning or a tragic meaning. In the former case, it is supposed to be the path to a holy existence; in the latter case, being is counted as holy enough to justify even a monstrous amount of suffering. The tragic man affirms even the harshest suffering: he is sufficiently strong, rich, and capable of deifying to do so. The Christian denies even the happiest lot on earth: he is sufficiently weak, poor, disinherited to suffer from life in whatever form he meets it. The god on the cross is a curse on life [*ein Fluch auf das Leben*], a signpost to seek redemption from life; Dionysus cut to pieces is a promise of life: it will be eternally reborn and return again from destruction. (WP § 1052)

This revealing passage from *Der Wille zur Macht* (1888), which serves to establish the Nietzschean difference between "the religious man" (Jew/Christian) and "the pagan" (Greek) in non-dialectical terms, reveals also the intriguing ambiguity of Nietzsche's attitude towards religion. Although "the other" is reaffirmed as "different," nothing can be ultimately decided for either one as a higher affirmation of "the same" (in this case, the religious, for both Dionysus and the Crucified are types of "religious man"). As Nietzsche writes in grand style,

> ...Is the pagan cult not a form of thanksgiving and affirmation of life? Must its highest representative not be an apology for and deification of life? The type of a well constituted and ecstatically overflowing spirit! The type of a spirit that takes into itself and *redeems* the contradictions and questionable aspects of existence! It is here I set the *Dionysus* of the Greeks: the religious affirmation of life, life whole and not denied or in part; (typical --that the sexual act arouses profundity, mystery, reverence). (WP § 1052)

Even though I do not intend to reexamine Nietzsche's critique of religion in this section, I must briefly recall the place of Nietzsche's "genealogy of Christianity" in his project of an "*Umwertung aller Werte*." Nietzsche's *Der Antichrist* (1888), ambiguously bearing both an apocalyptic sense ("the Antichrist") and a more programmatic aim of deconstruction ("the anti-Christian"), describes the Christian Church as "the highest of all conceivable corruptions," both Catholic and Protestant, "the one great curse," "the one immortal blemish of mankind":

> Parasitism is the *only* practice of the Church [*als einzige Praxis der Kirche*]; with its ideal of anemia, of "holiness," draining all blood, all love, all hope for life; the beyond as the will to negate every reality; the cross as the mark of recognition for the most subterranean conspiracy that ever existed --against health, beauty, whatever has turned out well, courage, spirit, *graciousness* of the soul, *against life itself* [*gegen das Leben selbst*]. (AC § 62)

The Christian religion is to be opposed precisely because of its binary opposition to life as a sickly faith, as if suffering itself were not a natural component of the vital flux, a necessary moment of the innocent becoming, the true measure of the will to power. Nietzsche's *polemos* against Christianity, like Kierkegaard's "Attack upon Christendom," has to be read in the light of his own writings as a corpus, the living body of thoughts that constitutes his autobiography. For Nietzsche's polemic corresponds to the very hermeneutical thrust of his genealogy of Christianity, from *The Birth of Tragedy* to *The Will to Power*: here is Nietzsche the man, *ecce homo*, reflecting on the staging of his greatest works. Such is the ambiguous unveiling of the divine, as the absence/ presence interplay with Dionysus, "the god of darkness" (EH GM), seems to allow for the myths of return after the death of God. Aestheticism seems to imply that new forms of mythology and religion will inevitably emerge in the revaluation of values. And yet, it would be misleading to merely resort to the young Nietzsche's ideal of the artist-philosopher or to the earlier interplay of Dionysian and Apollinian motifs so as to grasp how his reaction to Schopenhauer's aestheticism tacitly gives way to another one.[8] David Allison has convincingly shown the impossibility of reducing Nietzsche's reading of Kant to Schopenhauer's appropriation of the latter. As Allison argues, not only is it inadmissible to read Kant's noumenal thesis into Nietzsche's conception of the will, but his account of the Dionysian "corresponds to a fully empirical order" and is decisive for his reformulation of the modern conception of subjectivity.[9] In effect, the antithesis of the Dionysian and the Apollinian, which first appears as an "idea" (like Hegel's *Idee*), is "translated into the realm of metaphysics,"

---

[8] That seems to be Habermas's point in his criticism of Nietzsche as a "utopian" aestheticist. Cf. PDM 83-105.
[9] Cf. D. Allison, "Nietzsche Knows no Noumenon," in Daniel O'Hara (ed.), *Why Nietzsche Now?*, (Bloomington: Indiana University Press, 1985), 295-310.

developed and historically "sublimated [*aufgehoben*] into a unity." (EH BT § 1) Nietzsche's account of the tragic destiny of the Greek splendor announced already its decomposition into Platonic, Christian morality. As Nietzsche reviews it in his autobiography:

> The two decisive innovations of the book are, first, its understanding of the Dionysian phenomenon among the Greeks... Secondly, there is the understanding of Socratism: Socrates is recognized for the first time as an instrument of Greek disintegration, as a typical decadent. "Rationality" *against* instinct. "Rationality" at any price as a dangerous force that undermines life. Profound, hostile silence about Christianity throughout the book. That is neither Apollinian nor Dionysian; it negates all aesthetic values --the only values recognized in *The Birth of Tragedy*: it is nihilistic in the most profound sense, while in the Dionysian symbol the ultimate limit of affirmation is attained. (EH BT § 1)

One may argue that the Nietzschean "affirmation of life," "even the harshest suffering," is indeed the affirmation of Nietzsche's own tragic destiny. According to a "religious" reading of Nietzsche, this gospel of tragedy did not mean to dispense with religion, but it sought to come to a "second innocence" (*zweite Unschuld*) --as unveiled in the mythical aestheticism and life-become-artwork of Nietzsche himself ("How one becomes what one is"). As his early writings foresaw,

> Yes, my friends, believe with me in Dionysian life and the rebirth of tragedy. The age of the Socratic man is over; put on wreaths of ivy, put the thyrsus into your hand, and do not be surprised when tigers and panthers lie down, fawning, at your feet. Only dare to be the tragic man; for you are to be redeemed. You shall accompany the Dionysian pageant from India to Greece. Prepare yourselves for hard strife, but believe in the miracles of your God. (BT § 20)

Nietzsche's ambiguity, as I have suggested, certainly has to do with an "intellectual honesty" (*Redlichkeit*), a complexity in the constitution of everything given (*data*) to us, not as an ultimate truth fallen from heaven, but as something to be interpreted, revalued in its constitution by subjective relations --and eventually ruminated, organically incorporated as food for thought. If the aesthetic must stand between and against any polarization of subject and object, Nietzsche's recognition of Christianity as a source of untruth (*pia fraus*) would thus point to the unveiling of his own search for an absent *arché*, an anarchic genesis of the divine. "The general first probability one encounters," Nietzsche wrote, "as one contemplates holiness and asceticism is this: their nature is *complicated*." (MAM § 136) Nietzsche did not establish a rational method for his lifelong research, for his own life provided the *meta-hodos* for his "self"-deconstruction (the calling into question of his psychological identity, the undermining of the cogito as self-consciousness, the decentering of the metaphysical "subject"), as he willed only one thing, viz., to remain true to the untruth/truth of this self-overcoming "self," always "on the way" to the "truth" of his own becoming, aesthetically conceived. That is why Christianity, as the historical rationalization of an archic "God" through the sedimentation of Christian dogmas, appears as the antipodal expression of the aesthetic, in its moralization of *ursprüngliche* values and in its idolatry of an ascetic "God" *faute de mieux*:

> The truth of the *first* inquiry [i.e. expression, *Ausdruck*, in the *Genealogie der Moral*] is the birth of Christianity: the birth of Christianity out of the spirit of *ressentiment*, not, as people may believe, out of the "spirit" -- a counter-movement by its very nature, the great rebellion against the dominion of *noble* values. (EH GM)

Christianity is thus identified with a "slave morality" (as opposed to a "master morality"), born of *ressentiment*.[10] "The slave revolt in morality," Nietzsche writes, "begins when *ressentiment* itself becomes creative and gives birth to values: the *ressentiment* of natures that are denied the true reaction, that of deeds, and compensate themselves with an imaginary revenge." (GM I § 10) The "action" of Christian morality is, for Nietzsche, "fundamentally reaction," and, like the Jews, "the priestly nation of *ressentiment* par excellence," will not escape the fateful overcoming of its own ascetic ideal, beyond good and evil (GM I § 16). In effect, this reactive genealogy of Christianity was eschatologically constituted for its own overcoming (*Selbst-aufhebung*), from the outset, by the very *arché* of its theonomy:

> All great things bring about their own destruction through an act of self-overcoming: thus the law of life will have it, the law of the necessity of "self-overcoming" in the nature of life --the lawgiver himself eventually receives the call: "*patere legem, quam ipse tulisti*." In this way Christianity *as a dogma* was destroyed by its own morality; in the same way, Christianity *as morality* must now perish, too: we stand on the threshold of this event.

---

[10] Nietzsche always employs the word in French, to express "le fait de se souvenir avec animosité des maux, des torts qu'on a subis --comme si on les 'sentait' encore," "le fait d'éprouver, de ressentir --un chagrin, une douleur." Paul Robert, *Dictionnaire alphabétique et analogique de la langue française*, "Le Petit Robert," (éd. 1973), 1540.

After Christian truthfulness has drawn one inference after another, it must end by drawing its *most striking* inference, its inference *against* itself; this will happen, however, when it poses the question "*what is the meaning of all will to truth?*" (GM III § 27)

Nietzsche's critique of religion can be thus placed within the very self-overcoming of human nature that aestheticism seeks to unveil, allowing for a nonreligious conception of artistic self-affirmation, explicitly opposed or indifferent to every religious form of asceticism. Hence we may contrast religious readings of Nietzsche, such as the ones proposed by Marion, Valadier, and Altizer,[11] with the nonreligious interpretations by Deleuze and Foucault. To be sure, as Deleuze has argued, even if we concede that Nietzsche's genealogy allows for an active religion --as opposed to the reactive religion of *ressentiment* and bad conscience-- the essence of religion is such that, besides being a force, it is also and above all an effect of the will to power, so that it always already "finds itself subjugated by forces of an entirely different nature from its own and cannot unmask itself." (NP 144; JGB § 62) At any rate, one point of agreement shared by all interpreters of Nietzsche's critique of religion is the strength of his historical-critical arguments for the genealogy of Christianity, in particular, his analyses of the Jewish descent of Christianity and its ascetic foundations in Pauline theology --rather than in Jesus' deeds. To be sure, as Girard and Glucksmann have argued, the three *maîtres du soupçon* (Marx, Nietzsche, and Freud) have all ironically failed to suspect that the Hegelian view of the Jews as a pariah people and of Judaism as a slave religion (giving birth to Christianity) was itself a hermeneutical problematic involving both cultural kinesis (history of Israel and ancient peoples) and translation (Hebrew into Greek), a legacy which Hegel the theologian inherited from German Romanticism without much criticism.[12] It is certain, on the other hand, that Nietzsche opposes the grand style of the Old Testament to the rococo of the New. (JGB § 52; GM III § 22) For between the Old and the New Testaments an entire history of interpretation comes into being, a Christian story

---

[11] Cf. Thomas J.J. Altizer and William Hamilton, *Radical Theology and the Death of God*, (New York: Bobbs-Merril, 1966); Jean-Luc Marion, *L'idole et la distance*, (Paris: Grasset, 1977), *Dieu sans l'être*, Coll."Communio," (Paris: Fayard, 1982), Paul Valadier, *Nietzsche et la critique du christianisme*, (Paris: Cerf, 1974), *Nietzsche. L'athée de rigueur*, (Paris: Desclée, 1975); NN 217-261.

[12] Cf. André Glucksmann, *Les Maîtres Penseurs*, (Paris: Grasset, 1977), 257ff; René Girard, *Things Hidden Since the Foundation of the World*, trans. S. Bann and M. Metteer, (Stanford University Press, 1987), 265: "Relations between God and man re-enact the Hegelian scheme of 'master' and 'slave.' This notion has been docily accepted, even by those who claim to have 'liberated' themselves from Hegel. We find it in Marx, in Nietzsche and in Freud. People who have never read a single line of the Bible accept it unquestioningly."

which has changed the world, dividing it in a "before" and an "after," like Nietzsche's own interpretive destiny:

> The uncovering of Christian morality is an event [*ein Ereignis*] without parallel, a real catastrophe. He that is enlightened about that, is a *force majeure*, a destiny [*ein Schicksal*] --he breaks the history [*die Geschichte*] of mankind in two. One lives before him, or one lives after him. (EH "Why I Am a Destiny" § 8)

"Christianity," Nietzsche wrote, "has become something fundamentally different from what its founder did and desired." (WP § 195) From the beginnings of its institution as a religious "faith" (Paul and the primitive εκκλησια) up to its Platonic development into metaphysics (Augustine, medieval philosophy, Kant) and to its ethical ideal of asceticism (enmity toward "nature," "reason," "the senses"), Christianity has betrayed the *ursprüngliche* ethos of Jesus, who alone incarnated the genuine Christian:

> I go back, I tell the *genuine* history of Christianity. The very word "Christianity" is a misunderstanding: in truth, there was only *one* Christian, and he died on the cross. The "evangel" *died* on the cross. What has been called "evangel" from that moment was actually the opposite of that which he had lived: "*ill* tidings," a *dysangel*. It is false to the point of nonsense to find the mark of the Christian in a "faith," for instance, in the faith in redemption through Christ: only Christian *practice*, a life such as he *lived* who died on the cross, is Christian. (AC § 39)

However, Nietzsche is certainly not concerned about the *Ursprung* of this historical phenomenon called Christianity.[13] For Nietzsche, we must always start from where we are, from what we are, flesh and blood. As Foucault has shown, genealogy as an analysis of descent starts from our bodily existence. (FR 80-83) That is the very reason why genealogy diagnoses the social body of the Church (where Christ is the head and every Christian a member) as a sick body. (AC § 17, 18) The *skandalon* of Jesus the Idiot (AC § 29), nailed to the cross as if humankind were to be healed from an incurable disease, remained indeed madness for the Madman, who could sign "The Crucified" in a letter to his friend Peter Gast (1889):

---

[13] Cf. Nietzsche's Preface to the *Genealogy of Morals*, where he attacks Paul Rée's search for *Ursprung*; VFJ chapter 1.

Sing me a new song: The world is transfigured and all the heavens are full of joy.[14]

Nietzsche's ambiguity is thus expressed by his oscillation between theological criticism and pathological empathy vis-à-vis the Crucified.[15] If Nietzsche has imitated the kerygmatic style of Jesus, he has also refused his Christian messianism:

> I *want* no "believers;" I think I am too malicious to believe in myself; I never speak to masses. --I have a terrible fear that one day I will be pronounced *holy*: you will guess why I publish this book [*Ecce Homo*] *before*; it shall prevent people from doing mischief with me. I do not want to be a holy man [*Heiliger*]; sooner even a buffoon [*Hanswürst*]. --Perhaps I am a buffoon... But my truth is *terrible* [*furchtbar*]; so far one has called *lies* truth. (EH "Why I Am a Destiny" § 1)

From the clown to the madman, from Dionysus to the Crucified, Nietzsche's *Selbstüberwindung* turns, like Heidegger's *Holzwege*, into a labyrinthine interplay with the concealment of otherness, as life runs out of presence and absence becomes a true becoming. Whether this is the end or just a beginning in the horizon of the Same/Other, no truth can decide --at least on the autobiographical level of Nietzsche's interplay between Dionysus and the Crucified. In his "Attempt at Self-Criticism" (1886), added to a new edition of *The Birth of Tragedy*, Nietzsche had addressed an enigmatic question to his readers, "Who could claim to know the rightful name of the Antichrist?" The response was overtly assumed by his autobiographical unmasking, in his provocative *Ecce Homo*: "I am, in Greek, and not only in Greek, the *Antichrist*." (EH "Why I Write Such Good Books" § 2) The "anti- Christian" in Nietzsche's metaphorics has been translated, as he wrote in the same "Attempt," by "the name of a Greek god: I called it Dionysian." One question has nevertheless remained undecided --at least by Nietzsche's autobiography--, namely, "what is Dionysian?" Of course, Nietzsche immediately adds, in the same "Attempt," "This book [i.e. *The Birth of Tragedy*] contains an answer: one 'who knows' is talking, the initiate and disciple of his god." That is why I refrained from identifying Nietzsche's *Lebensphilosophie* with an aesthetic return to nature as *arché*. Granted, Nietzsche's critique of Platonism as the reversal of nature's *phainomena* into a

---

[14] *Portable Nietzsche*, op. cit., p. 685. Postmarked Turin, Jan. 4, 1889. *Selected Letters of Friedrich Nietzsche*, ed. Christopher Middleton, (Chicago: The University of Chicago Press, 1969), n. 201, p. 345.
[15] Cf. GM III § 137, MAM I § 235, JGB § 269, AC § 32.

deceptive "reality" of *eidé* (WP § 572) reminds us of a Heraclitean *kosmos* that lets the *physis* come into being as the *Schauspiel* of opposites. Yet Nietzsche prefers to dwell on the surface (FW § 256) precisely because genealogy has shown the mechanism of deception in humans' deepest convictions about things held to be true (FW § 354). And the death of God turns out to be the most revealing effect of this genealogical reversal. Nietzsche's radical reversal is to be thus distinguished from both Feuerbach's and Marx's in that Nietzsche is not simply switching back from "reality" to "appearances" --or from a metaphysical-spiritualist to a materialist-bodily conception of the world-- but he is ridding the world of any origin beyond its own historical, bodily-subjective becoming. The bodily-subjective becoming of the world appears then as a "natural revelation" of the death of God. Nietzsche's unmasking of the death-of-God motif --a theological motif which had already been invoked by both Luther and Hegel-- is, above all, a deconstruction of the christological idolatry, i.e. the christological motif of redemption which seeks to legitimize the transvaluation of "original sin," "spiritual death," and "alienation from God" -- externalizing moments that were philosophically reconciled in Hegel's trinitarian dialectic. Thus Nietzsche read and criticized the Tübingen theologians of his time (David Friedrich Strauss, Ferdinand Christian Baur), as well as Ernest Renan, only to radicalize their views on "historical criticism." The death of the historical (*historische*) Jesus on the cross coincides thus with the death of the confessional (*geschichtliche*) Christ, i.e., the death of God *tout court*. Since the body of Christ survived Jesus' death on the cross --through the Church and its sacraments--, Christian theology relied on the historical handing down of popular accounts and rituals to legitimize its hermeneutics. This "history of traditions" (*Überlieferungsgeschichte*) has ironically translated and betrayed the very transcendent, supra-historical origins of theology. That has been a veritable betrayal of the body, insofar as the history of the body unveils the Christian, Western spiritualization of everything that essentially belongs to the body: *eros*, *pathos*, intellect, existence, life, and death. A bodily aesthetics alone can do justice to Nietzsche's carnivalesque genealogy. The decaying Body of Christ, the Church, as a living Holy Sepulcher that cannot control the effects of its theological contaminations must be left to decompose itself --there is no need for atheists to engage in theology. Even in Nietzsche's time, liberal theologians, under the influence of Hegel and the historicist school, already realized that the writing of the New Testament presupposed an interpretative translation of Hebrew motifs into a Greek, universal framework. The betrayal of a Jewish messianism was seen then as the universal hope for both Jew and gentile, both slave and free. Such was indeed the triumphalist outcome of a universal ideal to be epitomized in Hegel's theological writings. Nietzsche's critique of idealism unmasks the world of the spirit so as to unveil the primacy of the body and to review history in the service of life.

3. AESTHETICISM AND MORAL SUBJECTIVATION

Morality is preceded by *compulsion*, indeed it is for a time itself still compulsion, to which one accommodates oneself for the avoidance of what one regards as unpleasurable. Later it becomes custom, later still voluntary obedience, finally almost instinct; then, like all that has for a long time been habitual and natural, it is associated with pleasure --and is now called *virtue*. (MAM I § 99)

Just as Nietzsche's genealogy of morals unveils the pagan sources of Judaeo-Christian morality, Foucault's genealogy of modernity will unmask the humanist hope at the heart of the teleology of history. The Nietzschean-Foucauldian conception of power as bodily or field interplay of forces (active and reactive) and its displacement of self-identity (flux and reflux) must thus be regarded as a consequence of the death of God. If the problematic of values in Foucault is obviously connected to Nietzsche's genealogy and his critical overcoming of Kantian philosophy, it is also important to comprehend how Nietzsche's revaluation of values may contribute to a genealogical account of individualization, normalization, and an ethics of self-care that defies disciplinary powers that be. Christianity, through its slave revolt against Rome, strikes us as a major paradigm of Nietzsche's rapprochement between subjectivation and moralization. Christian asceticism is regarded by Nietzsche as the best example of hypostatizing a morality of customs into a sacred set of norms and practices (*kanon, regula fidei*). Of course, Nietzsche's analysis is equally applied to Ancient Judaism, though in the latter ethnic identity and oral traditions (e.g., reciting in Hebrew) still played an important role in the processes of assimilation, internalization, and socialization, undermining its universalist claims to a moral standard of conduct. Nietzsche has convincingly shown how early Christianity appropriated the moralizing principles of Judaism and, *nollens volens*, combined them with Roman universalism so as to defeat, out of *ressentiment*, the noble morality of the oppressor. Tertullian's apologetic war opposing Jerusalem and Athens is thus displaced by the decisive battles of "Rome against Judea" and "Judea against Rome" until the Christian conversion of the latter. (cf. GM I § 15, 16) Nietzsche's genealogical critique of herd-morality unveils the problem of social control of individuals through massive moralization. For Nietzsche, the origin of custom is linked to the correlative notions that "the community is worth more than the individual" and that "an enduring advantage is to be preferred to a transient one." (MAM II § 89) Thus he defines *Sittlichkeit* (morality) as "nothing other than simply a feeling for the whole content of those customs under which we live and have been raised --and raised, indeed, not as an individual, but as a member of the whole, as a cipher in a majority." And he adds the revealing remark that "through his morality the individual *outvotes* himself." If Nietzsche's critique of power departs from socialism and democracy, as Keith Ansell-Pearson has shown, his aristocratic individualism should not be confused with liberalism insofar as for the latter politics is a means to peaceful coexistence of individual agents, while "for Nietzsche it is a means to the production of human greatness."[16] As Nietzsche himself wrote, his "philosophy aims at an ordering of rank (*Rangordnung*), not at an individualistic morality." (WP § 287) The conception of a cultural aristocracy is also found in William Connolly's thesis that Nietzsche's "brave ethics" does not preclude social, political engagement.[17] According to Connolly, the will to power can be either construed as a Hobbesian-like play of forces that bring about domination and mastery (over nature, persons, and things) or as a Foucauldian-like device that recognizes and affirms forms of otherness.[18] Foucault's merit, as far as political thought is concerned, thus consists in having rescued this Nietzschean aesthetic model of subjectivity so that, by giving style to one's character (FW § 290), political existence is ethically constituted through different processes of self-overcoming that resist massive normalization (State-controlled ideology, religious faith). A self-stylizing *askésis* implies a unity of character (*ethos*) that cannot be reduced to any particular institutionalized discourse or practice. As Ansell-Pearson has put it, "this unity of the self is not a *moral* unity, but an *aesthetic* one --more, it is one which is truly beyond the oppositions of moral judgment, that is, *beyond good and evil*."[19] In the *Genealogy of Morals*, particularly in the second essay (§ 16), Nietzsche clearly states his thesis of "the internalization of man" which would be later reformulated as the Foucauldian critique of individualizing normativity.

Morality, in the last analysis, is the outcome of political disciplining and training, stemming from a codification of customs and shifting towards a

---

[16] Cf. "Nietzsche's 'overcoming' of morality," editor's introduction to Friedrich Nietzsche, *On the Genealogy of Morality*, trans. Carol Diethe, (Cambridge: Cambridge University Press, 1994), x. Includes ET of "The Greek State" and "Homer on Competition."
[17] Cf. W. Connolly, "Beyond Good and Evil: The Ethical Sensibility of Michel Foucault," *Political Theory* 21/3 (1993) 365-389; *Political Theory and Modernity*, op. cit.
[18] W. Connolly, op. cit., 161.
[19] K. Ansell-Pearson, "The Significance of of Michel Foucault's Reading of Nietzsche: Power, the Subject, and Political Theory," *Nietzsche-Studien* 20 (1991) 282.

spiritualization and rationalization of human conduct. (GM II § 2) In MAM I § 45, Nietzsche speaks of a twofold pre-history of "good and evil," namely, "firstly, in the soul of ruling tribes and castes" and "then, in the soul of the subjected, the powerless." As he remarks, for a long time, good and evil are respectively identified with noble and base, master and slave. (cf. GM I § 4-9, 11, 13, 16) In Homer, for instance, both the Greek and the Trojan are always good. Nietzsche's thesis is that "our morality has grown up in the soil of the *ruling* tribes and castes." The same can be said about the conceptions of justice and fairness. (MAM I § 92) In brief, according to Nietzsche, to be moral first meant "to practice obedience towards a law or tradition established from of old." (MAM I § 96) Such was the tradition-directed "morality of mores" (*Sittlichkeit der Sitte*) which gave birth to the moralization of human nature. (cf. GM Preface § 4, III § 9; M I § 9) This is an accurate description of the meaning of ethics, especially from the standpoint of a philologist or cultural historian. What becomes more problematic is to bring this definition to a meta-ethical field, or to theorize about the meaning of conforming to certain patterns of conduct and to justify determinate actions and procedures. It could be said that neither Nietzsche nor Foucault was, after all, concerned about this kind of ethical theory, in that their work refers us to the historical field of the formation of moral subjects rather than the meta-ethics and ethical theories of contemporary analytical philosophy. Moral subjectivation stands thus for a genealogical account of the modes of subject-formation by which the self is made a moral individual within a given social group (tribe, clan, people, nation, society). Nietzsche's genealogy establishes a complex, typological relation between *ethnos* and *ethos*, which is appropriated by Foucault in his cultural, historical diagnosis of modern subjectivity. As will be seen in the next chapter, Foucault's conception of subjectivation in a genealogical analysis is best understood in light of the third axis (ethics) which concurs with truth and power to constitute modes of self-formation.

Chapter Five

FOUCAULT'S GENEALOGY OF MODERNITY

INTRODUCTION

"What are we in our actuality?" You will find the formulation of this question in a text written by Kant... a new pole has been constituted for the activity of philosophizing, and this pole is characterized by the question, the permanent and ever-changing question, "What are we today?" (Michel Foucault, TS 145)

The field of analysis which Foucault called "the formal ontology of truth" has been dealt with by different thinkers of modernity, such as Kant, Marx, Nietzsche, Weber, Heidegger, and the *Frankfurterschule*. As they examined the general framework of what Foucault termed the "technologies of the self," they subtly shifted away from the traditional, philosophical questions on the nature of the world, man, truth, and knowledge, so as to inaugurate a new conception of rationality, no longer based on an all-embracing, foundational metaphysics but on an integrated view of human activities --living, speaking, working-- that allowed for "man" to become "an object for several different sciences."[1] This was precisely what Foucault's archaeology aimed at, as we have seen, although on a discursive level of the formation of knowledges (*savoirs*), whose patterns and regularities were analyzed and reconstructed in *Les mots et les choses* and systematized, with the aid of linguistic and semiological descriptions, in *L'archéologie du savoir*. Now, although Foucault avowed that there was indeed a shift of focus, say, from the archaeology of *Les mots et les choses* (1966) and *L'archéologie du savoir* (1969) to the genealogy of *Surveiller et punir* (1975) and

---

[1] Cf. M. Foucault, "The Political Technology," in TS 145-162.

La volonté de savoir (1976), and from these to the practico-social analyses of subjectivation in the other two volumes of *L'Histoire de la sexualité* (*L'usage des plaisirs* and *Le souci de soi*, 1984), he also insisted on the pervasive, interpretive meaning of his genealogical method. Indeed, the one thing in common among Foucault's most important *maîtres à penser*, acknowledged in the inaugural lecture at the Collège de France, was precisely "historicity" --Georges Dumézil was a historian of religions, Georges Canguilhem a historian of science, and Jean Hyppolite a Hegelian historian of philosophical thought.[2] It is well known that from 1970 until his death in 1984, Michel Foucault taught in the prestigious Collège de France. What has been perhaps overlooked is that the name of this chair had been changed, following Jean Hyppolite's death in 1968. What used to be called "History of Philosophical Thought" (*Histoire de la pensée philosophique*) became, on November 30, 1969, the chair of "History of Systems of Thought" (*Histoire des systèmes de la pensée*) to be occupied by Foucault.[3]

We can thus speak of a Foucauldian conception of history that underlies his three different ways of analyzing discursive and nondiscursive practices of *savoir* (archaeology), *pouvoir* (genealogy), and *subjectivation* (interpretive-analytics). And yet, Foucault denied that he was ever elaborating on a new theory of history, although he conceded that he was doing a different kind of history in his main works. He went as far as to admit, in a 1982 interview, that he had written "two kinds of books," namely, one "concerned with scientific thought" (and he cites *Les mots et les choses* as an example), and the other "concerned with social principles and institutions" (e.g., *Surveiller et punir*). Neither should be identified with a "history of science." (TS 14) Later on, he admitted that he was writing still another kind of history, explicitly hermeneutic, a "history of ourselves," for which he was planning a monumental seven-volume *Histoire de la sexualité*.[4] These "methods" must not, however, be conceived as the overcoming of their previous counterparts, as if there were epistemological breaks leading from one method to the other, but they are complementary just as knowledge, power, and subjectivation presuppose and determine one another. It has been, therefore, my contention in this book that Foucault's conception of history is precisely what accounts for an apparent inflation of the power-genealogy axis, beyond the

---

[2] It is also interesting to remark that Foucault's main writings, from the three phases, were published in the "Bibliothèque des Histoires" of Parisian "Éditions Gallimard."

[3] Cf. Michel Foucault, *Résumé des cours, 1970-1982*, Conférences, essais et leçons du Collège de France, (Paris: Julliard, 1989), "Note liminaire."

[4] Besides the three volumes published thus far, the fourth is forthcoming, *Les aveux de la chair*. According to Miller's book, based on conversations with Daniel Defert, Foucault abandoned the original plan for a seven-volume work as early as 1975, after his visit to California. PMF 250 ff.; cf. MF 273f., 290; PPC 242f.

epistemological task traditionally assigned to the interpretation of historical events. As will be seen, Foucault's conception of history proves indeed helpful to understand the tension between a *critical* and a *genealogical* account of power relations.

Foucault was admittedly influenced by great contemporary philosophers, such as Heidegger, Husserl, Sartre, and Merleau-Ponty, and by modern thinkers alike, such as Kant, Hegel, and, above all, Nietzsche.[5] As Foucault avowed in his last interview, published three days after his death in 1984, if his "entire philosophical development was determined by [his] reading of Heidegger," it was Nietzsche who "outweighed" Heidegger --"*c'est Nietzsche qui l'a emporté*".[6] Deleuze has shown that Nietzsche's influence was decisive in Foucault's rejection of the Heideggerian myth of the pre-Socratic paradigm of *Ursprünglichkeit, à la mode* during the French reception of Heidegger in the 1950s. (F 113)[7] As early as 1961, Foucault wrote in the preface to *Folie et déraison* that he was conducting his inquiries "under the sun of the great Nietzschean quest [*sous le solei de la grande recherche nietzschéenne*]." (FD iv-v) In 1964, when he delivered the now celebrated lecture on "Nietzsche, Marx, Freud" at Royaumont, Foucault publicly consolidated his pact with the Nietzschean *daimon*. The fate of the genealogist of modernity was thus inscribed on the boundaries of critique and hermeneutic. It was also by that time that Gilles Deleuze and Pierre Klossowski published their seminal works on Nietzsche, which Foucault regarded as the most valuable French contributions to philosophy during the structuralist *belle époque*.[8]

In this study, I have tried to show how Foucault's reading of Kant and Nietzsche are decisive for a full understanding of a Foucauldian genealogy of modernity, where the term "genealogy" is understood *lato sensu*, as Foucault himself used it in his 1984 essay "On the Genealogy of Ethics." (BSH 237ff.; FR 340-343) Like Aristotle's classification of the sciences --which presupposes both a broad and a narrow conception of *episteme*[9]--, Foucault conceives of genealogy

---

[5] See the 1982 interview with Rux Martin, "Truth, Power, Self" in TS 9-15;

[6] "The Return of Morality," interview conducted by Gilles Barbadette and André Scala on the occasion of the French publication of volumes 2 and 3 of *The History of Sexuality*; *Les Nouvelles littéraires*, June 28, 1984; ET: PPC 242-67.

[7] The best example of Foucault's indebtedness to both Heideggerian phenomenology and French existentialism is certainly his 1954 introduction to the French translation of Ludwig Binswanger's *Le rêve et l'existence*, (Paris: Desclée de Brouwer, 1954).

[8] Gilles Deleuze, *Nietzsche et la philosophie* (Paris: PUF, 1962), and Pierre Klossowski, *Nietzsche et le cercle vicieux*, (Paris: Mercure de France, 1965). Cf. Didier Eribon, *Michel Foucault (1926-1984)*, (Paris: Flammarion, 1989), 175 ff.

[9] Cf. *Nicomachean Ethics* vi.1; *Metaphysics* vi.3: *episteme lato sensu* refers to all human, cognitive inquiries, comprising both the theoretical and the practical sciences (including thus

as the most general conception of history, and yet he also opposes this term to archaeology, on the one hand, and to critique, on the other, in what seems to be a *stricto sensu* use of the term. To be sure, there is no metaphysics underlying his formulation of genealogy, though Foucault emphatically uses the word "ontology" associated with it. Since my major concern in this study has been with the question of method in philosophy, especially in ethics and political philosophy, and with reference to the problem of history, I have only signaled these points and will postpone them for a properly ontological investigation. In brief, what I have termed Foucault's "genealogy of modernity" can be expressed by the articulation of his archaeological and genealogical analyses of the regimes of truth, power relations, and ethical practices that have constituted modern subjectivity. I have deliberately omitted a third dimension to this study, namely, the psycho-analytical approach to subjectivation, which has been undertaken by several authors in the last two decades.[10]

Following this *remise en scène* of the Foucauldian problematic, I will proceed to investigate the development of his conceptions of critique and genealogy, so as to complement the *exposés* of his reading of Kant's critique of metaphysics and Nietzsche's critique of modernity, in the first and second chapters. Foucault's approach to the *questions de méthode*, which translated the German *Methodenstreit* into existentialist, Marxist, and structuralist strategies for the French *intellectuels* of the 1960's, will be examined first, so as to address some of Habermas's criticisms. This chapter has been structured, to a certain extent, so as to respond to Habermas's three charges of relativism, *Präsentismus*, and cryptonormativism, to be dealt with in the following sections on truth, power, and ethics, respectively. The Foucauldian conception of modernity, his answer to the Kantian question of the *Aufklärung*, and Nietzsche's critique of modernity will lead us to what I understand to constitute a Foucauldian response to Habermas's accusation of "transcendental historicism." The overcoming of the *homo metaphysicus* will operate the transition to Foucault's critique of power, articulated with his Nietzschean-inspired conceptions of genealogy and the hermeneutics of subjectivity. I will conclude this chapter with an account of what Foucault has termed a "genealogy of ethics."

---

ethics and politics), while by *episteme stricto sensu* Aristotle of course means scientific knowledge.

[10] Cf. Patrick H. Hutton, "Foucault, Freud, and the Technologies of the Self," in TS 121-144; Ernani Chaves, *Foucault e a psicanálise*, (Rio de Janeiro: Zahar, 1978); Michael Mahon, *Foucault's Nietzschean Genealogy*, (Albany: SUNY Press, 1992).

1. FOUCAULT, HABERMAS AND THE "QUESTIONS OF METHOD"

> Entre l'entreprise critique et l'entreprise généalogique la différence n'est pas tellement d'objet ou de domaine, mais de point d'attaque, de perspective et de délimitation. (Michel Foucault, *L'ordre du discours* 68f.)

In this section, I will embark on my response to Habermas's critique of Foucault, dealing with specific problems regarding the problem of method, in connection with the latter's articulation of critique and genealogy. I will argue that the problems of continuity and discontinuity, archaeology and genealogy, in Foucault's works cannot be dissociated from his elaboration on new approaches to history and a critique of power. As announced from the outset, it was by taking Habermas's criticisms seriously that I was impelled to reexamine Foucault's genealogy of modernity, so as to deal with the problems of historicism and rationality which, according to Habermas, undermine Foucault's critique of power. Since the purpose of this study is to analyze Foucault's rather than Habermas's conception of power, I will use the latter's remarks and criticisms only as a way of articulating Foucault's project. Before anything, I would like to recall the background to Foucault's *questions de méthode*, namely, the debate that took place in postwar France since existentialists and marxists were challenged by the structuralist attack on humanism in the sixties.[11] It is in this context that I intend to pave the way for a discussion of Foucault's view of power relations as an ensemble of *dispositifs*, in the third section.

When Jean-Paul Sartre published in 1960 an essay-preface for his polemical *Critique of Dialectical Reason*[12], the choice of the title "Question de Méthode," translated more than a personal interest or the strategy of a fashionable existentialism. It came to no one's surprise thus that, twenty years later, one of Sartre's archi-rivals, contributed to a debate on penitentiary systems of France with a discussion strategically entitled "Questions de Méthode."[13] The "questions of method," in the plural, translated for Foucault the different levels of

---

[11] Cf. Mark Poster, *Existential Marxism: A Study of French Social Theory Since World War II*, (Princeton, NJ: Princeton University Press, 1976); Vincent Descombes, *Le même et l'autre: Quarent-cinq ans de philosophie française, 1933-1978*, (Paris: Minuit, 1979).
[12] J.-P. Sartre, *Question de méthode*, in *Critique de la raison dialectique*, (Paris: Gallimard, 1960).
[13] M. Foucault, "Questions de méthode," in Michelle Perrot (ed.), *L'impossible prison*, (Paris: Seuil, 1980) [ET in FE]. Cf. J.-P. El Kabbach's interview with Foucault on Sartre and the question of method, in *La Quinzaine littéraire* of March 1-15, 1968.[ET in FL]

problematization of a method (archaeological, genealogical, analytico-interpretative) in his work, distinguishing his multiform analyses from the Sartrean project that envisaged the only historical category capable of unifying individuals out of a common structural interest, the "practico-inert" field. As over against Sartre's pretense to "the truth of history," Foucault's critical reading of Kant and Nietzsche called into question the existential-Marxist "prolegomena to any future anthropology." In spite of all conceptual divergences, both Sartre and Foucault situated thus the questions of method at the heart of their philosophical investigations on history, truth, and human nature.

After all, the French reception of Husserl's phenomenology and the Hegelian renaissance constituted the common background of both thinkers, in their response to Heidegger's and structuralist critiques of humanism. Foucault's archaeological critique seems to aim as much at the transparency of Sartre's subject as Husserl's transcendental subjectivity. In the OT, Foucault undertakes the discursive analysis of how the different conceptions of method in the classical age would pave the way for the Kantian critique understood as method to rehabilitate metaphysics vis-à-vis the emerging sciences of nature. One has only to recall all the scientific inquiries and investigations of Bacon, Galileo, Newton and, above all, Descartes's *Rules for the Direction of the Mind* (1621) and his *Discourse on the Method of Conducting One's Reason Well and of Seeking the Truth in the Sciences* (1637). Although the Greek word *methodos* --in the sense of an "investigation," akin to *historia*-- is already found in classical texts such as Aristotle's *Nichomachean Ethics*, it was only in the seventeenth century that an ever-growing, methodic differentiation between the conception of metaphysics and the sciences of nature would lead to the autonomy of modern sciences in the nineteenth century. Hence the significance of the epistemic break which, according to Foucault, separates authors such as Descartes, Newton, and Leibniz --who still extended the usage of a rational, universal method to the diverse fields of human inquiry, including theology-- from Kant's critique of rationalist metaphysics, allowing for the emergence of empirical fields of positivities peculiar to all modern sciences, on the one hand, and the transcendental grounds of human cognition and freedom, on the other. This modern dualism, according to Foucault, would accompany all the adventures of the dialectic of reason, from Hegel and Marx to Husserl and Sartre.

As Gérard Lebrun has shown, Foucault's archaeology in *Les mots et les choses* succeeds in showing how phenomenology failed to do justice to Kant insofar as Husserl underestimated Kant's critique, by placing it within the same rationalist field of "objectivism" where Descartes, Leibniz, and Galileo belong.[14] As Lebrun sums it up, "the essential point of the *Critique* is the advent of a subject who possesses a priori knowledge to the extent that he is deprived of intellectual intuition; that is, to the extent that he is finite." (MFP 44) Foucault speaks thus of the phenomenological conception of "*le vécu*" (alluding to the *Lebenswelt*) as a prerequisite to the epistemic field and he appropriates Merleau-Ponty's circularity between the transcendental and the empirical only to arrive at the impasse of representational thinking after Kant's analytic of finitude. Foucault's strategy aims, in the last analysis, at the undermining of the transcendental subject, precisely by introducing the representation-anthropology divide that problematizes post-Kantian attempts to ground knowledge in a philosophical a priori. If Husserl's suspension of the thesis of the world failed to provide us with a presuppositionless method, Foucault's double suspension --i.e., the *epoche* of reference and meaning (BSH 49)--establishes the historicity of every form of cognition, a history of truth, as it were. This was indeed a radical attempt to extend phenomenology so as to fill the gaps left by the structuralist attack on the becoming of human subjectivity. For Foucault, structuralism was indeed the most systematic of all efforts to "evacuate the concept of the event," (PK 114) an extreme case for history. In this sense, Foucault was the self-proclaimed anti-structuralist and the radical hermeneute par excellence.

Now, I must remark in passing that it was also as part of the legacy of German idealism that the *Methodenstreit* opposing natural sciences (*Naturwissenschaften*) and human sciences (*Geisteswissenschaften*) emerged in the last century, and was renewed by the debate between Habermas and Karl Popper, on the one hand, and between Habermas and the new historicism, on the other.[15] As we have seen in the first chapter, it was precisely in his earlier writings that Foucault focused on the questions of method in his archaeology of knowledges so as to establish the historicity of all truth. Although Habermas gives many convincing reasons for his attack upon Foucault's systematic ambiguity, i.e., between what he sees as the critical and meta-theoretical claims of genealogy, he is not justified in imposing a critical-theoretical framework on a thinker who was not after all seeking to establish a social theory. That is why the Foucault-Habermas debate will only profit us by recasting its intrinsic problematic of

---

[14] Cf. G. Lebrun, "Note sur la phénoménologie dans *Les mots et les choses*," MFP 33-53; E. Husserl, *Krisis*, op. cit., § 25, 112.

[15] Cf. the writings on scientific methodology by Wilhelm Dilthey, Wilhelm Windelband, and Max Weber; J. Habermas, *Knowledge and Human Interests*, (Boston: Beacon Press, 1989); *The New Conservatism: Cultural Criticism and the Historians' Debate*, (Cambridge, Mass.: MIT Press, 1989).

historicity and power. Thus Habermas has discerned, for better or for worse, a double role played by the Foucauldian staging of power, in the ideal thought of a transcendental synthesis and the presuppositions of an empirical ontology. While the empirical research of the genealogist carries out the documentary interests of a *positiviste heureux* in his unearthed archives, Habermas condemns Foucault's "functionalist sociology of knowledge" for its implicit "transcendental-historicist concept of power." (PDM 269) In effect, in Foucault's own words, "[t]he forces operating in history are not controlled by destiny or regulative mechanisms, but respond to haphazard conflicts." (FR 88) The "concerted carnival" of Foucault's genealogical method consists thus of an ongoing compilation and process of bodies of power/ knowledge, the cultural productions of truth, which have been marginalized by previous historiographies.

With Foucault's discussion of regimes of jurisdiction and veridiction ("Questions of Method," *L'impossible prison*), the genealogy of modernity comes full circle in its radical critique of rationality and historicism, renewing the classical question of freedom and necessity in Western thought. It also attests to Foucault's lifelong concern with the historicity of scientific production, the history of systems of thought, and its discursive discontinuities vis-à-vis other forms of discourse and practices, such as literature, art, etc. Thus Kant and Nietzsche provide together the critical-genealogical background against which Foucault's social analyses of human discourses are effected. If the Kantian *Grenzbegriff* dualism of faculties leads to the Foucauldian limit-attitude between law-abiding and its transgression, it is Nietzsche's metaphorics of *wahr-sagen* that provides Foucault with the problematic of truth, values, and the self-overcoming of critical reflexivity. This "Nietzschean return to Kant" guides indeed Foucault's social interest in the study of *practices* rather than theories or ideologies. As he remarked on the question of method in history,

> To analyze "regimes of practices" means to analyze programmes of conduct which have both prescriptive effects regarding what is to be done (effects of "jurisdiction") and codifying effects regarding what is to be known (effects of "veridiction"). (FE 75)

Nevertheless, Habermas contends that Foucault's "genealogy of knowledge" is "grounded on a theory of power" (PDM 104), so that the latter will inevitably lead to performative contradiction. I shall arrive at another conclusion, with an alternative reading of Foucault's philosophical discourse of modernity, which I think to be in accordance with his overall conception of truth, power, and ethics. In my own attempt to address Habermas's threefold critique of Foucault's supposed relativism, presentism, and cryptonormativism, I will argue that the respective questions of truth, value, and norm are implicitly met by the historical a priori of a genealogy of subjectivity. It will be of fundamental importance to articulate Foucault's critique-genealogy binomial with his knowledge-power-subjectivation triangle in such a way as to deal with the problem of power without reducing it to an ontic category, not even to an ontological concept à la Heidegger, since power relations, like material relations of production, always already take place in history, in the very "eventalizing" of social practices.

2. TRUTH, ARCHAEOLOGY, AND GENEALOGY

> There is a battle "for truth," or at least "around truth"--...by truth I do not mean "the ensemble of truths which are to be discovered and accepted," but rather "the ensemble of rules according to which the true and the false are separated and specific effects of power attached to the true"... (Michel Foucault, PK 132)

Following the methodological question that permeates my study, I proceed now to show how Foucault's conjugation of the two approaches (i.e. the critical and the genealogical) runs parallel to his articulation of archaeology and genealogy. In order to reexamine Foucault's project in the methodological correlation[16] it establishes between his critical conception of power and his genealogical view of history, I decided to start from Habermas's charges that Foucault is doomed to performative contradiction and relativism. The first thing that must be pointed out here is that neither Foucault nor Nietzsche would question the truth that is at stake, say, in truth games and their rules, such as *modus ponens*, or concluding 'Q' from the premises 'P $\rightarrow$ Q' and 'P.' In effect, suspicion only arises on the level of referentiality, namely, on what 'P' stands for. Since for neither Nietzsche nor Foucault truth can be naively reduced to an *adaequatio* theory of sorts (i.e., the correspondence either between things and words, or between facts and their posterior interpretations), the notion of "regimes of truth" plays, for Foucault, the social, political role of the "will to truth," as every society accepts certain types of discourse and makes them function as true. (PK 132, PDM 270) According to Habermas,

---

[16] I am indebted to Deleuze's essay in MFP 185ff, as well as to Roberto Machado's preface to the fourth edition of *Microfísica do Poder*, (Rio de Janeiro: Graal, 1979).

> Foucault cannot adequately deal with the persistent problems that come up in connection with an interpretation approach to the object domain, a self-referential denial of universal validity claims, and a normative justification of critique. The categories of meaning, validity, and value are ... eliminated... (PDM 286)

As we shall see, the problem of truth refers us to the other problems of the critique of power and ethical normativity, which will be dealt with in the next sections. To a certain extent, Habermas has rightly framed his criticism of Foucault in terms of the three genealogical axes. And yet, as I will argue, he fails to correctly represent Foucault's genealogy of modernity as a historical, practical critique of modern subjectivity. As Dominique Janicaud has shown, it seems that "Habermas did not understand Nietzsche"[17] and to the extent that he applies the same criticism of signification to that of truth and value, he failed to do justice to Foucault's writings, which are quoted only to be dismissed as an aporetic critique of power. To start with, the Nietzsche appropriated by Foucault is not exactly the author of *Zarathustra* but the one of *The Birth of Tragedy*, of the *Genealogy of Morals*.[18] In the same vein, Foucault's appropriation of Kant's critique, as we have seen, departs from the *Aufklärung* ideal of rationality but preserves its emancipatory interest and grounds it in everyday history rather than in a transcendental freedom. Perhaps, to borrow Ricoeur's formula, we find here "a Kantianism without a transcendental subject." As Foucault writes in the preface to the *Birth of the Clinic*,

> For Kant, the possibility and necessity of a critique were linked, through certain scientific contents, to the fact that there is such a thing as knowledge. In our time --and Nietzsche the philologist testifies to it-- they are linked to the fact that language exists and that, in the innumerable words spoken by men --whether they are reasonable or senseless, demonstrative or poetic-- a meaning has taken shape that hangs over us, leading us forward in our blindness, but awaiting in the darkness for us to attain awareness before emerging into the light of day and speaking. (NC xv-xvi)

Thus, while Habermas starts with the assumption that philosophy has articulated the ideals critical theory must make practical, as John Rajchman remarks, "Foucault starts with the assumption that ideals and norms are always

---

[17] "Rationalité, puissance et pouvoir," in MFP 341: "Ce pseudo-résumé de la pensée de Nietzsche manifeste que Habermas *n'a pas compris* Nietzsche (en tout cas, qu'il n'a pas compris les pensées les plus intéressantes et les plus surdéterminées de Nietzsche." (emphasis in the original)

[18] Interview with Giulio Preti, "Un dibattito Foucault-Preti" in *Bimestre* 22-23 (1972) 2.

already 'practical;' the point of critique is to analyze the practices in which those norms actually figure, and which determine particular kinds of experience."[19] As we have seen in our exposés of Kant's and Nietzsche's conceptions of knowledge and truth, the very critical task of philosophy is radically diverse in these thinkers and that will certainly reflect in both Habermas's and Foucault's conceptions of philosophy. Foucault writes as a philosopher, and yet he is always solicited by the other of philosophical inquiry as he sets out to think from the outside, as it were, *la pensée du dehors*:

> But what is philosophy today, I mean philosophical activity, if it is not work which is critical of thought itself? And what is it, if instead of legitimizing that which we already know, it does not consist in finding out how and how far it might be possible to think differently? There is always something laughable about philosophical discourse when it attempts, from the outside, to lay down the law for others, to tell them where their truth really lies, and how to find it, or when it takes it upon itself to make clear what it is in their procedures which can be seen as naive positivity. Yet it is the right of philosophical discourse to explore that which, in its own thought, can be challenged by the use of a form of knowledge which is alien to it. (HS2 15)

Foucault's conception of philosophy as *askesis*, "*un exercice de soi dans la pensée*," reveals the archaeological-genealogical doublet that characterizes his "history of truth." While the archaeological dimension accounts for the analyses of the forms of problematization (*les formes mêmes de la problématisation*), the genealogical dimension allows for their formation from practices and their changes (*leur formation à partir des pratiques et de leurs modifications*). (HS2 17f.) Although this cross-fertilization of archaeology and genealogy is only explicitly formulated towards the end of his life, Foucault has applied it to earlier works, so as to suggest that there is indeed a quasi-systematic, three-axial approach to his *histoire de la vérité*. In his inaugural lecture at the Collège de France, quoted above, Foucault opposes archaeology to genealogy so as to contrast their complementary strategies in a radical attempt to avoid reducing historical analyses to a theory of knowledge or to a theory of infrastructural determinations. (OD 68-72) Thus, in the 1976 lecture at the same Collège, Foucault defines archaeology as "the appropriate methodology of this analysis of local discursivities," while genealogy "would be the tactics whereby, on the basis of the descriptions of these local discursivities, the subjected knowledges which

---

[19] John Rajchman, *Michel Foucault: The Freedom of Philosophy*, (New York: Columbia University Press, 1985), 79.

were thus released would be brought into play." (PK 85) In a 1984 interview conducted by Paul Rabinow, Foucault situated his "history of problematics" between a "history of ideas" and a "history of mentalities," since one must grasp "problematization not as an arrangement of representation but as a work of thought." (FR 390) And he defined thought as "freedom in relation to what one does, the motion by which one detaches oneself from it, establishes it as an object, and reflects on it as a problem." (FR 388) If Kant inspired Foucault's interest in the subjective constitution of reflection and its discursive, positive finitude, it was Nietzsche's unmasking of truth that ultimately guided his archaeological and genealogical approaches to history.

Since archaeology deals with discourses, "discourse" also acquires different meanings for Foucault and Habermas. In a 1968 essay on "Politics and the Study of Discourse,"[20] Foucault presents the criteria of formation, transformation, and correlation of discourses in the discursive analyses employed in the OT. He emphasizes then his concern with the problem of the *individualization of discourses* --always in the plural. (FE 54) And Foucault proceeds to remind his readers that "the *episteme* is not *a sort of grand underlying theory*, it is a space of *dispersion*, it is an *open and doubtless indefinitely describable field of relationships*." (FE 55) The dissemination of discursivity allows, at once, for the delimitations and displacements operated by the different epistemic formations. This usage of the word is therefore to be contrasted with Habermas's normative *Diskurs*, which follows Kant's discursive-intuitive opposition, in that validity claims are to be grounded in reason and reflective thinking. To be sure, both *discours* and *Diskurs* stem from the Latin *discursus* and are related to the verb *discurrere*, "to run hither and tither." As we have seen in the first chapter, the limits of representation in the critique would eventually motivate Foucault to replace the metaphoric of the *discours* with that of the *savoir*, and the *episteme* with the *dispositif*. But we must bear in mind that Foucault is indeed radicalizing the critique, under the sign of Nietzsche's genealogy, so as to conceive of both discursivity and non-discursivity in his radical attempt to overcome the Kantian opposition between theory and practice. Manfred Frank reminds us that a common-sense definition would have that "a discourse is an utterance, or a talk of some length (not determined), whose unfolding or spontaneous development is not held back by any over-rigid intentions." (MFP 126)[21] In the OT, discourse stands for a symbolic order of a state of affairs which makes it possible for all subjects who have been socialized under its authority to speak and act together.

---

[20] Originally appeared in *Esprit* 371 (May 1968) 850-874. ET, edited by Colin Gordon, in FE 53-72.
[21] Cf. M. Frank, "Sur le concept de discours chez Foucault," in MFP 125-134.

(MFP 133) The word "discourse" is used thus by Foucault's archaeological analyses as a second-degree order, situated between the reversible order of "language" (*langue*) and the irreversible order of "word" (*parole*). (OT 12; FE 56-63) Contrasting with the homogeneous ordering of the discourse in OT, the *Archéologie du savoir* and *L'ordre du discours* emphasize the *événements singuliers* ("specific events") which cannot be reduced to a "linear schema," as they do not conform to "a single law, often bearing with them a type of history which is individual to itself, and irreducible to the general mode of a consciousness which acquires, progresses and remembers itself." (AS 16) Discourses are therefore external to any totalizing, universalizing concept. Discourses are broken down into "statements" (*énoncés*), which are neither propositions nor sentences, and account for the impossibility of subordinating discourses to the "structure-becoming opposition" (*opposition structure-devenir*)(AS 20). Foucault places them between structure and event: "The *énoncé* is obviously an event which cannot be repeated; it has a situational singularity which cannot be reduced." (AS 133) Foucault resorts to the metaphors of verticality and horizontality in order to conjugate, on the same mobile, diagonal line, the singular grouping of énoncés with the ordering of institutional conventions and codifications. In the AS, Foucault already anticipates the nondiscursive practices that will be shown to be interdependent and correlative to their discursive counterparts: he speaks of an *ordre d'institution* to which discourses are subject as elements identical to one another and a *champ d'utilisation* in which the *énoncé* is invested. (AS 136, 137) The archive appears thus as the totality of all discursive regularities, within a vertical system of interdependence. (AS 96) As Frank remarks, Foucault claims in his inaugural lecture at the Collège de France, "that discourses are not ordered *per se*, but through the intervention of a will to power." (MFP ET 113)[22] Now, in opposition to a Hegelian semiology which, as we have seen, presupposes the reconciliation of a conceptual logic of *Aufhebung* with historical becoming, Foucault employs *savoir* to replace the order of the *discours*. At any rate, discourse is ultimately comprised by Foucault's later use of the broader term "practices" comprising both discursive and nondiscursive dimensions.

> I have sought to show how archaeology and genealogy are to be articulated in Foucault's conception of regimes of truth and jurisdiction, at the heart of his critique of power and ethics. In effect, truth already points to a

---

[22] The third section of Frank's paper was not included in the French original edition of MFP. Cf. the ET, *Michel Foucault Philosopher*, trans. Timothy J. Armstrong, (New York: Rouledge, 1992), 113 ff.

questioning of the status of knowledge, i.e., that the very possibility of knowledge is regarded as a problem for philosophy. Hence Deleuze's allusion to Foucault's "pragmatism" (F 81), insofar as truth appears as the outcome of problematizations of *savoir* and problematizations themselves are made from practices of saying and seeing. Foucault sought "to make visible the unseen," that is, to unveil "a change of level, addressing one self to a layer of material which had hitherto had no pertinence for history and which had not been recognized as having any moral, aesthetic, political or historical value." (PK 51)

Thus Foucault's genealogical critique follows a Nietzschean overcoming of Kant's critique, insofar as it brings to light a historically constituted subjectivity that had been concealed and silenced by the correlated constitutions of knowledge and power. The will to truth is always already an expression of a will to power, even on a discursive level, as one of the dispositifs of control, selection, and organization of discourse. It is this context that Foucault proceeds to speak of a "true discourse" (*le discours vrai*), "incapable of recognizing the will to truth that pervades it." (OD 22) Habermas mistakenly quotes this passage to stress "the methodological paradox of a science that writes the history of the human sciences with the goal of a radical critique of reason." (PDM 248) To be sure, Habermas's point is that a second-order truth, a mere effect of power relations, can neither account for an archaeology nor stem from genealogy's positivism with the objectivity of truth claims. However, just as Habermas accuses Foucault of imposing an ontological reading of power into the concept of truth, he fails to realize that it was this very "objectivism" that came under attack in archaeology and genealogy. Furthermore, as it will be shown, there is no ontology of power underlying Foucault's genealogy, nor is truth ultimately subordinated to power, even though it remains an effect of power. It seems that the same problem of a "performative contradiction" had been raised in the Foucault-Chomsky debate around the problem of human nature.[23] How can one articulate ethics and political philosophy without referring to a presupposed conception of human nature and rationality? This problem, as I have tried to show, dates back to Aristotle, but was only fully expressed in the modern conception of freedom that is associated with German idealism and the critical philosophy of Kant. Foucault qua philosopher is not concerned with some social theory, "an ideal social model for the functioning of our scientific or technological society." After all, this "will to know" has only masked the real mechanisms of power relations that underlie social, political theorizations:

It seems to me that the real political task in a society such as ours is to criticize the working of institutions which appear to be both neutral and independent; to criticize them in such a manner that the political violence which has always exercised itself obscurely through them will be unmasked, so that one can fight them. (FR 6)

Of course there remain several questions to be addressed, such as, Why should one oppose violence? Why should the oppressed resist? On which grounds should one social group fight and stand for their rights and freedom? Nancy Fraser has formulated this problem with a single question, "Why ought domination to be resisted?," and she is approvingly cited by Habermas. (PDM 283)[24] Foucault does not dismiss these questions, but he leaves them unanswered. For Foucault, it is only by actually engaging in political struggles that one takes part in processes that seek to subvert and alter power relations --but theory and knowledge are not external to these practices, let alone above them.

3. MODERNITY AND THE CRITIQUE OF POWER

These two questions --"What is the *Aufklärung*? What is the Revolution?" -- are the two forms under which Kant posed the question of his own present. They, are also, I believe, the two questions that have not ceased to haunt, if not all modern philosophy since the nineteenth century, at least a large part of that philosophy. After all, it seems to me that the *Aufklärung*, both as a singular event inaugurating European modernity and as a permanent process manifested in the history of reason, in the development and establishment of forms of rationality and technology, the autonomy and authority of knowledge, is for us not just an episode in the history of ideas. It is a philosophical question, inscribed since the eighteenth century in our thoughts. (Foucault, "The Art of Telling the Truth," PPC 94)

I have contended that Foucault's genealogy of modernity hinges on a critique of power that combines his reading of Kant's response to the *Aufklärung* with his appropriation of Nietzsche's radical philosophy. Foucault's own understanding of the Enlightenment as the modern, philosophical response to that question (FR 32)

---

[23] "Human Nature: Justice versus Power" (in *Reflexive Water: The Basic Concerns of Mankind*, ed. Fons Elders, London: Souvenir Press, 1974). Cf. P. Rabinow's Introduction to FR 1-27.
[24] N. Fraser, "Foucault on Modern Power: Empirical Insights and Normative Confusions," in *Unruly Practices: Power, Discourse, and Gender in Contemporary Social Theory*, (Minneapolis: University of Minnesota Press, 1989).

reveals the genealogical thrust of his approach. Like modernity itself, the *Aufklärung* cannot be reduced to a past period in the history of ideas, but rather defines a perennial challenge, a critical task, an ethico-political problem for our own age. Rationality and freedom are indeed philosophical themes whose nonphilosophical openings and implications have been accompanying the history of Western civilizations since their first beginnings. And yet it is only in modernity that reason is said to have come of age, so as to attain true freedom. Foucault characterizes the modern attitude by four main features, namely, its self-consciousness of the break with tradition, its will to "heroize" the present, its self-relation to itself, and its self-realization through art. (FR 39-42) Foucault invokes Baudelaire as the epitome of modernity, just as Habermas sees in Schiller's *Letters on the Aesthetic Education of Man* the aestheticist model that influenced Hegel, Schopenhauer, Nietzsche, and all the generation of post-modernists who in effect radicalize the fourth feature of Foucault's account. We had seen that, for Foucault, the threshold of our modernity is "situated not by the attempt to apply objective methods to the study of man, but rather by the constitution of an empirico-transcendental doublet which was called man." (OT 319) Now, Foucault sets out to define the modern ethos, first of all, in terms of a "permanent critique of ourselves" that breaks away from the "blackmail of the Enlightenment," as the only way to carry out the practical intent of Kant's *sapere aude* without falling back into dogmatic rationalism and humanism. Both are caricatures of the *Aufklärung*, since whatever is human about "human nature" is itself a human creation, a historical invention that bears the stamp of its own time. To rid ourselves of the for-or-against Enlightenment blackmail, we must "be at the frontiers," so as to analyze and reflect on the limits of human experience, "a critique of what we are saying, thinking, and doing, through a historical ontology of ourselves." (FR 45) Since there is no such a thing as a "golden age" of Enlightenment, neither past nor future, the philosophical ethos of modernity is a historico-practical critique of today. It is neither a theory nor a permanent body of knowledge, but only an attitude, an ethos, "a philosophical life in which the critique of what we are is at one and the same time the historical analysis of the limits that are imposed on us and an experiment with the possibility of going beyond them." (FR 50)

As over against the modern humanist traditions that draws the line between knowledge and power, Foucault sets out to show "a perpetual articulation of power on knowledge and knowledge on power." (PK 54) It is largely assumed that, following the May 1968 revolts in France, Foucault turned to more explicit analyses of power, moving therefore away from archaeology toward genealogy. The contrast between his last major text on archaeology, *L'archéologie du savoir*, and *Surveiller et punir*, is obvious. And yet there is a Foucauldian spacing that brings archaeology and genealogy together, precisely in his metaphor of space.[25] As we have seen, visibilities made possible the study and classification of, say, plants by Linneas, in the archaeology of OT. As for the genealogy, "space is fundamental in any exercise of power." (FR 252) In effect, space accounts for the power/ knowledge continuum. As Foucault says in the same interview, "the spatialization of knowledge was one of the factors in the constitution of this knowledge as a science." (FR 254) And as much could be said about the space of subjectivation in psychotherapy, medical clinics, and psychoanalysis. For Foucault,

> Mechanisms of power in general have never been much studied by history. History has studied those who held power --anedoctal histories of kings and generals; contrasted with this there has been the history of economic processes and infrastructures ... histories of institutions, of what has been viewed as a superstructural level... (PK 51)[26]

In order to make visible the constant articulation of power on knowledge and vice-versa, Foucault resorted to the *dispositif* metaphor.[27] We have alluded to Deleuze's book on Foucault, where the latter's philosophy is compared to a threefold (or fourfold, if we include the historical-time coordinate) of *dispositifs* defining the regimes of truth, mechanisms of power, and modes of subjectivation. As I will argue in this section, the conception of power *dispositifs* in Foucault is a felicitous formula to respond to Habermas's criticism. Habermas's systematic attack on the chimerical grounding of philosophy apart from the social world has revived the great Marxian tradition of "radical critique." Thus, his critique of Foucault remains much too complex to be dismissed as lacking philosophical magnitude. If I will be focusing on one single aspect of this "critique of power," namely the method that links micro-analyses to genealogical historiography, it is only for the sake of preserving the communication between the genealogy of power and critical theory. For Habermas, this link between the social order as

---

[25] I think that Gaston Bachelard's metaphoric of space, together with Heidegger's conception of the *Geviert* and Mallarmé's *espacement*, exerted a tremendous influence on both Foucault and Derrida.

[26] For an interesting analysis of Foucault's use of "anecdote" as a sign of order, see Adi Ophir, "The Semiotics of Power: Reading Michel Foucault's *Discipline and Punish*" *Manuscrito* 12/2 (1989) 9-34. I am grateful to Professor Michael Kelly for bringing my attention to Ophir's essay on Foucault's "semiotics of power."

Lebenswelt, on the one hand, and as *System*, on the other, is never articulated in Foucault. Hence Habermas praises Axel Honneth for having worked out this problematic feature of Foucault's social thought, namely the elaboration of a model of strategic action that defies the State as a network of power, that breaks away from the institutionally sedimented disciplines and power practices already presupposed in his early writings. As Habermas sums it up,

> When, like Foucault, one admits only the model of processes of subjugation, of confrontations mediated by the body, of contexts of more or less consciously strategic action; when one excludes the any stabilizing of domains of action in terms of values, norms, and processes of mutual understanding and offers for these machanisms of social integration none of the familiar equivalents from systems or exchange theories; then one is hardly able to explain just how persistent local struggles could get consolidated into institutionalized power. (PDM 287)

I have pointed out that Habermas charges of presentism, relativism, and cryptonormativism aim at Foucault's "attempt to preserve the transcendental moment proper to generative performances in the basic concept of power while driving from it every trace of subjectivity." (PDM 295) For Habermas, the main problem with Foucault's concept of power is that it cannot "free the genealogist from contradictory self-thematizations." Now, the critical questions of signification, truth, and value, raised by Habermas, are indeed critical in the context of social practices. If what Foucault aims at is not the social struggles between oppressors and oppressed (as in classical Marxism), but an asymmetrical ensemble of tensions between disciplinary powers and tacit bodies, then to invoke "the possibility of a new form of right," at once antidisciplinary and liberated from the principle of sovereignty, betrays a "value-free historiography" inherent in his genealogical method. (PDM 284)[28] Nevertheless, as Foucault asserts in "The Subject and Power,"

> Power exists only when it is put into action, even if, of course, it is integrated into a disparate field of possibilities brought to bear upon permanent structures. (BSH 219)

---

[27] As mentioned above, the French word "dispositif" has been translated as either "apparatus" (which misleads to confusing it with the Marxist term "appareil") or "device" (which seems to be a better translation, but is too reminiscent of a formalized, mathematical procedure).

[28] Habermas quotes from Foucault's lecture on "Sovereignty and Discipline," at the Collège de France (January 14, 1976), repro-duced as the second of "Two Lectures" in PK 92-108. In Foucault's own words: "If one wants to look for a non-disciplinary form of power, or rather, to struggle against disciplines and disciplinary power, it is not towards the ancient right of sovereignty that one should turn, but towards the possibility of a new form of right, one which must indeed be anti-disciplinarian, but at the same time liberated from the principle of sovereignty." (PK 108)

Furthermore, if instead of *puissance* Foucault prefers to speak of *pouvoir*, he also speaks more often of *discours* than of *rationalité*, not to mention "rationalization." He even goes as far as to say that "the word *rationalization* is dangerous. What we have to do is analyze specific rationalities rather than always invoking the progress of rationalization in general." (BSH 210) In this same context, Foucault reiterates the Nietzschean view of power as the acting upon other actions, "an action upon an action." (BSH 220) The metaphors of active and reactive forces also points to the discursive mechanism that evaluates their magnitude, the differential device that accounts for multiple forms of rationality which are historically contingent discursive formations and practices. In this regard, as Foucault said to Raulet, it would be unfair to characterize his enunciation of the problematic of knowledge/power relations as a "theory of power." (PPC 43; BSH 209) In effect, according to Foucault, power is never substantive (*le pouvoir*), since it cannot be reduced to a focus of possession or even agency (e.g. the State, social classes, ideological apparatuses), but is itself a diffuse complex of relations, involving thus both knowledges and modes of subjectivation. As he remarked in a 1976 lecture in Brazil, "there is not *one* power, but several powers [*il n'existe pas un pouvoir, mais plusieurs pouvoirs*]."[29] Foucault contends thus that society is not a unitary body on which one single power is exerted, but "an archipelago of different powers." Hence the juridical model of Grotius, Pufendorf, and Rousseau, which centralizes power in the sovereignty of the State or even in the civil society, tends to eclipse the techniques of power that defy superstructural functions of conservation and reproduction of power:

> Il existe une véritable technologie du pouvoir ou, mieux, des pouvoirs, qui ont leur propre histoire ...Privilégier l'appareil d'État, la fonction de conservation, la superstructure juridique, est, au fond, 'rousseauiser' Marx. C'est le réinscrire dans la théorie bourgeoise et juridique du pouvoir...[30]

Foucault undertakes thus the writing of a "history of powers in the West" (*une histoire des pouvoirs dans l'Occident*), where the different mechanisms of

---

[29] "Les mailles du pouvoir," in *Magazine littéraire* 324 (September 1994) 64. Forthcoming in Michel Foucault, *Dits et Écrits 1954-1988* (Paris: Gallimard, 1994). It is interesting to remark that Foucault delivered this lecture in Brazil at the zenith of the military dictatorship, and alluded to the Second Book of Marx's *Capital* so as to stress that the army itself was just one of the several regional, specific spheres of power that lead up to the juridical, State apparatus.

[30] M. Foucault, "Les mailles du pouvoir," art. cit., p. 65.

power are analyzed in light of their interactions with the diverse levels of power relations and their correlative *dispositifs* of truth and subjectivation. That is why Deleuze's model for power relations as *dispositifs* that at once constitute and are constituted by a network of *dispositifs* is indeed such a felicitous one. For, as Deleuze argues, the real boundary in Foucault is that between constants and variables (MFP 193), so that the lines which form the *dispositifs* only affirm the continual variations, and all we are left with are the lines of variation. And this is precisely the point of rupture between Foucault and every form of historicism that prevails even in neo-Marxist systems of culture like Gramsci's hegemony, in that Foucault leaves no room for teleology. In contrast with Althusser, who maintained that there are no ideological apparatuses that are not at the same time State apparatuses (*appareils d'État*), Foucault develops a veritable "philosophy of practices" in his analyses of concrete devices (*analyses des dispositifs concrets*) that displace the foci and agency of power. Above all, the Foucauldian device appears as a multilineal ensemble, composed of lines of different nature forming non-homogeneous systems: each line is divided, submitted to variations of direction, submitted to derivations. The *énoncés* which can be formulated are like vectors or tensors. Thus the three fields that Foucault often distinguishes (*savoir, pouvoir, subjectivation*) have no fixed contours, but are like chains of variables acting upon one another. Hence the prison device, for instance, as a panoptical machine that allows for the disciplinary agent to see without being seen. What accounts for social movements are neither subjects nor objects but regimes of statements (*régimes d'énoncés*) that, in contrast with nondiscursive devices, serve to determine new archives and new historical media such as the seventeenth-century General Hospital, the eighteenth-century clinic, the nineteenth-century prison, or Ancient Greek technologies of subjectivation.

Habermas fails thus to acknowledge that the reception of Nietzsche in France cannot be reduced to fashionable aestheticism nor to some structuralist contextualism à la Heidegger. As Foucault sets out to discuss (and reappropriate) Nietzsche's nonjuridical notion of power, he also embraces his conception of "history" and explicitly problematizes the historian's taken-for-granted *use of historiography*. As Habermas rightly put it, Foucault's reappropriation of Nietzsche's "Second Unmodern Observation" can be described as a threefold attack on modern historicism:

(a) the attack on modernity's presentist consciousness of time;
(b) the attack on hermeneutical methodology;
(c) the attack on global historiography. (PDM 249-251)

From Nietzsche's first essay on the *Genealogy of Morals*, Foucault concludes that, since nothing lies at the origin of things and there is no substratum, genealogy is the "union of erudite knowledge and local memories which allow us to establish a historical knowledge of struggles and to make use of this knowledge tactically today." (PK 83) It has been shown, and this cannot be overemphasized, how Nietzsche's influence on Foucault accounts for a "technological," nonjuridical conception of power. For Foucault regards Nietzsche as *the* philosopher of power. (PK 53) Besides the two known texts on Nietzsche mentioned above (NFM and FR 76-100), Foucault's 1973 lecture on "Truth and Juridical Forms" (VFJ) delivered in Brazil constitutes an important source to understand his microphysics of power. Foucault finds in Nietzsche the very kind of discourse where historical analyses of "the formation of the subject" refers to the "birth of a certain form of knowledge without ever admitting the pre-existence of a subject of cognition." (VFJ 163) Foucault suggests thus that we follow Nietzsche's work as a model for his archaeological, genealogical analyses. According to Foucault, one of the most important features of Nietzsche's genealogy is the usage of the term "invention" --in German, *Erfindung*--, which frequently recurs in his writings, and should be always opposed to "origin," *Ursprung*, to stress the fabricated character of human morality, its social codifications, in spite of endless metaphysical attempts to ground it in a divine or intelligible origin. After all, since every ideal has no origin but has also been invented, cognition itself is a human creation, and does not constitute the oldest instinct of human beings. The will to truth, the will to know, stems from the struggle and the compromise among instincts, so that cognition is just an effect of surface. "A genealogy of values, morality, asceticism, and knowledge," writes Foucault, "will never confuse itself with a quest for their 'origins,' will never neglect as inaccessible the vicissitudes of history." (FR 80) Hence the *rapprochement* between history and medicine --as opposed to metaphysical philosophy. We can also see here the betrayal of morals in the very search for a historical knowledge that does not hinge on some kind of subjective formation. Genealogy, as a historical analysis of the lowly, sordid beginnings of human inventions, seeks thus to overcome the moral of ressentiment that assigns to the doer (the subject) the good or evil of actions that we value morally (e.g., the goodness of founding fathers) --hence the need of a critique of moral values. Contra Kant's critique, genealogy is not after the transcendental conditions of possibility, but like Marx's *Kritik der Kritik*, it simply unveils the concrete, historical conditions of human beginnings. Once again, we can spot here Foucault's positive reading of the Kantian critique, inherited by Marx, inasmuch as "the *Aufklärung* is the age of critique." (FR 38)

In effect, Nietzsche's criticism of Paul Rée's utilitarian use of history (GM Preface 4, 7),[31] as Foucault points out, was aimed not only at Rée's own evolutionary version of historicism but at the entire suprahistorical, metaphysical traditions of thought that preceded him. One of the greatest contributions of Nietzsche's genealogical critique of Christianity and Western metaphysics lies precisely in the unmasking of history as a transcendental standpoint from where everything else can be understood. Just as Marx and Freud denounced masking structures of false consciousness and conscious behaviour, Nietzsche shook the metaphysical foundations of truth and reality so as to unveil the transvaluation of all values in the historical self-overcoming of human becoming. Unlike the other two "masters of suspicion," however, Nietzsche's hermeneutic is not after a deeper, hidden structure of meaning but remains on the very surface of appearances, where opposites always already operate the return of the same. As in Deleuze's reading of Nietzsche, Foucault interprets the "return of the same" in terms of a non-dialectical, differential interplay of forces. (NP 167-189) That is why, contra Althusser, Foucault goes on to warn against the political marriage of "hermeneutics" and "semiology."[32]

Foucault not only appropriates Nietzsche's conception of genealogy but he also applies it to Nietzsche's own corpus, thus betraying the double gesture of a Nietzschean metaphoricity, an "interpretation of the interpretation" (i.e. Foucault's and Nietzsche's interpretation of "facts") that cannot be reduced to the "outside" it seeks to unmask *as interpretation*.[33] In effect, the Nietzschean opposition of *Entstehung* and *Herkunft* to *Ursprung*, Foucault points out, translates the true objective of genealogy *qua* analysis of beginnings, at once unveiling the intricacies of discursive formations and undermining the illusion of self-identity in the very writing of history:

---

[31] Cf. Paul-Laurent Assoun, "Nietzsche et le Réelisme," in Paul Rée, *L'origine des sentiments moraux*, trans. Michel-François Demet, (Paris: PUF, 1982).

[32] Cf. M. Foucault, "Nietzsche, Marx, Freud" (1964), in *Nietzsche*, Cahiers de Royaumont, (Paris: Minuit, 1967), 183-200.

[33] Cf. M. Foucault, "La pensée du dehors," in *Critique* 229 (June 1966); M. Blanchot, *L'entretien infini*, (Paris: Gallimard, 1969). As Deleuze points out, exteriority (speaking and seeing) and the outside (thinking) are differentiated in both Blanchot's and Fou-cault's appropriation of Nietzsche's metaphoricity; cf. *Foucault*, op. cit., "Strategies or the Non-stratified: the Thought of the Outside (Power)," 70-93. Nietzsche's irreducible metaphoricity can be understood as the historical fact that there are only interpretations, since truth is nothing less than the "sum of human relations" which can be "transposed" (Greek verb *metaphorein*) into the legal, political, cultural codes that make them institutionally and historically true. Cf. "On Truth and Lie in an Extra-Moral Sense" (1873), in *The Portable Nietzsche*, ed. Kaufmann, pp. 42 ff.

Where the soul pretends unification or the self fabricates a coherent identity, the genealogist sets out to study the beginning --numberless beginnings, whose faint traces and hints of color are readily seen by a historical eye. The analysis of descent permits the dissociation of the self, its recognition and displacement as an empty synthesis, in liberating a profusion of lost events. (FR 81)

Descent implies also the inscription of historical events in the body, the domain par excellence of *Herkunft*, the locus of social manipulation, division, and reconstitution, the medium that records past experiences and generates desires and errors as well. Foucault's interest in the articulation of body and event becomes more explicit in his later writings, notably as an effect of the power relations that act indirectly upon the body (subjecting it to time, e.g., in *Surveiller et punir*), but it is already expressed in this text, in the powerful language of spacing surfaces:

The body is the inscribed surface of events (traced by language and dissolved by ideas), the locus of a dissociated self (adopting the illusion of a substantial unity), and a volume in perpetual disintegration. Genealogy, as an analysis of descent, is thus situated within the articulation of the body and history. Its task is to expose a body totally imprinted by history and the process of history's destruction of the body. (FR 83)

The dissolution of self-identity, in the very decomposition of the body, shows that Nietzsche's reversal of the Cartesian domination of the mind over the body, or even his reversal of the Kantian noumenal rupture, is not a dialectical solution to an old pattern of rationalist and idealist aspirations, but a radical expression of a materialist, immanent critique. There is nothing above human becoming that accounts for the fate of individuals and the social body in their striving to preserve life and make it better or worse. In effect, "[n]othing in man --not even his body-- is sufficiently stable to serve as the basis for self-recognition or for understanding other men." (FR 87f.) Thus what Marx's reversal of Hegel's dialectic fails to accomplish in his social, historical critique from below, Nietzsche's affirmation of *Wirklichkeit* operates a formidable return to the surface of appearances (the *real* effects, for there is no *Ding an sich*) that at once are structured by and structure the social struggles *effected* by the will to power. The *wirkliche Historie* written by the genealogists is to be opposed to traditional history in that the former defies the established relationship between the eruption of events and a necessary continuity in the unfolding of "historical facts." History becomes "effective" insofar as it introduces "discontinuity into our very being," depriving "the self of the reassuring stability of life and nature." (FR 88) What used to point to a certain interpretation of a' historical, natural process manifest in the *event*, becomes now an arbitrary moment in the yet-to-be-decided play of forces:

> An event, consequently, is not a decision, a treaty, a reign, or a battle, but the reversal of a relationship of forces, the usurpation of power, the appropriation of a vocabulary turned against those who had once used it, a feeble domination that poisons itself as it grows lax, the entry of a masked "other." The forces operating in history are not controlled by destiny or regulative mechanisms, but respond to haphazard conflicts. (FR 88)

The three uses of history invoked by Nietzsche (monumental, antiquarian, and critical) are inevitably recurrent in the genealogist's recast of historical knowledge, for power and knowledge always operate in history and, as Foucault maintains throughout, they cannot take place apart from each other. The critical use of history leads thus to "the destruction of the man who maintains knowledge by the injustice proper to the will to knowledge" (FR 97), just as the veneration of monuments becomes a parody and the respect for ancient continuities becomes systematic dissociation. The "concerted carnival" of this genealogical method consists of an ongoing compilation and process of bodies of power/knowledge, the cultural productions of truth, which have been marginalized by previous historiographies. Now, the main theses of Foucault's conception of power can be summarized as follows, in light of *Surveiller et punir* and his interviews in *Power/Knowledge*. We have seen that modernity is marked by the era of anthropology, following the analytic of finitude of Kant's critique of metaphysics. Nietzsche's critique of Kant, according to Foucault, has shown that modern man's awakening from the dogmatic slumber has not evaded an anthropological sleep that characterizes our own age of uncertainty. Foucault's main thesis in *Surveiller et punir* is that the prison was linked to the transformation of individuals. (PK 39) The analysis of the carceral society is also related to other institutions of disciplinary power (the cell, the workshop, the hospital), that provide it with three great schemata, namely, "the politico-moral schema of individual isolation and hierarchy; the economic model of force applied to compulsory work; the technico-medical model of cure and normalization." (DP 248) Power is thus shown to be co-extensive with the social body, as power relations play at once a conditioning and a conditioned role. (PK 142) For Foucault, these relations are of multiple forms, besides those of prohibition and punishment, and although their interconnections delineate general conditions of domination, one cannot reduce it to a binary structure opposing "dominators" to "dominated." For the multiform "relations of domination... are partially susceptible of integration into overall strategies," as power relations can indeed be used positively as strategies and "there are no relations of power without resistance." (PK 142) Bentham's panoptical device appears thus as a paradigm of the modern disciplinary institutions of bio-power and normalizing technologies of control. According to Foucault,

> In this central and centralized humanity, the effect and instrument of complex power relations, bodies and forces subjected by multiple mechanisms of "incarceration," objects for discourses that are in themselves elements for this strategy, we must hear the distant roar of battle.

And he hastens to add,

> At this point I end a book that must serve as a historical background to various studies of the power of normalization and the formation of knowledge in modern society. (DP 308)[34]

According to Habermas's reading of this last paragraph (or footnote), confronted with Foucault's initial remark that he would "study the birth of the prison only in the French penal system," *Surveiller et punir* aims at modern society as a whole, even though the study is indeed confined to late 18th-, early 19th-century prison systems in France. (cf.SP 35 n. 1; ET: 309 n.3) I agree with Habermas's contention here, although I do not think Foucault's genealogy implies that modern society is simply a Great Confinement or that a local, microphysical analysis can be extended to a global macropolitics of sorts. After all, as Deleuze puts it, we find two complementary theses in Foucault's conception of a "local" power, namely, that "power is local because it is never global" and that "it is not local or localized because it is diffuse." (F 26) In brief, I will argue that the problematic at issue is rather methodological than textual-analytical, having to do with Foucault's overall genealogical project, especially with his conception of a "new history" that allows for an overlapping of the empirical and the transcendental in the very analysis of facts said to be "historical"-- in full agreement with his earlier formulation of the *a priori historique*.

---

[34] In the French original, the last paragraph is a footnote at the very end of the text: "Dans cette humanité centrale et centralisée, effet et instrument de relations de pouvoir complexes, corps et forces assujettis par des dispositifs d'"incarcération" multiples, objets pour des discours qui sont eux-mêmes des éléments de cette stratégie, il faut entendre le grondement de la bataille." And, in footnote, "J'interromps ici ce livre qui doit servir d'arrière-plan historique à diverses études sur le pouvoir de normalisation et la formation du savoir dans la société moderne." (SP 315)

As we have seen, the State already presupposes other existing power relations, precisely on the multiform, non-homogeneous levels of a "microphysics of power." (PK 122) The complex of those power relations presuppose thus technologies of power that relate individuals to the very normalizing techniques that make them subjects within social groups such as the family, neighborhoods, local communities, associations, schools, the workplace, hospitals, and diverse religious, social, and political institutions, etc. As Paul Patton has shown, there must be some way of making sense of Foucault's conception of power --even if it does not provide us with a clear-cut theory of power-- so as to understand how and to what extent we can believe, with Foucault, in the inevitability of resistance to domination. As we have sought to show in this study, Foucault's reading of Kant and Nietzsche has taken us beyond humanist, traditional conceptions of political philosophy and human nature. And yet, as Patton remarks,

> This human material is active; it is an entity composed of forces or endowed with certain capacities. As such it must be understood in terms of power, where this term is understood in its primary sense of capacity to do or become certain things. This conception of the human material may therefore be supposed to amount to a "thin" conception of the subject of thought and action: whatever else it may be, the human subject is a being endowed with certain capacities. It is a subject of power, but this power is only realized in and through the diversity of human bodily capacities and forms of subjectivity. Because it is a "subject" which is only present in various different forms, or alternatively because the powers of human being can be exercised in infinite different ways, this subject will not provide a foundation for normative judgment of the kind that would satisfy Fraser or Habermas: it will not provide any basis for a single universal answer to the question, "Why ought domination to be resisted?"[35]

Foucault himself has never denied human agency or that human beings are the subject of power, although he radically refuses to hypostatize it or to reduce the subject to the cause of human actions. In his essay on "The Subject and Power," Foucault reiterates his commitment to a philosophical ethos that takes seriously the task of a "history of today":

> When in 1784 Kant asked, *Was heißt Aufklärung?*, he meant, What's going on just now? What's happening to us? What is this world, this period, this

---

[35] P. Patton, "Foucault's Subject of Power," *Political Theory Newsletter* 6/1 (May 1994) 61. An earlier version of this paper was published in French in *Sociologie et Sociétés*, Vol. XXIV, no.1, April 1992.

precise moment in which we are living? Or in other words: What are we? as *Aufklärer*, as part of the Enlightenment? (BSH 216)

Foucault contrasts Kant, Hegel, and Nietzsche's "engaged" attitude ("we") with Descartes's solipsist, a-historical *ego* ("I"). Habermas and Foucault agree thus on the self-determination of the modern philosopher who can no longer remain indifferent to the political, historical events of her own times. And yet, what Habermas's charges of *Präsentismus* completely miss is precisely the anti-historicist attitude of Foucault's recasting the Kantian *Antwort* to the question *Was ist Aufklärung?* Just as Kant publicly addressed the readers of the *Berliner Monatschrift* with an alternative philosophical discourse of modernity --for Moses Mendelssohn had offered a different reply two months earlier--, so Foucault published his interpretation of Kant's text two hundred years later, in the *Magazine littéraire*, so as to affirm "philosophy as the discourse of modernity on modernity." (PPC 88)[36] The historical ontology of ourselves means, according to Foucault, that although we still live under the sign of reason and revolution, we are no longer within the same framework of truth, power, and moral coordinates that shaped Kant's optimism, since there are no fixed stars above us or eternal laws within. In effect, Foucault will argue that modern political philosophy itself is a child of its own time, as the juridical conception of power will be preserved from Hegel and Marx's dialectics of domination to the psycho-analytical theories of repression. Power struggles cannot be thus reduced to practices of domination (ethnic, social, religious) and forms of exploitation (of individuals in function of production), but must also address the problems of subjection and subjectivation. (BSH 212) Although Habermas has rightly articulated the problem of values with normativity, he failed to comprehend the political thrust of Foucault's genealogy of modern subjectivity.

As it will be disclosed in the next section on normativity, one of the greatest merits of Foucault's critique of power lies in his revaluation of power relations in their diffuse, non-reducible modes of human subjectivity. To be sure, it was the Nietzschean conception of a history of bodily relations that enlightened, as it were, Foucault's analyses of individualizing techniques of power in SP. To begin with, we can conceive of both punishment and surveillance as forms of discipline, both being historically constituted as institutionalized, individualizing mechanisms of control within society that allow for its self-regulation --in both

---

[36] Foucault's "The Art of Telling the Truth" (PPC 86-95) was a revised version of a 1983 lecture at the Collège de France; "Qu'est-ce que les lumières?" was first translated and published in English as "What is Enlightenment?" in the 1984 Rabinow edition of the *Foucault Reader* (FR 32-50).

liberal and socialist societies. Needless to say, it is the dynamic ensemble of such techniques of control that, for Foucault, determine discipline as a positivity within power structures that can be analyzed, for instance, through disciplinary techniques of examination and writing. Although there might be good and bad forms of discipline and punishment, Foucault does not advocate some forms of discipline in detriment of others, since his concern is strictly descriptive. Thus he has shown how Bentham's Panopticon (1791) was devised as a technology of power to solve the problems of surveillance. (DP 195 ff.; PK 148) The panoptical model is then described as a *"laboratoire de savoir et de pouvoir"*, *"une manière de définir les rapports du pouvoir avec la vie quotidienne des hommes"* (SP 201-207), *"une microphysique du pouvoir," "un pouvoir qui s'exerce plutôt qu'il ne se possède."* (31) Government thus appears as a function of technology: the government of individuals, the government of souls, the government of the self by the self, the government of families, the government of children. That links the genealogies of the prison to the genealogy of bio-power in the *Histoire de la sexualité*, as Foucault takes a radical stand against "the government of individualization," as totalizing techniques of disciplinary power. (BSH 212) That the Roman *patria potestas* granted the father of the Roman family the right to "dispose" of the life of his children and slaves in modern times, according to Foucault, is contrasted with the disciplinary politics of the modern State, which no longer keeps the sovereignty relation that, for instance, the medieval sovereign had over his subjects, but exerts a form of power that is at once individualizing and totalizing. This "political double bind," according to Foucault, is the direct legacy of the Christian institution of pastoral techniques. (BSH 213ff.) If Hobbes saw power as the transfer of rights from the prince to the natural right possessed by each individual (HS1 177f.), Foucault contends that bio-power is no longer associated with the new juridical being, the sovereign, but rather with the "power over life and death," a conception of power as "a right of seizure: of things, time, bodies, and ultimately life itself; it culminated in the privilege to seize hold of life in order to suppress it." (HS1 179; FR 259) It is of fundamental importance to signal that Foucault draws a distinction between *société disciplinaire* and *société disciplinée*, so that the panoptical model, like the *Grand Renfermement*, belongs to the *"ordre du discours"* inasmuch as it unveils the *"ordre des institutions."* As Foucault remarks in an interview,

> The point is not to construct a system, but an instrument: a *logic* appropriate to the power relations and the struggles which are going on around them; this sort of research can take place only one step at a time, on the basis of

reflections (which of necessity have to be historical in some respects) on given situations.[37]

It is only within the broader framework of this "economy of power relations" that both the singular State and the pluralist society belong together in the same analysis of social control. Michael Walzer concedes that Foucault has succeeded in unveiling the complex mechanisms of discipline that link macro- and micro-levels of social life, but remains skeptical about the latter's claims to avoiding "anarchism/nihilism" or falling prey to some form of conservatism. In a nutshell, Walzer does not think that local resistance can ever be effected without the normative claims that in one way or another refer us back to the State and/or its institutions.[38] What makes all the difference, in the last analysis, is the form of government or the political model at stake, namely, a liberal State as opposed to authoritarian and totalitarian ones. I think Foucault would agree with part of this contention, although he would immediately add that the very process of subjectivation is precisely what accounts for the sedimentation of certain regimes of veridiction and jurisdiction as certain power mechanisms prevail over others in the formations of self-governance and government.[39] What Walzer, like Habermas, fails to acknowledge is that Foucault's critique of normativity does not ultimately deny the norm-subject relation but turns it into a problematic correlation, inasmuch as subjectivity and normativity are both established through power-related valuations of truth and moral values. It is in this sense that Foucault assumes the diffusion of the norm through the social body in the seventeenth and eighteenth centuries, operated according to three main modalities, namely,

1. the functional inversion of disciplines, which neutralize the dangers, to make the large social groups play a positive role and increase the possible utility of individuals;
2. the swarming of disciplinary mechanisms, the massive, compact disciplines are decomposed into flexible procedures of control, every institution becomes susceptible of utilizing the disciplinary schema;

---

[37] "Power and Strategies: A Discussion with Michel Foucault," *Les Révoltes Logiques* n. 4 (1977) 76.
[38] Cf. M. Walzer, "The Politics of Michel Foucault," in David Couzens Hoy (ed.), *Foucault: A Critical Reader*, (New York: Basil Blackwell, 1986), 51-68.
[39] Cf. M. Foucault, "Omnes et Singulatim: Towards a Criticism of 'Political Reason'." Lectures delivered at Stanford University on Oct. 10 and 16, 1979. In Sterling McMurrin (ed.), *The Tanner Lectures on Human Values II*, (Salt Lake City: University of Utah Press, 1981), 225-254; FE 87-104.

3. the state-control of the mechanisms of discipline, through the organization of a centralized police, permanent, omnipresent surveillance that renders everything visible. (SP 211-213; DP 210-13)

Thus, Foucault's overall concern with the writing of a history of the body, together with the political technologies of the body, its strategies and tactics, accounts for the formation of what he called the *société disciplinaire*. (SP 211) Foucault concludes his study on power with the ironic question, "Is it surprising that prisons resemble factories, schools, barracks, hospitals, which all resemble prisons? [*Quoi d'étonant si la prison ressemble aux usines, aux écoles, aux casernes, aux hôpitaux, qui tous ressemblent aux prisons?*]" (DP 228; SP 229) What is at stake in this form of social structure is what Foucault calls "the synaptic regime of power," an invention of the eighteenth century, "a regime of its exercise *within* the social body, rather than *from above* it." For Foucault it is thus understandable that capitalism had to fabricate the mechanisms that would secure the protection of wealth, through the moralization of the working subjects, just like the institution of the police, based on the fear of the criminal:

> ...it was absolutely necessary to constitute the populace as a moral subject and to break its commerce with criminality, and hence to segregate the delinquents and show them to be dangerous not only for the rich but for the poor as well, vice-ridden instigators of the gravest social perils. (PK 41)

4. SUBJECTIVITY AND THE GENEALOGY OF ETHICS

> L'homme, tel qu'il est observé, démembré, décomposé par toutes les biométries et les anthropométries du monde, atteste incontestablement l'existence de l'Homme. L'objectivation normative de l'homme vient au secours des droits de l'homme: les hommes sont tous égaux, manifestant tous les mêmes qualités, à quelques différences près, accidentelles, nécessairement accidentelles puisque ne renvoyant jamais à la consistance d'une essence. (François Ewald, "Michel Foucault et la norme," 217)

As we undertake a close examination of Foucault's conception of power, we immediately realize that it cannot be dissociated from his history of truth, on the one hand, and from his genealogy of subjectivity, on the other. This becomes particularly clear in the last writings, on the "hermeneutics of the subject" and throughout the four volumes of the *Histoire de la sexualité*. In the 1980 lectures he delivered in the United States, Foucault explicitly endorsed a transition from studying systems of power relations to studying the creation of ethical agency, completing thus the three-axial genealogy of ourselves. It is very instructive to note that Foucault insists that, although there has been a shift of focus in his analyses, he has not departed from the original project of writing a "history of the present." In one of his Dartmouth lectures, Foucault remarks that contemporary philosophy has been concerned, from Husserl to the neo-Marxists, with the overcoming of a metaphysics of the subject.[40] This question betrays already the very link that Foucault, inspired by Nietzsche, was seeking to establish between subjectivity and truth, following the self-overcoming of the *homo metaphysicus*. According to Foucault, the philosophy of self-consciousness has both "failed to found a philosophy of knowledge" and "failed to take into account the formative mechanisms of signification and the structure of systems of meaning."[41] That is why Foucault set out to study government in relation to the way individuals conduct themselves, in techniques of production, signification, and domination. In his 1978 lecture on "Governmentality," Foucault cites Le Vayer's typology of government, which devises three forms in accordance with a particular discipline: "the art of self-government, connected with morality; the art of properly governing a family, which belongs to economy; and finally the science of ruling the State, which concerns politics." (FE 91) The governmentalization of the modern State, for Foucault, was made possible thanks to the Christian pastoral, the diplomatic-military technique, and the seventeenth- and eighteenth-century *police*. (FE 104) Of particular interest is Foucault's contention that the salvation paradigm of the Christian pastoral techniques of self-sacrificial asceticism and self-awareness of communitarian identity gave way, with the decline of ecclesiastical institutions and an ever-growing process of secularization, to the State technologies of welfare, health insurance, and social security, that would characterize our own age.

Both in the second and in the third volumes of the *Histoire de la sexualité*, Foucault explores the *techniques de soi* and the *technologies de soi* so as to thematize the general genealogy of the *rapports de soi à soi*.[42] It is "the kind of relationship you ought to have with yourself," says Foucault, "*rapport à soi*, which I call ethics, and which determines how the individual is supposed to constitute himself as a moral subject of his own actions." (FR 352) As we have seen in Foucault's reading of Kant, the critical genealogy of modernity provides

---

[40] Cf. M. Foucault, "About the Beginning of the Hermeneutic of the Self: Two Lectures at Dartmouth," edited by Mark Blasius, in *Political Theory* 21/2 (1993) 198-227.
[41] Ibidem, p. 202.
[42] Cf. also the course descriptions on "Subjectivité et vérité," in the *Résumés des cours* for 1980-81 at the Collège de France.

us with a new understanding of ethics as well, beyond the traditions of ethical codifications and their moral practices. Once again, the self-overcoming of morality announced by Nietzsche's genealogy is at full work in Foucault's *dispositifs* of sexuality and normativity. In a nutshell, we realize that Foucault shifts away from the traditional conception of a "human nature" as the outcome of normalizing processes, imposed by the human sciences and practices of disciplinary power, and espouses the concept of a bodily subjectivation, so as to devise new technologies of the self that affirm the self without the exclusion of its other, "as strategic games of liberty." (FR 50) By subjectivation Foucault meant "the way a human being turns him- or herself into a subject," (BSH 208), that is, the ensemble of techniques through which individuals act so as to constitute themselves as such. As I will argue here, Foucault presents us with a self-overcoming, non-universalizable ethics that responds to the very charges raised by Habermas that the crypto-normativism of genealogy was doomed to political nihilism. Although he has been called "the founding father of our *Kathedernihilismus*,"[43] Foucault's "return of morality" implies an ethics "against ethics" --to paraphrase John Caputo,[44]-- on the level of the very ethical principle of transgression. In effect, as Patton has remarked, according to this Nietzschean-Foucauldian ethic, values are always already internal to types of individual and social being, hence the absence of an articulated political theory does not preclude activism and resistance.[45] On the contrary, as Connolly has convincingly shown, Foucault attacks the utopian dream of the "whole of society" insofar as it requires the destruction, the exclusion, or the repression of the other.[46] Precisely because it cannot promise universal liberation, an aesthetic "ethic of care for the self" reminds us that "liberty is the ontological condition of ethics" and that the freedom of the other presupposes the imperative *epimeleia seautou*,"care for yourself." (FF 4f.; FR 359 ff.; TS 19)[47]

Foucault takes "norm" as an ontological category, as a characteristic of an ontology of present, through the different institutions of a normative order in his archaeological, genealogical analyses of the rise of psychiatry, medicine, the human sciences, the penal code, and sexuality. The disciplines analyzed in SP, as one of the main technologies of power of modern societies are in effect defined as

---

[43] J.G. Merquior, *Foucault*, (London: Fontana Books, 1985).
[44] J. Caputo, *Against Ethics*. Bloomington: Indiana University Press, 1993.
[45] Cf. Paul Patton, art. cit., 61.
[46] Cf. William Connolly, "Beyond Good and Evil: The Ethical Sensibility of Michel Foucault," *Political Theory* 21/3 (1993) 365-389.
[47] M. Foucault, "The Ethic of Care for the Self as a Practice of Freedom," interview conducted by Raúl Fornet-Betancourt, Helmut Becker, and Alfredo Gomez-Müller, in FF 1-20.

"pouvoir de la norme." (SP 186) *La volonté de savoir* institutes the *dispositif de sexualité* as normative power, on the level of the State and the society thereby administered. I will follow François Ewald's highly original study on the Foucauldian conception of normativity in order to make sense of the ethical implications of his genealogy of the modern subjectivity.[48] Even before we proceed to understand such a conception of norm, it is important to clarify what is meant by ethics in this context. In *L'usage des plaisirs*, the articulation between sex and ethics is undertaken so as to investigate how patterns of sexual behavior become the object of moral concern, for instance, how a moral reflection in Ancient Greece --which was rather a question of stylizing freedom (HS2 111)-- gives way to a moral problematization in later Christianity, or how the historical constructs of sexuality and sex can be better understood against the framework of confessional technologies for the discipline and control of the bodies. (HS3) Foucault speaks of at least three different ways of approaching morality, namely:

1. morals (*morale*) can denote a set of values and rules of action which are proposed to individuals or social groups through several prescriptive apparatuses such as the family, educational institutions, churches, etc.; morality is regarded here as a code;
2. it can also be understood as "the actual behavior of individuals in their relation to rules and values that are proposed to them," that is, as a set of practices;
3. and finally --as we have seen, this is the definition that interests Foucault- -it can be understood as the way one must conduct oneself, i.e., "the way one must constitute oneself as moral subject acting in relation to the prescriptive elements that constitute the code [*la manière dont on doit "se conduire," c'est-à-dire la manière dont on doit se constituer soi-même comme sujet moral agissant en référence aux éléments prescriptifs qui constituent le code*]" (HS2 32-33) This field of historicity where human beings are constituted as subjects of morality, through the relation of the self to itself, is precisely what determines the field of Foucault's ethic of self-care. This field emerges thus as a response to the Nietzschean challenge of nihilism:

When all the customs and the morals on which the power of gods, priests, and redeemers depend are finally reduced to nothing, when, therefore,

---

[48] François Ewald, "Michel Foucault et la norme," in Luce Giard (ed.), *Michel Foucault: Lire l'oeuvre*, op. cit., 201-221.

morality in the ancient sense of the word is dead: what will come?...Well, what exactly will come? (M I § 96)

Foucault says in an interview that he views politics as an ethics (FR 375), in accordance with the notions seen above of the philosophical ethos and of an aesthetics of existence. At any rate, Foucault is interested in the self-constitutive character of subjectivity rather than in a theoretical formulation or calculus of ethical propositions. Foucault conceives of a fourfold of subjectivity, or the four "causes" of "interiority" in its relation to itself. (HS2 33-35) The first "cause" is the "ethical substance" (*substance éthique*), such as passions, feelings, sexual desire; for the Greeks, the ethical substance was not sexuality (modernity) or the flesh (Christianity), but the *aphrodisia*, the works of Venus, at once acts, desire, and pleasure. (FR 353) The second "cause" is the *mode d'assujettissement* of the moral subject, mode by which individuals have to recognize the moral obligations imposed to them. In the Greek aesthetics of existence, based on free choice, our work is indeed our own life and ourselves --as opposed to an object, a text, a fortune, an invention, or an institution. The third cause, analogous to the Aristotelian fourfold, is the efficient: the elaboration of an ethical work that is effected on oneself so as to transform oneself in the moral subject of one's conduct ("*[le] travail éthique qu'on effectue sur soi-même...pour essayer de se transformer soi-même en sujet moral de sa conduite*," HS2 34). In a word, a self-praxis or self-aesthetics of moral existence. Asceticism is thus regarded as *techne* (a set of techniques, such as the technologies of the body, marriage, love courting). And finally, the fourth teleological cause (*la téléologie du sujet moral*), what kind of being should one become? That is how one can proceed then to situate the questions of *askesis*, ascetic techniques, as well as the *enkrateia*, the dominion of oneself.

Now, if there is a condemnation of normalizing power in SP, in that norms seem to conform to rationalities, habits, and traditions of individualizing panopticism, it is also the case that Foucault proposes no alternatives. Foucault insists that he is not after "a history of solutions" and that is the reason why he cannot even accept the word "alternative." Norms may be said to be inevitable, as long as ethics and politics demand that habits and modalities of human relations be codified. And yet, do we have to ground them in a metaphysic of morals? Is the task of philosophy, after all, to ground norms? For Foucault, if there is one norm, that must be freedom itself, the only prerequisite of ethics. The critical ontology of ourselves requires indeed "a patient labor giving form to our impatience for liberty." (FR 50) Ethics, in this sense, implies commitment and yet no complicity vis-à-vis the norm. The first difficulty arises, of course, with Foucault's usage of the word "norm," which as Ewald shows, acquires a new philosophical thrust that was not there before. The common-sense connotation is that of "standard," "rule," and "mean," as opposed to the abnormal, the pathological, the extreme. Thus Georges Canguilhem remarks in *Le normal et le pathologique*,

> Quand on sait que *norma* est le mot latin que traduit équerre et que *normalis* signifie perpendiculaire, on sait à peu près tout ce qu'il faut savoir sur le domaine d'origine du sens des termes norme et normal.[49]

According to Ewald, Foucault takes the opposite procedure of the norm when he makes the production of truth into an event, so as to challenge a universal, general, a-historical conception of norm. For instance, that sexuality was a social pleasure for both Greeks and Romans (FR 251) defies our modern translation of sexuality into social relations. Foucault was interested in the complex dispositif of sexuality that, in its three-axial constitution of subjectivity, points to different normalizing mechanisms, making thus possible a comparison that would be otherwise impossible. For Ewald, the norm is the institutionalized reference for a social group that is objectified as an individual: "*La norme est au principe d'une communication sans origine et sans sujet.*"[50] Hence the asymmetry of comparing an Ancient, Greek homosexual to his or her counterpart in modern societies can only be understood in terms of the normative reference, which for each case is found in a complex ensemble of dispositifs that combines both the normalizing insertion of the individual in a dense social milieu and the normativity resulting from his or her moral technologies of the self.

The same applies to Foucault's conception of power. As Ewald remarks, Foucault did not turn disciplinary society into a society of generalized confinement; on the contrary, the diffusion of disciplines implies that confinement is no longer segregating, but rather homogenizes the social space, as the disciplines constitute society itself, with a common language to all institutions, or at least, translatable between themselves.[51] That includes the penitentiary systems, which are integrated into society and whose administration of punishment is exclusive to and legitimized by the disciplinary act. There is indeed an empty juridical split with the privation of liberty that serves to mask disciplinary facts. The norm is precisely what accounts for the transitions from discipline *en bloc* to disciplinary mechanism, from negative to positive discipline, and the generalization of institutional discipline. The norm articulates thus the disciplinary

---

[49] G. Canguilhem, *Le normal et le pathologique*, (Paris: PUF, 1966), 177.
[50] F. Ewald, art. cit., 206.
[51] Ibidem, 205.

institutions of production, knowledge, wealth, making them interdisciplinary and homogenizing the social space --if not uniting it.[52] In SP, Foucault describes three great disciplinary instruments, namely, the hierarchical surveillance, the normalizing sanction, and the examination (Part III, chapter 2: Les moyens du bon dressement, 172 ff). These are tools that envisage to solve some traditional problems of power, to ordain multiplicities, to articulate the whole and its parts, to put them in relation among themselves. As we have seen, discipline fabricates individuals, it is the specific technique of a power that is given to individuals: "*le pouvoir disciplinaire, lui, s'exerce en se rendant invisible; en revanche il impose à ceux qu'il soumet un principe de visibilité obligatoire.*" (SP 189) If power was traditionally conceived of as that which is seen (SP 189), with discipline, according to the Foucauldian "logic" of the norm, the subjects are the ones to be seen, allowing for the reversal of the political axis of individualization ("*le renversement de l'axe politique de l'individualisation,*" 194) and the *individualisation normative*, without any reference to a nature, a metaphysics, a substance, but as a pure relation, purely comparative. The norm (*la norme*) is the measure which at once individualizes, allowing for endless individualization, and makes comparison possible. (209)

> Un principe de comparaison, de comparabilité, une commune mesure, qui s'institue dans la pure référence d'un groupe à lui-même, lorsque le groupe n'a plus d'autre rapport qu'à lui-même, sans extériorité, sans verticalité. (209)

Normative individualization has no exterior, as normative space has no "outside," so the abnormal belongs within, since the exception is always already within the rule. And yet, of course, the abnormal is opposed to the normal, but this is rather a matter of limits. When disciplines become normative, disciplinary institutions become isomorphous. When society becomes normative, institutions such as the army, school, prisons, become redundant vis-à-vis each other. Hence one should not confuse "norm" and "discipline": while the former is a common measure, the latter envisages the body with a function of *dressage*. That means that disciplines are not necessarily normative. That is why what characterizes modernity, according to Foucault, is precisely the advent of normative disciplines, the normalization of disciplines, and hence the formation of disciplinary societies. Thus, both the rise of capitalism and the emergence of a modern State embody this shift away from a juridical system and from a system of personal power, toward the disciplinary technologies of bio-power. In effect, all the analyses of

---

[52] Ibidem, 206.

social control in SP seem to converge to the remarks on the "right to death and power over life," which as we have seen, attest to the new mechanisms that inaugurate the era of bio-power, "*disciplines de corps et contrôles régulateurs de populations.*" (HS1 177) As Foucault himself remarks, "*le développement du bio-pouvoir, c'est l'importance croissante prise par le jeu de la norme aux dépens du système juridique de la loi.*" (HS1 189) In this enigmatic remark, Foucault does not mean that bio-power implies a process of the decline of law, since the formation of a normalizing society will actually lead to a legislative proliferation. And yet, as he hastens to add, in relation to the seventeenth century we have entered an era of the regression of the juridical. Ewald argues that it is not a matter of announcing an eminent disappearance of right or doing a critique of bio-power in the name of right. Foucault is rather concerned with the relations between the juridical and the political, right and power, from the standpoint of an adequate analysis of the mechanisms of power. Since the norm is opposed to the juridical mode of the law, which legitimizes the power of the sovereign, the bio-power is expressed by the normative mode of constitutions, codes, "*toute une activité législative permanente et bruyante.*" (HS1 190)

Thus the normative and the juridical constitute two different modalities of the exercise of power, as power is no longer confined nowadays to the traditional forms of wars, struggles, *interdits*, confrontations, but is above all the management of resources and of the lives of entire populations. And Ewald sees here the contrast between the monarchical State and the "Providence-State" (welfare State). What Habermas does not acknowledge is that for Foucault the norm is indeed a principle of communication rather than confinement or incarceration. Thus, for Foucault, the subject at stake is not the subject of right but the modern subject of the norm. As Ewald points out, according to Foucault, "*L'individu est toujours déjà normalisé.*" The normative is therefore a power without outside (*un pouvoir sans dehors*) since there is no human essence: all individuals are comparable, they are only differentiated by differences of quantity.[53] Foucault draws an important distinction between law and right, as he inscribes the norm among the acts of judgment. The norm is rather characterized by its logic, a "new economy of power," allowing for life to become the object of power, by giving form to the bio-power.

By way of conclusion, Foucault's response to the challenge of modernity problematizes "the relations between the growth of capabilities and the growth of autonomy" (FR 48), which seemed to be inevitably progressing toward universal emancipation. The dark dialectic of the *Aufklärung*, in our very century, proved

---

[53] Ibidem, 215.

that power relations of different forms and through diverse technologies have made efficient the most inhuman procedures of normalization. If human beings have been made the subjects of normalizing techniques of disciplinary power, they can also resist. Because they are endowed with bodily capabilities for action, human freedom appears not only as a precondition for the exercise of power but also as resistance which can always take place out of power relations. "Power is exercised only over free subjects," observes Foucault, "and only insofar as they are free." (BSH 221) Hence we should conceive of an agonistic ethic of freedom, according to which institutional, juridical dispositifs that foster domination, exploitation, and normalization can be subverted through concrete practices of ethical transgression, on different microlevels of power relations. After all, far from being reducible to State and political institutions, "power relations are rooted in the system of social networks." (BSH 224) Foucault's aestheticist ethic of self-care, together with his conception of individualization and normalization, betrays a departure, as Connolly remarks, from morality to ethics, insofar as it undermines the normative grounds of the good, human nature, the social contract, or the useful. And yet, Foucault's refusal to resort to metaphysics or hegemonic identities, as Connolly suggests, "is not to liquidate ethics, but to become ashamed of the transcendentalization of conventional morality. It is to subject morality to strip searches."[54] In effect, Foucault's ethical articulation of subjectivity and normativity betrays, in the last analysis, a skeptical ethos that one finds in Sextus Empiricus and in every genuine philosophical *skepsis* vis-à-vis the concealed dogmatism of established theories. Foucault avows that, in his permanent critique of the *dire vrai*, he has adopted "the radical but unaggressive skepticism which makes it a principle not to regard the point in time where we are now standing as the outcome of a teleological progression which it would be one's business to reconstruct historically." And he adds, "that skepticism regarding ourselves and what we are, our here and now, which prevents one from assuming that what we have is better than --or more than-- in the past." (PK 49)

---

[54] William Connolly, "Beyond Good and Evil," art. cit., 366.

CONCLUSION: TRUTH, POWER, ETHICS

> My objective for more than twenty-five years has been to sketch out a history of the different ways in our culture that humans develop knowledge about themselves: economics, biology, psychiatry, medicine, and penology. The main point is not to accept this knowledge at face value but to analyze these so-called sciences as very specific "truth games" related to specific techniques that human beings use to understand themselves. (Michel Foucault, TS 17, 18)

To speak of unity in the corpus of Foucault's writings is, to say the least, a misleading procedure. Not only did he warn us --his readers-- against interpretations that presumed the coherent, perfected unity of an author behind his writings, but he actually devoted many of his works to unmask taken-for-granted assumptions of continuities, identities, and self-contained truths in the interpretation of texts. "The author," wrote Foucault, "is not an indefinite source of significations which fill a work; the author does not precede the works... The author is therefore the ideological figure by which one marks the manner in which we fear the proliferation of meaning." (FR 118f.) Foucault also warned us against the temptation to assign him theories and methods that his texts did not authorize --witness the tentative theses and anti-systematic, scattered researches of his unfinished projects. And yet, we have seen that there is a discursive continuity in Foucault's own texts and interviews --despite the discontinuity of methods and topics dealt with. And this "metacritical" continuum, binding together archaeology, genealogy, and hermeneutics, on the one hand, and knowledge, power, and subjectivation on the other, proved to be an enlightening access to the Foucauldian space of the history of the systems of thought. The "historical a priori" was shown to support the main thesis of this study "on the genealogy of modernity," namely, that truth, power, and ethics have made modern subjectivity possible through a historical, ontological self-constitution of ourselves. How this Foucauldian "philosophical discourse of modernity" avoids the relativism, presentism, and cryptonormativism of what Habermas denounced as "transcendental historicism" is precisely what I set out to show in this study.

I will conclude this study with a final revaluation of Foucault's conception of history, neither reducible to an archaeology nor to a genealogy *stricto sensu*, neither a history of science nor an intellectual history, neither *histoire des idées* nor *histoire des mentalités*, "neither Marxist nor Annaliste."[1] We have seen how the conception of an "ontological history of ourselves" effected a methodological shift from the critique of the critique (archaeology, *epistemé*) towards the genealogy of subjectivity (power *dispositifs*). It has been shown that Foucault himself described his overall project of undertaking a genealogy of who we are by alluding to the three axes of truth, power, and ethics. I will review in conclusion how the specificity of each axis is said to be interdependent and correlated to each other, just as their interweaving points to new ways of doing history that, although nominalist and aestheticist in their narrative style, are far from being transcendental, historicist, and apolitical.

For Foucault, a régime of truth points to a conception of "truth" as "a system of ordered procedures for the production, regulation, distribution, circulation and operation of statements (*énoncés*)." (PK 133) As Deleuze would insist, there is no universality of the true in Foucault, since truth itself designates the ensemble of productions within a given "device" (*dispositif*), which comprises the truths of enunciation (*énoncés*, statements), truths of luminosity and visibility, truths of force, truths of subjectivation. After all, there is no such a thing as a *constant* will to truth in Foucault.[2] To extract a "will to truth" from this ensemble of devices, to deduce a "theory of power" from Foucault's writings and interviews turns out to be an imposition of a preconceived thesis on a tacit corpus of diffuse variables. In effect, even though Habermas's criticism of Foucault's "utterly unsociological concept of power" (PDM 249) succeeds in showing its critical displacements vis-à-vis modernity, it fails to elucidate the philosophical relevance of Foucault's articulation of history and power *dispositifs*. We have seen that Foucault's *histoire de la vérité* challenged both philosophical conceptions of truth and the way historians have traditionally approached their task:

---

[1] Cf. Paul Veyne, "Foucault révolutionne l'histoire," appendix to *Comment on écrit l'histoire*, 2nd ed., (Paris: Seuil, 1978); Hayden White, *Tropics of Discourse*, (Baltimore: Johns Hopkins University Press, 1978), pp. 230-260; Mark Poster, *Foucault, Marxism and History*, (London: Blackwell, 1984); Allan Megill, "The Reception of Foucault by Historians," *Journal of the History of Ideas* 48 (1987) 117-141.

[2] Cf. G. Deleuze, "Qu'est-ce qu'un dispositif?," in MFP 193.

Historians, like philosophers and literary historians, have been accustomed to a history which takes in only the summits, the great events. But today, unlike the others, historians are becoming more willing to handle 'ignoble' materials. (PK 37)

Foucault has shown that the idea of a corpus of source data is much more problematic than one might assume. For instance, when one studies the history of madness, "it will never be possible to constitute the ensemble of discourses on madness as a unity, even by restricting oneself to a given country or period." (PK 38) Thus, one of the main tasks of history, according to Foucault, consists more in "making all these discourses visible in their strategic connections than in constituting them as unities, to the exclusion of other forms of discourse." (PK 38) Discursive analyses have been decisive to the interpretive fusion with new horizons of nondiscursive analyses.

As Foucault announces at the introduction to his second study on the *Histoire de la sexualité*, he is concerned with sexuality as an *experience*, that is, understood as the correlation in a culture, between domains of knowledge (*savoir*), types of normativity (*normativité*), and forms of subjectivity (*subjectivité*). (HS2 10) Of course, the novelty of bringing truth, power, and ethics together may be regarded as arbitrary a procedure as other possible triangles, suggested by Foucault himself, such as truth, power, subjectivation, or knowledge, power, right. What is certainly most instructive is that Foucault displaces the juridical from the sphere of power towards the domain of truth, since regimes of veridiction and regimes of jurisdiction belong together, just as knowledge and power do. Moreover, the conception of subjectivity may be said to bind them all together, in a "historical ontology," very similar to the one Heidegger assigns to Nietzsche's will to power. One may find such an "epochal" reading of Foucault's critique of power in Reiner Schürmann's study of Heidegger's *principe d'anarchie*.[3] And yet, Foucault's Nietzschean-inspired diagnostic genealogy is neither opposed to modernity nor does it reduce events to ontological configurations. Hence, the relation of ethics to politics remains always contingent on a historical complex that already entails its own regimes of truth.

Although recognizing the difficulty of classifying Foucault's concepts within the mapping of his own fictions and regimes of truths, we have seen that those concepts are themselves bound up with the Foucauldian practical interest as an

---

[3] Cf. R. Schürmann, *Le principe d'anarchie: Heidegger et la question de l'agir*, (Paris: Seuil, 1982). I am indebted to François Raffoul for raising this issue. Cf. also Hubert Dreyfus, "On the Ordering of things: Being and Power in Heidegger and Foucault," *Southern Journal of Philosophy*, Supplement, 28 (1989) 83-96.

intellectual response to specific problems of his own age. Just as Habermas was caught up in the *Positivismusstreit* and *Historikerstreit* of methodological discussions, so Foucault was also drawn into the different problematics and sets of conceptualizations attached to phenomenology, structuralism, Marxism, and the *Annales* school. And yet, Foucault does not claim to any meta-critical level that would allow for his own conceptions to respond to the shortcomings of his opponents and interlocutors, inasmuch as there is no ideal-speech situation or ideal-language theory in Foucault. We have seen that there is nothing like a theory of power or a social theory in Foucault's overall project, as we must also discard any theory of history to be inferred from his *histoires*. Thus Habermas's charge of "transcendental historicism" misses the point, even though Foucault's reappropriation of Kant's *Ausgang* and Nietzsche's *Selbstüberwindung* might suggest such a hybrid notion. In effect, not only Kant's teleology comes under attack in Foucault's history of truth but Nietzsche's genealogy is also appropriated as an immanent critique of subjectivity. Habermas's attempt at a non-teleological regulative ideal is, therefore, doomed to revive Kant's transcendental subjectivity. Hence Foucault opposes his "historicist" approach to Habermas's "transcendental" precisely to reaffirm the impossibility of escaping the historicity of self-constitution:

> ...the problem for Habermas is, after all, to make a transcendental mode of thought spring forth against any historicism. I am, indeed, far more historicist and Nietzschean. I do not think that there is a proper usage of history or a proper usage of intrahistorical analysis...that works precisely against this ideology of the return. History protects us from historicism --from a historicism that calls on the past to resolve the questions of the present. (FR 250)

The Nietzschean thesis that subjectivity entails historicity is all that is at stake for Foucault in this endless debate over method and truth. Subjectivation is, in the last analysis, an effect of governmentality, for what we are and have become is the outcome of diverse procedures of governance --of ourselves and of others. Foucault's critique of modern subjectivity is, at once, an analysis of the contingent, historical effects that bind together truth, power, and self relations, and a genealogy of the different modes of subjectivation that objectifies "modernity." It is therefore misleading and unfair to characterize Foucault's shifts from archaeology to genealogy and hermeneutics as clear-cut breaks since there remains a genealogical-historical concern that underlies the changes of thematic emphases. As Michael Mahon's careful study of Foucault's genealogy has shown, it was under Nietzsche's influence that Foucault's conception of subjectivation was first outlined in the *Histoire de la folie* and paved the way for the elaborated formulations of his later works:

> On the basis of the moralization of madness modern man finds himself categorized, located in space, constrained by time, disciplined, normalized, and individualized. (FNG 5)

Hence the Foucauldian conception of an ascetic ethics operates a *rapprochement* between the subject of power and the moral agent that is very reminiscent of Nietzsche's own genealogy of morality. As Paul Veyne remarks, Foucault's aestheticism is not a historicist attempt to resuscitate Greek ethics but a modern diagnosis that rescues the classical, aesthetic conception of "a work of the self on the self."[4] As we have seen in the second and third chapters, Foucault reappropriates the Nietzschean *askésis* as a self-stylizing care for the self (*souci de soi, epimeleia heautou, cura sui*) so as to avoid the intellectualist, Socratic "know thyself" (*gnôthi seautou*) in its disdain for the body, the flesh, the *aisthesis* --in brief, the eclipse of the other self-imperative of the Delphic oracle, *méden agan*, "nothing in excess."[5] Thus both Nietzsche and Foucault conceive of the *ethos* as a mode of being, the self-becoming of a *daimon* which, as in Heraclitus' motto, presupposes no human nature --as opposed to Aristotle's metaphysical account of the rationality-sociability binomial. Humans become what they are by the dwelling of their self-constitution, that is, in accordance with their care for themselves. To be sure, Foucault hastens to add to this formula of self-governance the implicit ways the self is cared for by others, so as to avoid the aristocratic individualism of Heraclitus' and Nietzsche's *amor fati*. If by subjectivation Foucault means "the way a human being turns him- or herself into a subject" (BSH 208), he also insists that the techniques through which individuals act so as to constitute themselves as such are always already culturally, historically constituted. If truth, power, and ethics are the three modes of objectification of the subject, i.e., how human beings are constituted subjects of knowledge, power, and moral agency, it is through specific discursivities that such an objectification of self-formations comes into being, in their complex relations to non-discursive practices that concur to define Foucault's "historical a priori." That is why

---

[4] P. Veyne, "The Final Foucault and His Ethics," *Critical Inquiry* 20/1 (1993) 7.
[5] In a very interesting letter to his friend Carl von Gersdorff (Dec. 1, 1867), the young Nietzsche had remarked: "Only now am I really thankful for our Schopenhauer, now that I have a chance to practice a little *askésis*" --alluding to his one-year military service in mounted artillery, stationed in Naumburg. *Selected Letters of Friedrich Nietzsche*, ed. Christopher Middleton, (Chicago: The University of Chicago Press, 1969), 31.

Foucault set out to examine the "dividing practices" qua "techniques of domination" that isolated lepers in the Middle Ages, confined the mad and the poor in the classical age, classified diseases, institutionalized the practices of clinical medicine in the nineteenth century and psychiatry in modern times, in brief, normalized social deviances in Western societies. These dividing practices subtly imply and are implied by a certain logic of exclusion that claims to be grounded in some form of scientific discourse, in particular, the "sciences of man" thematized in Foucault's genealogy of modernity. As Mary Rawlinson sums it up,

> The universal individual, the normal man --the self that can be developed, educated, considered a "human resource," whose vote can be predicted, even as his labor and welfare can be projected and regulated-- is constituted, Foucault argues, in a specific history of discourse that begins in the late eighteenth century with the substitution of the self-dispensing authority of the state for a power organized around the family and the exercise of a personal will. (KPS 379)

The specificity of modern discourses on truth, power, and ethics is strategically rescued by Foucault's archaeological and genealogical analyses so as to undermine the civilizing processes of normalization and their universalistic claims. It is in this sense that Foucault opposes his own "specific" approach to that of the "universal" intellectual. Contrary to the universal intellectual's myths of the free subject above the State, the Capital and their subordinates (technicians, magistrates, teachers), the specific intellectual maintains a direct, localized relation to scientific knowledge and institutions. (PK 126) History and the social sciences are thus submitted to a critical genealogy of self-constitution. Foucault's questions of method, to use Colin Gordon's words, are guided by the genealogical question "How are the human sciences historically possible, and what are the historical conditions of their existence?" (PK 230-1) Foucault's new ways of processing historical knowledges (*savoirs*) have been exerting a tremendous impact on historians and social scientists alike. Although the reception of his work remains controversial among thinkers of different trends, it is unquestionable today that Foucault's problematization of method has constituted a lasting contribution for the social and behavioral sciences. Adi Ophir states three main consequences of Foucault's works for the methodology of the social theories:

1. Social theory no longer looks for "the meaning of what one wants to say (*vouloir-dire*) or intends to do, but for orders of acts, communicative and non-communicative alike;"

2. "Social theory must adopt a kind of 'critical positivism.' Interpreting various domains of social reality, social theory must posit its signified on the surface of social fields. Thus, social criticism must speak in terms of observable regularities of behavior and orders of relations among overt elements of social reality, discursive practices included."
3. "Critical discourse meets the discourse of power always already from within a conflicting system of power and on the battle ground between the two systems."[6]

As Foucault himself admitted, he was not so much creating new theoretical devices as providing the social sciences with new perspectives for approaching their fields of investigation:

Eventalizing singular ensembles of practices, so as to make them graspable as different regimes of "juridiction" and "veridiction": that...is what I would like to do. ...this is neither a history of knowledge-contents (*connaissances*) nor an analysis of the advancing rationalities which rule our society, nor an anthropology of the codifications which, without our knowledge, rule our behavior. I would like in short to resituate the production of true and false at the heart of historical analysis and political critique. (FE 79)

By way of conclusion, I should like to allude to the reception of Foucault's genealogical method by French historians, which can be summed up by Patricia O'Brien's felicitous formula to describe the Foucauldian approach to history as "neither Marxist nor Annaliste."[7] In Europe, history's shift towards the social in the 1950s was fostered by Marxism and the *Annales* school. The Marxist school effected a systematic attempt to write "history from below," as represented by the works of Georges Rudé on the Parisian crowd, Albert Soboul on the Parisian *sans-culottes*, and E.P. Thompson on the English working-class.[8] There was a substantial turn away from the traditional histories of political leaders and political institutions towards social analyses of the daily life of workers, servants, women, ethnic groups, etc. The *Annales* school, which found in Fernand Braudel its most important exponent, was characterized by the threefold analysis corresponding to its different units of time: the "structure" or *longue durée*,

---

[6] Cf. Adi Ophir, "The Semiotics of Power," art. cit., 31-32.
[7] Cf. P. O'Brien, "Michel Foucault's History of Culture," in *The New Cultural History*, ed. Lynn Hunt, (Berkeley: University of California Press, 1989), 25-46.
[8] George Rudé, *The Crowd in the French revolution* (Oxford, 1959); Albert Soboul, *Les Sans-culottes parisiens en l'an II*, 2nd ed., (Paris, 1962); E.P. Thompson, *The Making of the English Working Class*, (London, 1963).

dominated by the geographical milieu; the "conjuncture" or medium term, oriented toward social life; and the "event" (*événement*), articulating the political with the individual. It was the structural analysis of *longues durées* which prevailed over the others, defining its peculiar way of doing social history. The *Annales* became a school when it was institutionally affiliated with the École Pratique des Hautes Études, after World War II, having retained the name of the original journal, founded in 1929 by Marc Bloch and Lucien Febvre (*Annales d'histoire économique et sociale*, changed into *Annales: Economies, Sociétés, Civilisations*, in 1946). There has been, however, another shift in European history, to which both Marxists and *Annalistes* have decisively contributed with their recent writings on the linguistic problematic eclipsed by the structural domination of the economic motif (i.e., the infrastructure). This turn has been described as a shift from social history towards cultural history, as *mentalités* ("mentalities") no longer reflect the material conditions of a given society, but are themselves constituents of social reality. To this third generation belong names such as Jacques Le Goff, André Burguière, Michelle Perrot, and the *nouvelle histoire* that seeks to break away from the infrastructural towards the superstructural.[9] Fourth-generation *Annales* historians Roger Chartier and Jacques Revel are among those historians in France who welcomed Foucault's antipositivist critique of social history as a new problematic to guide this new conception of cultural history.[10]

This problematic, to my mind, lies precisely in the Foucauldian articulation of the technologies of power and the genealogical discourse of truth-formations. Although I cannot elaborate on this point here, I think the reception of Foucault by historians has decisively contributed to the refashion of historical understanding through practice rather than theory --and the same can be said about Michel de Certeau and Pierre Bourdieu's influence on the "new historians." In a nutshell, that also confirms the prophetic words of E.H. Carr who said, as early as 1961, that "the more sociological history becomes, and the more historical sociology becomes, the better for both."[11] In effect, the genealogical critique of historicism remains, at the end of this century, one of the greatest

---

[9] Cf. Jacques Le Goff et al., *La nouvelle histoire*, Paris: CEPL, 1978; Peter Burke, *The French Historical Revolution: The Annales School 1929-1989*, (Cambridge: Polity, 1990)

[10] Cf. Roger Chartier, *Cultural History: Between Practices and Representations*, trans. Lydia Cochrane, (Ithaca: Cornell University Press, 1988); *Modern European Intellectual History: Reappraisals and New Perspectives*, ed. Dominick LaCapra and Steven Kaplan, (Ithaca: Cornell University Press, 1982).

[11] Cited by Lynn Hunt's Introduction to *The New Cultural History*, op. cit., 1.

challenges for both philosophers and social scientists and historians alike, who tend to dismiss this problem as an overcome reductionism.

At any rate, Foucault's genealogy of modernity succeeds in making progress towards a "new economy of power relations," as questions of method in cultural history renew the often neglected articulation of ethics and politics, and the problematics of their relations. If genealogy seeks to uncover the struggles that have been forgotten in the process of formation of rationalities over subjugated knowledges, then the ensemble of devices that produce "veridiction" and "jurisdiction" can be used as a reversal operator that brings "subjectivation" back to a level of objectification. As Janicaud remarked, the guiding question for Foucault's articulation of *savoir*, *pouvoir*, and *subjectivation* is: "How can an objective or objectifiable structure structure itself?" (MFP 339) And this problematic was already anticipated in the early *doublet empirique-transcendental* which Foucault applied to his archaeological researches in the human sciences: genealogy does not thus represent an epistemological break but a strategic *coupure*, which Foucault later tries to account for in the methodological inflation of the power-genealogy relation. The use of certain Foucauldian metaphors, the interplay of domination and resistance in a context other than the social context of struggles for liberation, points to the persisting difficulties of coming up with a "final solution" to the genealogical staging of power relations:

> It consists of taking the forms of resistance against different forms of power as a starting point. To use another metaphor, it consists of using this resistance as a chemical catalyst so as to bring to light power relations, locate their position, find out their point of application and the methods used. Rather than analyzing power from the point of view of its internal rationality, it consists of analyzing power relations through the antagonism of strategies. (BSH 211)

Far from seeking refuge in historicism or irrational nihilism, Foucault's work, as Paul Rabinow maintained, is itself "a testament to sustained critical rationality with political intent." (FR 13) Foucault's genealogy thus combines the Nietzschean three-axial "historical a priori" with the Kantian critique of the present so as to account for political *engagement*. For Foucault, the reversibility of the external spaces of discursive and non-discursive practices is precisely what allows for strategies of resistance to take place on this very level of exteriority, where the conditions said to be constitutive of subjectivity will only then unveil their normative thrust, in the particularity of commitments made empirically by the self --both individually and collectively. Such is, indeed, the post-Nietzschean return to Kant operated by Foucault's genealogy of modernity. Foucault's ethics of care for the self as an aesthetics of existence is certainly closer to Nietzsche's *Selbstüberwindung* than to Kant's self-imposed *Ausgang*. But Foucault's strategy seeks to combine both in a permanent critique of normalization and disciplinary power, as the philosophical ethos of modernity denounces the *dispositif* networks that constitute our own subjectivity, drawing a return of morality through practices of freedom which offer no promise of liberation. Even though he opposed a universalizable conception of truth, power, and ethics, Foucault has decisively contributed to both history and the social sciences with a genealogy of subjectivity that, by combining the Kantian critique and the Nietzschean genealogy, can account for such a complex conception as culture and its political micromeshes. As Foucault himself points out:

> I think that the central issue of philosophy and critical thought since the eighteenth century has always been, still is, and will, I hope, remain the question: *What* is this Reason that we use? What are its historical effects? What are its limits, and what are its dangers? How can we exist as rational beings, fortunately committed to practicing a rationality that is unfortunately crisscrossed by intrinsic dangers? ...if it is extremely dangerous to say that Reason is the enemy that should be eliminated, it is just as dangerous to say that any critical questioning of this rationality risks sending us into irrationality. (FR 249)

LIST OF ABBREVIATIONS

1) IMMANUEL KANT

All works by Kant refer to the *Werkausgabe* edited by Wilhelm Weischedel in the "Suhrkamp Taschenbüchern Wissenschaft" collection in 12 volumes (Frankfurt am Main: Suhrkamp, 1989).

Anth	*Anthropologie in pragmatischer Hinsicht*. ET: *Anthropology From a Pragmatic Point of View*, trans. Mary J. Gregor. The Hague: Martinus Nijhoff, 1974.
GMS	*Grundlegung zur Metaphysik der Sitten*. ET: *Groundwork of the Metaphysics of Morals*, trans. Lewis White Beck. Indianapolis: Bobbs-Merrill Co., 1959.
OH	*Kant On History*. Edited by Lewis W. Beck. New York: Macmillan, 1963. Includes ET of "Idee zu einer allgemeinen Geschichte in weltbürgerlicher Absicht" and "Beantwortung der Frage: Was ist Aufklärung?"
KrV	*Kritik der reinen Vernunft*. ET: *Critique of Pure Reason*, trans. N. Kemp Smith. New York: St. Martin's Press, 1965.
KpV	*Kritik der praktischen Vernunft*. ET: *Critique of Practical Reason*, trans. Lewis White Beck. Indianapolis: Bobbs-Merrill Co., 1956.
KU	*Kritik der Urteilskraft*. ET: *Critique of Judgement*, trans. J.C. Meredith. Oxford: Clarendon, 1952.
MS	*Metaphysik der Sitten*. ET: *The Metaphysics of Morals*, trans. Mary J. Gregor. New York: Cambridge University Press, 1991.

Rel	*Die Religion innerhalb der Grenzen der bloßen Vernunft*. ET: *Religion Within the Limits of Reason Alone*, trans. T.M. Greene and H.H. Hudson. New York: Harper & Row, 1960.

2) FRIEDRICH NIETZSCHE

All works by Nietzsche refer to the *Kritische Gesamtausgabe*, edited by Giorgio Colli and Mazzino Montinari, (Walter de Gruyter & Co., 1967-78)

GT	*Die Geburt der Tragödie*. (1872; 1874; 1886) ET: *The Birth of Tragedy*, in *Basic Writings of Nietzsche*. Translated by W. Kaufmann. New York: Random House, 1968.
UB	*Unzeitgemässe Betrachtungen*. Erstes Stück: David Strauss, der Bekenner und der Schriftsteller (1873); Zweites Stück: Vom Nutzen und Nachteil der Historie für das Leben (1874); Drittes Stück:Schopenhauer als Erzieher (1874); Viertes Stück: Richard Wagner in Bayreuth (1876) ET: *Unmodern Observations*, ed. W. Arrowsmith, (New Haven: Yale University Press, 1990)
MAM	*Menschliches, Allzumenschliches*. Erster Band (1878; 1886); Zweiter Band: Erste Abteilung: Vermischte Meinungen und Sprüche (1879; 1886); Zweite Abteilung: Der Wanderer und sein Schatten (1880; 1886) ET:*Human, All Too Human*, trans. R.J. Hollingdale, (Cambridge: Cambridge University Press, 1982)
M	*Morgenröte* (1881; 1887) ET: *Daybreak*, trans. R.J. Hollingdale, (Cambridge: Cambridge University Press, 1982)
FW	*Die Fröhliche Wissenschaft* (1882; 1886). ET: *The Gay Science*, trans. W. Kaufmann, (New York: Vintage, 1987).
Z	*Also Sprach Zarathustra* (I-II: 1883; III: 1884; IV: 1884)
ET	*Thus Spoke Zarathustra*, trans. W. Kaufmann, in *The Portable Nietzsche*, (New York: Vintage, 1987).
JGB	*Jenseits von Gut und Böse* (1886) ET: *Beyond Good and Evil*, trans. W. Kaufmann, in *Basic Writings of Nietzsche*, ed. W. Kaufmann, (New York: Random House, 1968).
GM	*Zur Genealogie der Moral* (1887) ET:*On the Genealogy of Morals*, trans. W. Kaufmann and R.J. Hollingdale, in *Basic Writings*.
GD	*Götzen-Dämmerung* (prep. 1888; 1889) ET: *Twilight of the Idols*, trans. W. Kaufmann, in *The Portable Nietzsche*.

A	*Der Antichrist* (prep. 1888; 1895), in *The Portable Nietzsche*.
EH	*Ecce Homo* (prepared 1888; 1908) ET: *Ecce Homo*, trans. W. Kaufmann, in *Basic Writings of Nietzsche*.
WM	*Der Wille zur Macht* (Nachlaß 1880's; 1901; 1906) *The Will to Power*, trans. W. Kaufmann and R.J. Hollingdale, (New York: Vintage Books, 1968).

3) MICHEL FOUCAULT

SP	*Surveiller et punir: Naissance de la prison*. Paris: Gallimard, 1975. ET: *Discipline and Punish: The Birth of the Prison*. (DP) Translated by Alan Sheridan. New York: Vintage Books, 1979.
FR	*The Foucault Reader*. Edited by Paul Rabinow. New York: Pantheon Books, 1984.
MIP	*Mental Illness and Psychology*. Translated by Alan Sheridan. Berkeley, Los Angeles, and London: University of California Press, 1987.
HF	*Histoire de la folie à l'âge classique*. Paris: Gallimard, 1972.
AS	*L'archéologie du savoir*. Paris: Gallimard, 1969.
OT	*The Order of Things: An Archaeology of the Human Sciences*. New York: Vintage, 1973.
BC	*The Birth of the Clinic: An Archaeology of Medical Perception*. Translated by A. M. Sheridan Smith. New York: Vintage, 1975.
FE	*The Foucault Effect: Studies in Governmentality*. Edited by Graham Burchell, Collin Gordon, and Peter Miller. Chicago: The University of Chicago Press, 1991.
PPC	*Politics, Philosophy, Culture: Interview and Other Writings, 1977-1984*. Ed. Lawrence Kritzman. New York: Routledge, 1990.
PK	*Power/Knowledge: Selected Interviews and Other Writings by Michel Foucault, 1972-1977*. Ed. by Colin Gordon. New York: Pantheon Books, 1980.
OD	*L'ordre du discours*, Leçon inaugurale au Collège de France prononcé le 2 décembre 1970. Paris: Gallimard, 1971.
RC	*Résumé des cours, 1970-1982*, Conférences, essais et leçons du Collège de France. Paris: Julliard, 1989.
HS1	*Histoire de la sexualité 1: La volonté de savoir*. Paris: Gallimard, 1976.
HS2	*Histoire de la sexualité 2: L'usage de plaisirs*. Paris: Gallimard, 1984.
HS3	*Histoire de la sexualité 3: Le souci de soi*. Paris: Gallimard, 1984.

FL	*Foucault Live: Interviews, 1966-84*. Translated by John Johnston. Edited by Sylvère Lotringer. New York: Semiotext(e), 1989.
RM	*Remarks on Marx: Conversations with Duccio Trombadori*. Translated by R. James Goldstein and James Cascaito. New York: Semiotext(e), 1989.
TS	*Technologies of the Self: A Seminar with Michel Foucault*. Edited by Luther H. Martin, Huck Gutman, and Patrick H. Hutton. Amherst: University of Massachusetts Press, 1988.
VFJ	*La verdad y las formas jurídicas*. Barcelona: Gedisa, 1980.
GEM	"Généalogie de l'État Moderne," unpublished notes from lectures delivered at the Collège de France, Paris, 1984.

4) OTHERS

NN	David B. Allison, (ed.) *The New Nietzsche: Contemporary Styles of Interpretation*. Cambridge: MIT Press, 1985.
NGC	Kenneth Baynes, *The Normative Grounds of Social Criticism: Kant, Rawls, and Habermas*. Albany, NY: SUNY Press, 1992.
MFF	James Bernauer, *Michel Foucault's Force of Flight: Towards an Ethics of Thought*. Atlantic Highlands: Humanities Press, 1990.
FF	James Bernauer and David Rasmussen, *The Final Foucault*. Cambridge, Mass.: MIT Press, 1988.
AT	Donald Crawford, *Kant's Aesthetic Theory*. Madison: The University of Wisconsin Press, 1974.
F	Gilles Deleuze, *Foucault*. Translated by Seán Hand. Minneapolis: University of Minnesota Press, 1988.
NP	Gilles Deleuze, *Nietzsche et la philosophie*. Paris: PUF, 1962.
BSH	Hubert L. Dreyfus and Paul Rabinow, *Michel Foucault: Beyond Structuralism and Hermeneutics*, Second Edition, With an Afterword and an Interview with Michel Foucault. Chicago: The University of Chicago Press, 1983.
MF	Didier Eribon, *Michel Foucault*. Translated by Betsy Wing. Cambridge, Mass.: Harvard University Press, 1991.
MFP	*Michel Foucault Philosophe*, Rencontre Internationale, Janvier 1988. Paris: Seuil, 1989.
PDM	Jürgen Habermas, *The Philosophical Discourse of Modernity*. ET: Frederick Lawrence. Cambridge, Mass.: MIT Press, 1987.

List of Abbreviations

PhG	Georg W.F. Hegel, *Phänomenologie des Geistes*. ET: *Phenomenology of the Spirit*, trans. A.V. Miller. New York: Oxford University Press, 1977.
PMF	James Miller, *The Passion of Michel Foucault*. New York: Anchor, 1993.
RPh	Georg W.F. Hegel, *Grundlinien der Philosophie des Rechts*. ET: *Philosophy of Right*, trans. T.M. Knox. Oxford: Oxford University Press, 1952.
CP	Michael Kelly, *Critique and Power: Recasting the Foucault/ Habermas Debate*. Cambridge, Mass.: MIT Press, 1994.
PFE	Jean-François Kervegan, "Le problème de la fondation de l'éthique: Kant, Hegel." *Revue de Métaphysique et de Morale* 95/1 (1990) 33-55.
TF	Herman Lebovics, *True France: The Wars Over Cultural Identity 1900-1945*. Ithaca: Cornell University Press, 1992
FNG	Michael Mahon, *Foucault's Nietzschean Genealogy: Truth, Power, and the Subject*. (Albany: SUNY Press, 1992).
KPS	Mary Rawlinson, "Foucault's Strategy: Knowledge, Power, and the Specificity of Truth."*Journal of Medicine and Philosophy* 12 (1987) 371-95.
DM	Denis L. Rosenfield, *Du Mal*. Paris: Aubier, 1990.

INDEX

A

aestethics, 37
aesthetic judgments, 37, 39, 46
aesthetic theory, 37
aestheticism, 7, 10, 32, 37, 73, 81, 90, 94, 99, 101, 102, 104, 107, 108, 110, 136, 159
Allison, David, 72, 107
Annales school, 5, 158, 161
antagonism, 27, 163
anthropology, 3, 10, 16, 20, 26, 31, 32, 42, 45, 59, 70, 77, 80, 90, 95, 122, 140, 161
anti-modernism, 86
archaeology, ix, 2, 8, 15, 17, 19, 20, 23, 25, 47, 117, 118, 120, 121, 122, 123, 125, 127, 128, 129, 130, 133, 155, 156, 158
Aristotle, 8, 31, 63, 69, 92, 119, 120, 122, 130, 159
asceticism, 109, 110, 111, 114, 137, 147
Aufhebung, 53, 58, 59, 62, 65, 129
Aufklärung, 16, 20, 62, 86, 87, 91, 94, 95, 96, 120, 126, 131, 138, 143, 153, 165
autonomy, 3, 10, 33, 34, 37, 46, 47, 48, 54, 56, 57, 60, 81, 95, 104, 122, 131, 153

B

Beaufret, Jean, 20
Beyond Good and Evil, 83, 85, 89, 95, 104, 115, 148, 154, 166
Birth of Tragedy, 107, 108, 112, 126, 166
Blondel, Eric, 72
Bourdieu, Pierre, 5, 162
Braudel, Fernand, 161
Brazil, vii, 135, 137
Burguière, André, 162

C

capitalism, 146, 152
Chartier, Roger, 5, 11, 162
Christianity, vi, 4, 76, 81, 83, 85, 86, 100, 103, 104, 106, 107, 108, 109, 110, 111, 114, 138, 149, 150
civil society, 58, 59, 135
Classical Age, 21, 25
cognitive faculties, 33, 40, 41, 74
cognitive truth, 15
Collège de France, 9, 94, 118, 127, 129, 134, 143, 147, 167, 168
communication, 134, 151, 153
Connolly, William, 93, 115, 148, 154
consciousness, 7, 15, 19, 26, 29, 30, 33, 34, 40, 53, 59, 60, 62, 63, 64, 65, 129, 136, 138
conventionalism, 82
cosmology, 77, 80, 90
Crawford, Donald, 36, 43, 168
critical enterprise, 2

Critique of Practical Reason, 15, 20, 25, 38, 165
cryptonormativism, 120, 125, 134, 156
cultural anthropology, 95
cultural values, 95
culture, 2, 5, 7, 11, 22, 68, 72, 77, 96, 97, 136, 155, 157, 164

D

Das Kapital, 9
David-Ménard, Monique, 16
de Certeau, Michel, 162
Deleuze, Gilles, 15, 36, 72, 119, 168
democracy, 115
democratization, 8
Derrida, Jacques, 7, 58, 72, 73, 74, 75, 87, 94, 104, 133
Descartes, Rene, 24, 93, 101, 122, 123, 143
determinism, 92
dialectical reason, 33
Dionysus, 106, 107, 112
dispositifs, 121, 130, 133, 136, 141, 148, 151, 154, 156
dogmatism, ix, 22, 102, 154
Donzelot, Jacques, 11

E

empirical behavior, 32
empirical knowledge, 22, 26
empirical sociability, 3, 10
Enlightenment, 5, 6, 16, 19, 24, 37, 86, 131, 143
Epicureanism, 28
Eribon, Didier, 20, 119, 168
ethics, vii, ix, xi, 1, 2, 3, 4, 5, 8, 9, 10, 11, 16, 18, 24, 31, 33, 37, 39, 44, 45, 47, 48, 49, 51, 52, 53, 55, 56, 57, 62, 74, 93, 94, 97, 103, 104, 114, 116, 120, 124, 130, 147, 149, 150, 154, 155, 156, 157, 159, 160, 163, 164
ethnology, 25, 95
Ewald, François, 11, 146, 149

existentialism, 119, 121
experimentalism, 3, 71, 88, 103

F

faculty of desire, 36
faculty of judgment, 14, 36, 41, 46
fatalism, 101
Feuerbach, Ludwig, 89
finalism, 10, 46, 51
formal purposiveness, 40, 41, 43, 46
formalism, 50, 52, 54, 62
Foucault, Michel, vi, 1, 5, 9, 13, 16, 17, 20, 72, 115, 117, 118, 119, 121, 125, 127, 129, 133, 135, 145, 146, 148, 149, 155, 161, 167, 168, 169
Foucault-Chomsky debate, 130
Foucault-Habermas debate, 5, 7, 123
foundation of ethics, 17, 47, 48, 50, 61, 97
France, 5, 13, 18, 21, 72, 75, 118, 119, 121, 133, 136, 141, 162, 169
Frankfurt School, 7
free play, 40, 102
free will, 56, 61, 86, 91
freedom, xi, 3, 10, 11, 14, 24, 26, 27, 31, 33, 34, 36, 38, 42, 45, 48, 49, 50, 51, 55, 56, 57, 59, 60, 62, 64, 65, 81, 85, 90, 91, 93, 95, 105, 106, 122, 124, 128, 130, 131, 132, 148, 149, 150, 154, 164
French Revolution, 62
Freud, Sigmund, 9, 75, 78, 99, 100, 104, 110, 119, 120, 138

G

Galileo, 122, 123
Gast, Peter, 82, 111
genealogy of ethics, 120
German idealism, x, 3, 10, 35, 37, 47, 48, 49, 85, 100, 101, 102, 123, 130
globalization, 8
God, 2, 4, 10, 16, 20, 51, 65, 76, 78, 79, 80, 81, 82, 83, 87, 88, 90, 94, 99, 101, 103, 105, 107, 108, 109, 110, 113, 114

Greece, 104, 108, 149
Guyer, Paul, 39, 43

H

Haar, Michel, 72
Habermas, Jürgen, vi, ix, x, 4, 5, 6, 7, 16, 18, 34, 47, 48, 49, 54, 70, 73, 100, 104, 107, 120, 121, 123, 124, 125, 126, 128, 130, 131, 132, 133, 134, 136, 141, 142, 143, 145, 148, 153, 156, 158, 168, 169
Heidegger, Martin, 2, 6, 13, 20, 21, 22, 23, 67, 69, 70, 71, 72, 73, 75, 78, 79, 80, 91, 101, 104, 112, 117, 119, 122, 125, 133, 136, 157
Henrich, Dieter, 48
historicism, 4, 6, 18, 63, 65, 86, 95, 101, 103, 104, 120, 121, 123, 124, 136, 138, 156, 158, 162, 163
historicity, 7, 11, 21, 22, 26, 63, 69, 78, 80, 86, 89, 92, 96, 99, 105, 118, 123, 124, 149, 158
Hobbes, 8, 91, 144
Honneth, Axel, 6, 134
human existence, 71, 77, 80, 90, 92, 105
human experience, 33, 59, 69, 105, 132
human knowledge, 22, 101
human nature, 1, 2, 3, 10, 17, 26, 28, 30, 31, 32, 42, 45, 46, 51, 68, 69, 76, 77, 82, 83, 88, 93, 94, 97, 105, 110, 116, 122, 130, 132, 142, 148, 154, 159
human sciences, 7, 15, 17, 25, 47, 123, 130, 148, 160, 163
humanism, 4, 121, 122, 132
humanity, 10, 15, 32, 76, 80, 82, 84, 85, 86, 87, 89, 93, 141
Hume, 21, 101
Husserl, 13, 17, 18, 21, 23, 26, 70, 72, 119, 122, 123, 147
Hyppolite, Jean, 7, 118

I

individual rights, 8
interpretive analytics, 2

irrationalism, ix, 5, 86, 104

J

Janicaud, Dominique, 126
Jaspers, Karl, 72
Jewish messianism, 113
Judaism, 83, 104, 110, 114

K

Kant, Immanuel, vi, 14, 15, 16, 20, 56, 101, 165
Kantian formalism, 43, 53
Kantian idealism, 53, 90
Kantian philosophy, 15, 102, 114
Kaufmann, Walter, 68, 72, 94
Kervegan, Jean-François, 48, 169
Kierkegaard, 107
Klossowski, Pierre, 72, 119
Kofman, Sarah, 72
Kuhn, Thomas, 21

L

language, 2, 18, 25, 72, 80, 105, 126, 129, 139, 151
laws of nature, 30, 36
laws of understanding, 24
Le Goff, Jacques, 5, 11, 162
Lebovics, Herman, 21, 169
Lebrun, Gérard, 18, 36, 122
Leibniz, 101, 122, 123
Locke, 101
Lyotard, Jean-François, 26, 36

M

Machiavelli, 8
madness, 13, 16, 78, 79, 81, 111, 157, 159
Maffesoli, Michel, 5

Marx, Karl, x, 9, 10, 42, 47, 75, 78, 80, 82, 84, 99, 100, 103, 104, 110, 113, 117, 119, 122, 135, 137, 138, 139, 143, 168
Marxism, 9, 121, 134, 156, 158, 161
Marxist structuralism, 5
mental faculties, 41
metaphysical subjectivity, 3
metaphysical teleology, 42
metaphysics, x, 1, 3, 4, 6, 10, 14, 15, 17, 20, 22, 25, 28, 29, 30, 32, 33, 46, 69, 73, 76, 78, 80, 82, 86, 89, 90, 91, 92, 95, 97, 99, 101, 102, 103, 105, 108, 111, 117, 120, 122, 138, 140, 147, 152, 154
Methodenstreit, x, 120, 123
moral action, 49, 61, 97, 105
moral agents, 1
moral anthropology, 20
moral consciousness, 33, 59, 61
moral judgments, 50
moral laws, 31, 34, 45, 51
moral subject, 4, 10, 52, 55, 58, 60, 62, 105, 116, 146, 147, 149, 150
moral subjectivity, 52, 55, 58, 60
moral values, 49, 71, 85, 137, 145
moralism, 37, 57, 62
morality, 2, 3, 4, 6, 10, 11, 27, 28, 31, 32, 34, 39, 41, 43, 45, 46, 48, 50, 51, 52, 53, 54, 55, 56, 57, 60, 62, 68, 70, 83, 85, 86, 87, 88, 90, 97, 99, 101, 102, 105, 108, 109, 111, 114, 115, 116, 137, 147, 148, 149, 150, 154, 159, 164
morals, x, 3, 7, 10, 11, 15, 27, 31, 50, 51, 52, 56, 60, 75, 85, 86, 87, 89, 93, 96, 97, 101, 103, 104, 114, 137, 149, 150

N

natural history, 63
Nazi genocide, 18
neocolonialism, 9
New Testament, 111, 113
Nietzsche, Friedrich, vi, 67, 102, 115, 166
Nietzschean genealogy, 3, 11, 76, 99, 164

nihilism, 4, 11, 73, 76, 78, 83, 84, 85, 87, 88, 91, 96, 97, 99, 101, 103, 105, 145, 148, 149, 163
normalization, 4, 11, 114, 140, 141, 152, 154, 160, 164
normativity, xi, 7, 115, 126, 143, 145, 148, 149, 151, 154, 157

O

objectivism, 123, 130
objectivity, 8, 57, 58, 59, 60, 62, 63, 104, 130
ontology, 1, 2, 4, 20, 75, 77, 94, 117, 120, 124, 130, 132, 143, 148, 150, 157
Order of Things, ix, 16, 24, 25, 167

P

patriotism, 60
Perrot, Michelle, 5, 11, 121, 162
personality, 10, 42, 102
perspectivism, 3, 71, 73, 74, 75, 90, 101, 103, 104
phenomenalistic idealism, 29
phenomenology, 17, 21, 22, 26, 59, 65, 119, 122, 158
Phenomenology of the Spirit, 52, 169
philosophical anthropology, 2, 20, 28
Philosophical Discourse of Modernity, ix, 6, 18, 168
philosophical knowledge, 25
Philosophy of Law, 62
Philosophy of Right, 49, 50, 52, 56, 169
Plato, 8, 69, 87, 90, 92, 101, 102
Platonism, 69, 112
political philosophy, vii, 2, 8, 16, 26, 93, 120, 130, 142, 143
political power, 8
political theory, 100, 148
politics, 5, 7, 56, 57, 62, 74, 81, 94, 115, 120, 144, 147, 150, 157, 163
Popper, Karl, 123
positivism, 7, 25, 130, 161
post-structuralism, 6, 104

power relations, 8, 95, 103, 119, 120, 121, 125, 130, 131, 135, 136, 139, 140, 141, 142, 143, 144, 145, 147, 154, 163
practical reason, x, 3, 14, 29, 32, 33, 34, 44, 46, 48, 50, 102
pragmatism, 130
presentism, 125, 134, 156
principle of subjectivity, x, 50, 66
psychiatry, 13, 18, 148, 155, 160
psychoanalysis, 9, 133
psychological idealism, 29
psychology, 13, 20, 25, 59, 80, 83, 90, 95, 104

R

racism, 9
radical critique, 2, 6, 68, 76, 81, 88, 92, 93, 100, 101, 124, 130, 133
radicalism, 90
rational foundationalism, 54
rationalism, 4, 6, 33, 100, 132
rationality, ix, 6, 7, 19, 24, 26, 48, 53, 55, 69, 70, 73, 75, 80, 81, 82, 91, 94, 117, 121, 124, 126, 130, 131, 135, 163, 164
reason, 3, 10, 14, 15, 26, 28, 31, 32, 33, 34, 36, 37, 38, 41, 45, 46, 48, 51, 53, 54, 55, 62, 64, 69, 70, 76, 80, 81, 88, 91, 93, 95, 101, 103, 111, 122, 128, 130, 131, 132, 143, 150
reflective thought, x
relativism, 97, 120, 125, 134, 156
religion, 3, 10, 64, 76, 80, 82, 83, 85, 87, 89, 92, 94, 99, 103, 104, 106, 107, 108, 110
Renaissance, 21, 25, 93, 96, 101
ressentiment, 4, 10, 83, 85, 109, 110, 114, 137
Revel, Jacques, 11, 162
Rohden, Valerio, 36, 37
Romanticism, 101, 110
Rosenfield, Denis, 28, 49, 50
Rousseau, 86, 91, 101, 135

S

Sartre, 18, 105, 119, 121, 122

Schopenhauer, 10, 22, 37, 76, 77, 86, 101, 102, 107, 132, 159, 166
Schürmann, Reiner, 157
science, 6, 14, 16, 19, 23, 30, 51, 58, 69, 71, 94, 118, 130, 133, 147, 156
self-affirmation, 11, 93, 96, 105, 110
self-consciousness, x, 22, 30, 33, 49, 57, 62, 63, 64, 75, 92, 109, 132, 147
self-determination, x, 22, 33, 49, 52, 54, 55, 58, 60, 143
self-differentiation, 53
self-foundation, 49
self-governance, 105, 145, 159
self-identity, 114, 139
self-understanding, 8
sensus communis, 27, 41
sexism, 9
sexuality, 148, 150, 151, 157
Sittlichkeit, v, 7, 34, 48, 50, 51, 52, 53, 55, 57, 59, 61, 62, 66, 115, 116
skepticism, ix, 154
slave morality, 83, 100, 104, 109
sociability, 27, 32, 44, 69, 75, 96
social control, 114, 145, 153
social groups, 142, 145, 149
social institutions, 1, 49
social order, 8, 134
social relations, 151
social sciences, 11, 160, 161, 164
social theory, 5, 6, 8, 16, 97, 123, 130, 158, 161
socialism, 115
sociology, 25, 89, 124, 162
Socratism, 108
Spinoza, 65, 101
Stoicism, 28
structuralism, 17, 123, 158
subjectivation, x, xi, 2, 8, 10, 19, 20, 22, 35, 76, 78, 105, 114, 116, 118, 120, 133, 135, 136, 143, 145, 148, 155, 156, 157, 158, 159, 163
subjective morality, 57
subjectivity, x, 1, 3, 4, 7, 11, 18, 19, 22, 24, 26, 33, 42, 50, 56, 58, 59, 60, 62, 63, 66, 68, 71, 91, 95, 97, 104, 107, 115, 116, 120,

122, 123, 125, 126, 130, 134, 142, 143, 145, 146, 149, 150, 151, 154, 155, 156, 157, 158, 163
sublime, 36, 44, 45

T

theology, 46, 59, 66, 79, 80, 90, 100, 110, 113, 122
theoretical reason, 10, 15, 32, 80
theory of power, 91, 97, 124, 135, 142, 156, 158
third world, 8
transcendental deduction, 27, 38, 39, 40, 41, 44, 102
transcendental freedom, 3, 10, 126
transcendental idealism, 3, 29, 42
transcendental intuition, 53
transcendental philosophy, 17, 23, 24, 25, 26, 39
Tugendhat, Ernst, 48, 49

U

United States, 146
universal freedom, 66
universal laws, 26, 45
unreason, 13, 16, 70, 78, 81

utilitarianism, 10

V

Veyne, Paul, 5, 11, 156, 159
Voltaire, 86

W

Warren, Mark, 93
wealth, 146, 152
Weber, Max, 103, 123
Western civilizations, 80, 132
Will to Power, vi, 68, 72, 77, 82, 89, 91, 99, 107, 167

Y

Young Hegelians, 42, 47
Yovel, Yirmiahu, 27

Z

Zaratustra, 81